The Multinational
Kingdom in Isaiah

The Multinational Kingdom in Isaiah

A Study of the Eschatological Kingdom
and the Nature of Its Consummation

Andrew H. Kim

WIPF & STOCK · Eugene, Oregon

THE MULTINATIONAL KINGDOM IN ISAIAH
A Study of the Eschatological Kingdom and the Nature of Its Consummation

Wipf & Stock
An Imprint of Wipf and Stock Publishers
199 W. 8th Ave., Suite 3
Eugene, OR 97401

www.wipfandstock.com

PAPERBACK ISBN: 978-1-7252-7092-3
HARDCOVER ISBN: 978-1-7252-7093-0
EBOOK ISBN: 978-1-7252-7094-7

Thank you,
Susan Kim, for being my best friend
and the love of my life.

Thank you,
Appa and Umma,
for being my greatest supporters
on earth and in heaven.

Contents

Preface

THE ROLE OF NATIONS in the eschatological kingdom is a topic that first piqued my interest during my ThM program. With the guidance of my advisor, Dr. Michael Vlach, I wrote my ThM thesis on God's redemptive plan for the nations. After writing my thesis, I started to notice a rise in interest on new creation theology and decided to write my doctoral dissertation on nations in the eschatological kingdom. I noticed that several recent biblical theology works claim that the OT prophets present a depiction of the eschatological kingdom as a singular corporate reality, comprised of Jews and Gentiles, rather than a multinational kingdom with the introduction of the New Covenant. In my study, I noticed that Isaiah provided multiple passages that depict national distinctions between Israelite and Gentiles, which undermines the argument that the NT church redefines national Israel in the eschatological kingdom. Though in the current work I charge some individuals as being inconsistent in their arguments about the eschatological kingdom, I am grateful for their contributions to this topic. It is my hope that the current work will play a role in helping people better understand the nature of the eschatological kingdom and God's redemptive plan for *all* nations, including Israel.

Acknowledgments

Since this work was originally my doctoral dissertation at Southwestern Baptist Theological Seminary, I must express my gratitude toward my colleagues, friends, and family who supported me in completing this work. I am grateful to my supervisor, Dr. Craig Blaising, for his guidance and insight from the prospectus stage through the completion of the project. I am thankful for Dr. Steven James and his continual support and prayers in encouraging me to finish this project.

Throughout this journey, I have felt the prayers of my church and family. The Bridge Church has been one of the greatest blessings in my life. They have continually prayed for me and graciously gave me the flexibility to be a full-time student and pastor. My godly parents have spent many hours interceding on my behalf throughout the writing of this project. They have sacrificed monetarily for me and my family and have been a testimony to the Lord's faithfulness in my life. In the midst of finishing my dissertation, on January 15, 2018, my dear father passed from this life into the presence of his Lord and Savior. Before he passed, he encouraged me to complete this work and his words gave me motivation to finish. I am thankful for the legacy he left me, and I dedicate this work to him.

The greatest support throughout this process has come from my wife, Susan. She has been a faithful companion throughout my entire journey. She worked full time to financially support our family so that I could focus on this work. There is no other individual who has sacrificed more, and I am forever grateful for her. My sons, Zachary and Levi, have provided me much relief during this process. They are living reminders of why the topic of the kingdom matters and I pray that one day they would love King Jesus and be a part of his multinational kingdom.

Finally, I thank the Lord, who has showered me with blessings. His word has given me hope after my father's passing by giving me a vivid picture of his multinational kingdom. My prayer is that this book would also help others look forward, with excitement, to the multinational kingdom that will consummate with the return of King Jesus, even while they endure through various trials.

Abbreviations

ABD	*The Anchor Bible Dictionary*
AB	Anchor Bible
ABRL	Anchor Bible Reference Library
ANE	Ancient Near Eastern
AJSLL	*The American Journal of Semitic Languages and Literature*
ATJ	*Ashland Theological Journal*
BibSac	*Bibliotheca Sacra*
BBR	*Bulletin for Biblical Research*
BECNT	Baker Exegetical Commentary on the New Testament
BDAG	Greek-English Lexicon of the New Testament
BNTC	Baker New Testament Commentary
BSL	Biblical Studies Library
CBQ	*Catholic Biblical Quarterly*
CC	Continental Commentaries
CTJ	*Conservative Theological Journal*
EDNT	Eerdman's *Exegetical Dictionary of the New Testament*
HALOT	*The Hebrew and Aramaic Lexicon of the Old Testament.*
HTR	*The Harvard Theological Review*
ICC	International Critical Commentary
JAOS	*Journal of the American Oriental Society*
JBL	*Journal of Biblical Literature*

JETS	*Journal of the Evangelical Theological Society*
JMT	*Journal of Ministry & Theology*
JSOT	*Journal for the Study of the Old Testament*
JSOTSup	Journal for the Study of the Old Testament: Supplement Series
JSS	*Journal of Semitic Studies*
JTI	*Journal of Theological Interpretation*
JTSA	*Journal of Theology for Southern Africa*
LD	Lectio Divina
MSJ	*The Master's Seminary Journal*
NAC	New American Commentary
NACBT	New American Commentary Studies on the Bible and Theology
NBD	*New Bible Dictionary*
NIB	*New Interpreter's Bible*
NIBC	New International Bible Commentary
NICOT	New International Commentary on the Old Testament
NICNT	The New International Commentary on the New Testament
NIGTC	New International Greek Testament Commentary
NIVAC	The New International Version Application Commentary
NovT	*Novum Testamentum*
NovTSup	Novum Testamentum Supplement Series
NSBT	New Studies in Biblical Theology
NTOA	*Novum Tesamentum et Orbis Antiquus*
NT	New Testament
NTS	*New Testament Studies*
OT	Old Testament
OTL	Old Testament Library
OtSt	Oudtestamentische Studiën
PRS	*Perspectives in Religious Studies*

PRTJ	*Protestant Reformed Theological Journal*
RTR	*Reformed Theological Review*
SBL	Studies in Biblical Literature
SJT	*Scottish Journal of Theology*
TDNT	*Theological Dictionary of the New Testament*
TDOT	*Theological Dictionary of the Old Testament*
TLOT	*Theological Lexicon of the Old Testament*
TOTC	Tyndale Old Testament Commentaries
TrinJ	*Trinity Journal*
TWOT	*Theological Wordbook of the Old Testament*
UBSHS	United Bible Societies Handbook Series
VT	*Vetus Testamentum*
VTSup	Supplements to Vetus Testamentum
WBC	Word Biblical Commentary
WLQ	*Wisconsin Lutheran Quarterly*
WTJ	*Westminster Theological Journal*
WUNT	Wissenschaftliche Untersuchungen zum Neuen Testament
ZAW	*Zeitschrift für die altetestamentliche Wissenschaft*
ZTK	*Zeitschrift für Theologie und Kirche*

Introduction

WORKS ON BIBLICAL THEOLOGY,[1] which assume a canonical narrative, explain the narrative in a variety of ways.[2] Some biblical theologians

1. In a 1787 lecture, Johann P. Gabler called for a distinction between biblical and dogmatic theology. Though not the first to use the term, "biblical theology," Gabler was the first to popularize the separation of biblical and dogmatic theology. See Wunch and Eldredge, "J. P. Gabler," 133–58. For an excellent analysis and introduction to Gabler's thought, see Boers, *What Is New Testament Theology?*, 23–38. Gabler defines biblical theology as a descriptive science which "transmits what the sacred writers thought about the things of God," while dogmatic theology "is didactic in nature and transmits the philosophizing of a particular theologian concerning godly things, in term of his mode of thinking, historical situation, place denomination and school." See Anderson, "Tradition and Scripture," 6. Charles Scobie provides a general definition for biblical theology: "Biblical theology thus ought to mean something like the ordered study of what the Bible has to say and his relation to the world and humankind." See Scobie, *Ways of Our God*, 4–5. David Baker provides four modern views for biblical theology: (1) the NT as the essential Bible; (2) the two testaments as equally Christian; (3) the OT as the essential Bible; and (4) the two testaments as one salvation history. See Baker, *Two Testaments, One Bible*. This work will utilize the second view, which Brevard Childs calls the "canonical" approach. See Childs, *Biblical Theology*, 70–80; Childs, *Biblical Theology in Crisis*. William Dumbrell gives a definition of the canonical approach: "Biblical theology is the progressive, descriptive, unfolding of the stages whereby the whole of the canonical 'story' develops from the basic deposit of Genesis 1–3 until the full purpose of God is reached in the descent of the new creation in Revelation 21–22." Dumbrell uses the canonical approach with the assumption that the new creation is the dominating theme throughout the canon. This assumption will affect his interpretation of God's eschatological kingdom and "Israel," in Isaiah. See Dumbrell, "Paul and Salvation History," 287.

2. Gerhard von Rad builds his OT theology on *heilsgeschicte*, or "saving history." See Rad, *Old Testament Theology*. Walter Brueggemann focuses on the process of conflict and disputation through which Israel arrived at complex truth-claims about Yahweh. See Brueggeman, *Old Testament Theology*. Desmond Alexander interprets the overall narrative of Scripture as a return to Eden. See Desmond, *From Eden to the New Jerusalem*. Christopher Wright writes that the canonical narrative is concerned primarily about God's mission to the world. God's mission is the framework that unlocks

interpret the narrative as a redemptive history. Many focus on the kingdom of God as the key theme that clarifies the direction of redemptive history.[3] As the narrative unfolds, God redeems people from all nations into his kingdom. When this redemptive process consummates, the kingdom enters a new phase that some have referred to as the "eschatological kingdom."[4]

The affirmation that God redeems people from all nations raises a question concerning the corporate status of nations in the consummate kingdom.[5] Does redemption concern individuals only or does it extend

---

the "grand narrative" of Scripture. See Wright, *Mission of God*. Von Rad, Bruggemann, Alexander, and Wright are a few examples of how those who assume a canonical narrative explain the canonical text in different ways.

3. Works which emphasize a kingdom theme in the canon include: Dumbrell, *Covenant and Creation*; Weiss, *Die Predigt Jesu vom Reiche Gottes*; Lundström, *Kingdom of God*; Perrin, *Kingdom of God*; Ladd, *Jesus and the Kingdom*; Schnackenburg, *God's Rule and Kingdom*; Beasley-Murray, *Jesus and the Kingdom*; Chilton, *Pure Kingdom*; Saucy, *Kingdom of God*; Caird and Hurst, *New Testament Theology*; Ridderbos, *Coming of the Kingdom*. Two recent biblical theologians who apply a kingdom of God theme throughout the whole canon include Eugene Merrill and Stephen Dempster. See Merrill, *Everlasting Dominion*; Dempster, *Dominion and Dynasty*.

4. Although the term "eschatological kingdom" is not frequently mentioned, the concept of a consummated kingdom is proposed by several biblical theologians. For example, George Ladd presents an inaugurated eschatology, which presents the eschatological kingdom as a present and future reality. He writes, "God's Kingdom in Jesus' teaching has a twofold manifestation: at the end of the age to destroy Satan, and in Jesus' mission to bind Satan." See Ladd, *Theology of the New Testament*, 64. God's kingdom is not only seen in the future consummation of the canonical narrative, but also in our present reality. Jürgen Moltmann informs his view of God's eschatological kingdom around the hope from Christ's resurrection. He writes that the cross of Christ and the resurrection point forward to the consummation of God's kingdom. According to him, the importance of the resurrection is not its past, accomplished reality but its eschatological nature. See Moltmann, *Theology of Hope*, 181. Dumbrell attempts to answer the question of how the canon arrives at the images presented in Rev 21–22. Dumbrell defines biblical theology with the presupposition that the rich diversity of Scripture serves its profound unity. This means that the canonical narrative finds its consummation in God's eschatological kingdom as depicted in Revelation. See Dumbrell, *The End of the Beginning*. The examples of Ladd, Moltmann, and Dumbrell affirm that the consummation of God's kingdom is the eschatological kingdom, even though there may be differences in how they understand the nature of this kingdom.

5. Works that comment on the topic of nations in God's kingdom include: McNicol, *Conversion of the Nations*; Thompson, *One Lord, One People*; Moessner et al., *Paul and the Heritage of Israel*; Konradt, *Israel*; Sherwood, *Paul*; Poulsen, *God, His Servant*; Carraway, *Christ Is God Over All*; Croatto, "Nations," 143–61; Grisanti, "Israel's Mission," 39–61; Grüneberg, *Abraham, Blessing and the Nations*; Hays, *Every People and Nation*; Kaiser, *Mission in the Old Testament*; Köstenberger and O'Brien, *Salvation*;

to national entities? The canonical narrative portrays God's dealings with humanity on both individual and corporate levels, which include ethnic, tribal, national, and territorial dimensions of human existence. However, does this narrative consummate only in a redemption of individuals from the nations or does it include the redemption of individuals identified with national distinctions?

This question relates to how one understands the role of Israel in the canonical narrative. Throughout the OT, Israel is a nation in relation to a territorial location among the nations of the earth. The biblical narrative speaks of Israel and the nations as well as various individuals among them. Many have claimed that in the overall canonical narrative, Israel is best read as a type of an eschatological consummation of individuals drawn from all nations.[6] It is a type of a corporate reality composed of peoples not only from national, ethnic Israel but also from all nations, tribes, and ethnic groups. In the consummation, the multiplicity of nations is replaced by a single corporate reality of individuals redeemed out of the multinational order. The promises to Israel on the national and corporate order are understood to be consummated typologically through a singular corporate reality, which is considered to be the eschatological kingdom of God.

Many have argued that the NT reveals this consummation for redemption history by introducing the church as a replacement for Israel. This common position has been challenged in a number of works.[7] However, some have claimed that even in the OT, the trajectory of the canonical narrative begins to move in this direction.[8] This work will address this

---

Lohfink and Zenger, *God of Israel*; Merrill, *Everlasting Dominion*; Odendall, *Eschatological Expectation*; Scott, *Paul and the Nations*; Vlach, *Has the Church Replaced Israel?*; Wright, *Mission of God*.

6. Works on biblical theology that argue for Israel as an OT type of the eschatological kingdom include: Vos, *Biblical Theology*; Alexander, *Eden*; Alexander, *Paradise*; Dumbrell, *Covenant and Creation*; Dumbrell, *End of the Beginning*; Dumbrell, *Search for Order*; Goldsworthy, *According to Plan*; Robertson, *Israel of God*; Dempster, *Dominion and Dynasty*; and Beale, *Temple*.

7. Works on biblical theology that challenge supersessionism include: Bauckham, *Restoration*; Blaising and Bock, *Dispensationalism*; Bock and Glaser, *The People*; Diprose, *Israel*; Horner, *Future Israel*; Feinberg, "Place That Israel Holds"; Feinberg, *Continuity and Discontinuity*; Frankel, *Land of Canaan*; Fruchtenbaum, *Israelology*; Fuller, *Restoration of Israel*; Fullerton, "Viewpoints"; Fusco, "Luke-Acts"; House, *Israel*; Grisanti, "Israel's Mission"; Kaiser, *Mission in the Old Testament*; Vlach, *Has the Church Replaced Israel?*; Soulen, *God of Israel*.

8. See Beale, *Biblical Theology*; Goldsworthy, *According to Plan*; Alexander, *Eden*;

issue by focusing on the book of Isaiah and how it is utilized in promoting the view that the eschatological kingdom will be a singular corporate reality, comprised of Jews and Gentiles. I will examine the assumption that the canonical narrative, in Isaiah, is best read with a view toward a kingdom consummation conceived as a singular corporate reality of individuals redeemed from the nations. Instead, I will argue that Isaiah's eschatological visions are consistent with a multinational consummate order where Israelites and Gentiles are identified with national and territorial distinctions.

Background

The focus upon the narrative of redemptive history can be traced to the late nineteenth-century works of Herman Bavinck and Abraham Kuyper.[9] Modern biblical theologians who follow the thought of Bavinck and Kuyper include Geerherdus Vos, O. P. Robertson, O. T. Allis, William Dumbrell, D. A. Carson, and G. K. Beale. A long tradition of works from the Reformed tradition utilizes a redemptive-history approach in interpreting the canonical text.[10] These writings evidence the widespread impact of this type of approach within Reformed theology.[11]

---

and Gentry and Wellum, *Kingdom through Covenant*. Dumbrell builds his argument for a mono-national kingdom from the Abrahamic Covenant, which is reiterated in Isa 40–66. See Dumbrell, *End of the Beginning*, 119–20. Hays affirms a multinational kingdom from the Abrahamic Covenant but sees Isaiah as a turning point in which national distinctions are erased in the eschatological kingdom with the introduction of the New Covenant. See Hays, *Every People and Nation*, 106. Whether one's argument begins from the Abrahamic Covenant or with the introduction of the New Covenant, there is agreement from several theologians that Isaiah predicts a mono-national kingdom made up of individuals from all nations.

9. See Bavinck, *Reformed Dogmatics* and Kuyper, *Sacred Theology*.

10. For a study on the trajectory of Herman Bavink and Abraham Kuyper's influence on Geerhardus Vos and later American biblical theologians, see Gaffin, "Systematic and Biblical Theology," and Engelsma, "Herman Bavinck."

11. A list of works that evidence a redemptive-historical approach include: Vos, *Biblical Theology*; Beale, *Biblical Theology*; Scobie, *Ways of Our God*; Goldsworthy, *According to Plan*; Alexander, *Eden*; Dumbrell, *End of the Beginning*; Robertson, *Christ of the Covenants*; Allis, *Prophecy and the Church*; Kline, *Kingdom Prologue*; Kline, *God, Heaven, and Har Magedon*; Gentry and Wellum, *Kingdom through Covenant*. A recent festschrift for O. Palmer Robertson reveals the influence of Robertson's redemptive history approach on Reformed theologians. Contributors of this festschrift include Richard Gaffin, Bruce Waltke, George W. Knight III, Simon J. Kistemaker, Robert L. Reymond, and Morton H. Smith. See Penny, *Hope Fulfilled*.

A common assumption proposed in these writings is that the multinational kingdom, predicted in the OT, is replaced by a corporate reality of individuals in the NT. Dumbrell foresees this already in the promise of a "great nation" in the Abrahamic Covenant.[12] He does not see this "great nation" as referring to the nation of Israel, whose coming into existence is arguably related to this promise in the ongoing biblical narrative, but rather to an eschatological reality that will replace all previously existing nations on earth, including Israel. This "nation" reveals Israel as a type in OT narrative that foreshadows a "final political unity" described in Rev 21–22.[13] Vos states that with the unfolding of the canonical narrative, Israel becomes redefined since her relationship with Yahweh is emphasized in the prophets as spiritual rather than literal.[14]

Many understand the NT proclamation of New Covenant blessings being given to Jews and Gentiles without distinction as indicating that national distinctions will be removed in the eschatological kingdom. Stephen Dempster explains the eschatological kingdom as encompassing the entire earth with a new "Israel," comprised of individuals from different nations.[15] Desmond Alexander proposes that the church, with the inclusion of Gentiles, replaces the multinational kingdom predicted in the OT prophets.[16]

Although the history of redemption approach argues that the NT gives evidence of the aforementioned shift in the canonical narrative,[17]

---

12. Dumbrell writes, "We may therefore look to the New Testament to fulfill the concept of Israel, which failed to be realized in the OT." See Dumbrell, *Covenant and Creation*, 28.

13. Dumbrell, *Covenant and Creation*, 66–67.

14. See the chapter entitled "The Place of Prophetism in OT Revelation" in Vos, *Biblical Theology*.

15. Dempster, *Dominion and Dynasty*, 233–34. Dempster adds that a promised Davidic king will mediate blessings to this future kingdom. He connects the Abrahamic Covenant with the new Adamic/Davidic king. The Davidic king will restore a new world order, which will end the cosmic battle between the seed of the woman and the serpent. Dempster draws upon Ps 2 to show how the new Davidic king will rule over the nations thereby fulfilling the Abrahamic Covenant. Dempster, *Dominion and Dynasty*, 176. Desmond Alexander also affirms a multiethnic people in the new creation because of his understanding of the Abrahamic Covenant. Alexander writes, "Citizens of the new earth will be drawn from all ethnic groups of this earth." Alexander, *Eden*, 165.

16. Desmond Alexander points to Acts 2 as foreshadowing the international dimension of the church in the New Jerusalem. See Alexander, *Eden*, 165.

17. For a survey of works that affirm a supersessionist reading of the NT, see Kaiser, "Assessment."

others allege that the OT itself gives evidence of a coming change in the direction of the narrative.[18] Daniel Hays writes that Isaiah envisions an "eschatological picture of people from all nations blending together with the remnant of Israel as the true people of Yahweh."[19] In Hays's discussion of Isa 66:18, he concludes that the eschatological kingdom "reverses" the national divisions resulting from Babel.[20] The new kingdom is to consist of a "multiethnic, multicultural, and multilingual" people.[21] Interestingly, Hays refrains from using the term "multinational" in his description. According to Hays, Isaiah's predictions point to a singular corporate reality of individuals drawn from the nations.[22]

In their book *Kingdom through Covenant*, Stephen Wellum and Peter Gentry employ Isaiah as evidence for a mono-national kingdom. They argue that with the introduction of the New Covenant, the picture for the kingdom of God becomes reconceptualized. When Gentry interacts with Isaiah's prophecies concerning the New Covenant, he sees a transformation

18. Peter Gentry cites several works that utilize Isaiah as evidence of a change in OT narrative. See the chapter entitled "The New Covenant: Introduction/Isaiah/Ezekiel," in Gentry, *Kingdom through Covenant*, 434–70. Daniel Hays also points to Isaiah as describing a new multiethnic kingdom where individuals come together without any national distinctions. See Hays, *From Every People and Nation*, 106.

19. Hays, *From Every People and Nation*, 106.

20. Hays, *From Every People and Nation*, 115.

21. Hays, *From Every People and Nation*, 199.

22. A tension exists between passages on universalism and nationalism in Isaiah's description of the kingdom. Some scholars agree that Yahweh has called Israel to be an active agent in dealing with nations (i.e., H. H. Rowley, P. Volz, and E. J. Hamlin). Other scholars, however, see Israel as a passive presence among the nations (i.e., Morgernstern and Martin-Achard). Yet a third group of scholars does not see Israel playing any beneficial role at all. Instead they place Israel against the nations (i.e., N. H. Snaith, P. A. H. de Boer, and H. M. Orlinsky). In his dissertation, Aschalew Kebede argues that the distinction between Israel and Gentile nations will be removed "in that day" when the nations are incorporated into the people of God. He resolves the tension between passages on universalism and nationalism by focusing on individualism in God's kingdom. See Kebede, "Universalism and Nationalism," 5–7. John McKenzie adds that the main teaching of Isaiah was not nationalism, but universal salvation of individuals from all nations. See McKenzie, *Second Isaiah*. By emphasizing individualism over nationalism, Kebede and McKenzie assume an eschatological kingdom consummation comprised of individuals alone. Daniel Hays also utilizes individualism in order to understand Isaiah's kingdom. This focus on individualism can be seen in Hays's interpretation of Isa 2. Although he acknowledges that a future mix of peoples, consisting of Jews, Assyrians, Egyptians, and Cushites, will exist in the kingdom, he argues that they will exist as individuals rather than individuals with national and territorial distinctions. See Hays, *From Every People and Nation*, 107.

in the nature and identity of Israel in the coming eschatological consummation. According to Gentry, with the introduction of the New Covenant, God redefines Israel's identity as inclusive of Gentiles and broadens her land to be coextensive with the new creation. A new multiethnic "Israel" replaces national Israel together with the whole multinational order.[23] In other words, the New Covenant introduces a "new people" with a "new place."[24] What God promised to Abraham becomes fulfilled in a "greater way" when God unites Jews and Gentiles into "one family."[25]

In his review of *Kingdom through Covenant*, Craig Blaising explains the problem of erasing national distinctions in God's eschatological kingdom. He writes, "A deficient anthropology will almost certainly leave one unprepared to grasp the holistic nature of the eschatological kingdom, since that kingdom is presented in Scripture as a multi-national not just multi-personal reality."[26] The fact that Gentiles are introduced into God's kingdom does not in itself mean that God redefines the nation of Israel or, for that matter, erases national distinctions. As Blaising observes, "A key feature of the biblical narrative from its appearance in Genesis 10–11 to the final eschatological scene in Revelation 22 is the multi-national reality of humanity."[27] If this is so, it would be more fitting to read Isaiah's universal and nationalistic passages as consistent with this narrative emphasis.

This has implications for how one understands Israel's role in Isaiah's eschatological visions. If the eschatological kingdom is composed only of individuals who are part of various national entities, then the assumption of a "new" multiethnic Israel may be possible.[28] However,

23. Peter Gentry writes, "This marriage relationship was broken by Israel's unfaithfulness, and God brought the curse of exile upon Israel, and so he forsook his unfaithful wife." See Gentry, *Kingdom through Covenants*, 442. Craig Blaising critiques Gentry's argument by writing, "Gentry believes that Israel is redefined in the new covenant such that the meaning content of the covenant promise establishing Israel's particular identity—the identity of the partner in the marriage covenant—is changed. . . . When the new covenant is established, it is established with a 'new [that is, different] Israel.'" See Blaising, "Hermeneutical-Theological Response," 119n14.

24. See Gentry, *Kingdom through Covenant*, 468. Gentry writes that the creation of the new heavens and the new earth parallel the creation of Jerusalem. The new Jerusalem is identical with the new heavens and the new earth. Gentry uses Isa 65:25 as stating that the new Zion has become the new Eden.

25. Gentry, *Kingdom through Covenant*, 460–61.

26. Blaising, "Hermeneutical-Theological Response," 121.

27. Blaising, "Hermeneutical-Theological Response," 120.

28. The reason why a "new" Israel, as opposed to a "new" Egypt, is necessary is because everlasting promises were given to national Israel in the OT. Thus, there needs

if the kingdom includes a multinational structure, then the inclusion of Gentile individuals, who remain identified with national and territorial distinctions from Israelites, should not redefine or replace national Israel.

Several works on biblical theology attempt to respond to the assumption that the new covenant community replaces national Israel by focusing on the integrity of national promises to Israel. These works affirm a national future for Israel in God's eschatological kingdom and deny the assumption that a "new" Israel, consisting of individuals from all nations, replaces national Israel. However, focusing on the role of Gentile nations in the OT may see the same result. Since several theologians utilize Isaiah as key to their reading of the biblical narrative, I will argue that a multinational kingdom is consistently pictured in Isaiah's visions of the eschatological kingdom.

A Roadmap for the Book

In chapter 1, I will look at anthropological studies concerning a definition of a nation(s). Although a nation is defined by several factors (i.e., common language, common economic life, and psychological makeup), two important elements for a nation are an identifiable ethnic core and a common historical homeland. For ancient Israel, their identity as a nation was informed by these two traits.

In chapter 2, I will transition to biblical word studies on nations. Within the canon of Scripture עַם, אֻמָּה, מִשְׁפָּחָה, גּוֹי and ἔθνος can all be translated as "nation," although they can also refer to a "family," "tribe," or "people" depending on the context. I will examine the contextual uses of גּוֹי and its relationship with מִשְׁפָּחָה, אֻמָּה, עַם and ἔθνος. In so doing, I hope to demonstrate that the OT canon portrays consistently a multinational paradigm, specifically in descriptions of the eschatological kingdom.

In chapter 3, a foundation for a multinational kingdom will be developed from Gen 10–12. Consistent with anthropological studies on nations, Gen 10 affirms the concept of land as foundational for a group of people to identify as a nation. Genesis 11 reveals that the diversity of nations did not simply result from sin. When understood within the context of Gen 10–12, Gen 11 is God's means to accomplish his intended

---

to be a new "Israel" from the NT who will receive these everlasting promises since these promises were originally given to national Israel. In order to maintain God's faithfulness to his promises, several theologians read national Israel as a type that is replaced by a "new" Israel—namely, the new covenant community.

plan for a multinational human reality. In Gen 12, the Abrahamic Covenant offers a paradigm of Israel's interaction with Gentile nations. In sum, Gen 10–12 provides a foundation for a multinational kingdom that the rest of the canon will develop.

In chapter 4, I will trace the theme of nations throughout the OT by highlighting passages that comment on nations in an eschatological, consummate, or idealized setting. I will examine several OT prophets, other than Isaiah, to demonstrate consistency in their vision of a multinational eschatological kingdom. The Writings will show a world order that has ideal and eschatological dimensions, which are multinational in its nature. Also, the Writings portray a future Davidic king who will mediate these blessings to a multitude of nations within a multinational paradigm.

In chapter 5, I will examine Peter Gentry's claim that Isaiah depicts a mono-national kingdom since his arguments represent others who also assert that Israel functions as an OT type of the eschatological kingdom. Isaiah's prophecies do not shift the multinational paradigm to a mono-national kingdom, but affirms a multi-personal and multinational kingdom with territorial and national distinctions. I will conclude by analyzing Gentry's hermeneutical assumptions and how it affects his reading of Isaiah's eschatological visions.

In chapter 6, I will propose an alternate reading of Isaiah's eschatological kingdom that interprets the kingdom consummation as a multinational reality. My interpretation of Isaiah will offer better explanatory power in dealing with the textual details of Isaiah than one that rejects national particularity. Three themes within Isaiah's eschatological visions contributes toward a multinational kingdom: (1) Zion, (2) Israel and Gentile nations, and (3) messianic king. Informed by these three themes, I will study several passages that present a multinational portrayal of Isaiah's eschatological kingdom.

In the conclusion, chapter 7, I will summarize the main points from this book and suggest that a canonical understanding of Gentile nations, specifically one that argues for a renewed multinational kingdom, should take into account Israel's identity and role. Biblical theologians inconsistently assume a multiethnic kingdom without affirming its national dimensions. Finally, I will present implications from this book on the modern discussion of ethnic diversity in the church and will also suggest other areas for further study.

1

Defining a Nation

Anthropological Perspective

BEFORE ARGUING FOR A multinational eschatological kingdom, a definition of a nation must be established. The purpose of this chapter is to
present a definition as discussed among anthropologists.[1] Anthony Smith
comments on the difficulty with arriving to a consensus for a definition:

> The study of nations and nationalism cannot be confined to a
> single disciplinary perspective. Historians long dominated the

---

1. For the purposes of this book, I will limit the scope of study on anthropological
works. I will reference anthropological works that note that a common homeland is
fundamental for any definition of both premodern and modern nations. The reason
for this limitation is because there is a debate among sociologists about defining premodern nations versus nation-states. Anthony Smith argues that premodern communities could be defined as a nation based on common cultural aspects. However,
Montserrat Guibernau critiques Smith's definition since it does not consider political
aspects. Guibernau thinks that distinguishing between nations with and without states
resolves the key dilemmas arising from Smith's classical definition of a nation and
other anthropologists' definition. Guibernau defines a "state" as a human community
that claims the monopoly of the legitimate use of physical force within a given territory. A "nation" refers to a human group conscious of forming a community with
shared culture and territory. Thus, "nations without states" refer to territorial communities with their own identity and a desire for self-determination included within the
boundaries of one or more states by which they do not identify. Guibernau proposes
five dimensions that define a nation: psychological, cultural, territorial, historical, and
political. See Guibernau, "Anthony D. Smith," 125–41. Guibernau's critique of Smith
shows the ongoing debate about the elements included in defining a nation. However,
both Guibernau and Smith agree that a nation, whether premodern or modern, must
include an attachment to a common homeland. This is what is relevant for this book.

field, but latterly they have been joined by anthropologists, political scientists, sociologists, social psychologists, students of linguistics, international relations scholars, geographers, philosophers, regional economists, international lawyers, and many others.[2]

In their respective works, Anthony Smith, Louis Snyder, and Karl Deutsch offer different defining characteristics of a nation.[3] They propose that a nation includes a common language, territory, government, economic life and psychological makeup.[4]

Anthony Smith argues that there is a process by which an ethnic group becomes a nation: (1) a group of people distinguish themselves from outsiders; (2) this group cultivates various shared memories, symbols, values, and traditions; (3) this group begins to reside and attach themselves to a certain territory and see it as their historic homeland; (4) this group creates a distinct public culture of rites and ceremonies, symbolic codes, and education for that community; and (5) this group observes standardized and uniform laws throughout a community.[5] According to Smith's outline, several elements develop over time within an ethnic group that changes its status to a nation: traditions, ceremonies, laws, education, and a historic homeland.

There are several anthropologists who criticize Smith's proposed outline because he does not differentiate between a nation from a nation-state. Walker Connor observes that Smith confuses nationhood with a state because elements of a state are included in his definition of a nation.[6] Connor instead defines a nation as "the largest group that can command a person's loyalty because of felt kinship ties; it is, from this

2. Smith, *Nationalism*, 3.

3. See Smith, *Nation in History*; Deutsch, *Nationalism*, 3–20; Snyder, *Meaning of Nationalism*, 55–70.

4. Max Weber writes that "a nation is a community of sentiment which would adequately manifest itself in a state of its own; hence, a nation is a community which normally tends to produce a state of its own." See Weber, "Nation," 25. Joseph Stalin argues that "a nation is a historically constituted, stable community of people, formed on the basis of a common language, territory, economic life, and psychological make-up manifested in a common culture." See Stalin, "Nation," 20. Anthony Smith understands a nation as "a named human population occupying a historic territory or homeland and sharing common myths and memories; a mass, public culture; a single economy; and common rights and duties for all members." See Smith, *Nation in History*, 3.

5. Leoussi, *Call of the Homeland*, 5.

6. Connor, "Nation," 39.

perspective, the fully extended family."[7] Daniele Conversi asserts that a distinction between a nation and nation-state must be carefully delineated because the inclusion of rights for citizens can only be granted by a state.[8] Conversi adds that Smith's definition of a nation includes ethnosymbolism, which confuses the distinction between a nation-state and a nation.[9] Ernest Gellner comments that nationalism, as a principle, holds the political and the national unit as congruent.[10] Although a nation and state were intended for each other, there remains a difference between the two. John Stone adds that if nationalism is seen as a socially constructed belief system, then a "nation" can be invented in the same manners as one could invent a "race."[11] Clearly, there remains a discussion about which factors distinguish a nation from a nation-state. However, there is a characteristic that all anthropologists agree that a nation must possess, namely a historic homeland.

Historic Homeland

Anthony Smith writes, "Nations are, by definition, territorialized communities, that is, communities the majority of whose members have come to reside in an historic territory or homeland and to feel a strong attachment to it."[12] Nations associate with a specific homeland even though the boundaries may change over time. They are bounded with mobility throughout that territory and view it as theirs.[13] While Anthony Giddens regards nationalism as primarily a political movement associated with the nation-state, he recognizes that a homeland is tied to "a myth of origin," which holds the ideals of a nation.[14] Frederick Hertz claims that

---

7. Connor, *Ethnonational*, 202; Connor, "Timelessness of Nations," 35–37.

8. Conversi, "Mapping the Field," 23.

9. For Smith's application of ethnosymbolism, see Smith, "Basic Themes of Ethnosymbolism," 23–40, and Conversi, "Reassessing Theories of Nationalism," 73–85.

10. Gellner, *Nations and Nationalism*, 55.

11. Stone and Rizova, "Ethnic Enigma," 31–32.

12. Smith, *Ethno-symbolism and Nationalism*, 29.

13. Smith writes, "What has mattered to *ethnie* is the possession, or at least association with, a 'homeland'—a territory which they and others recognize to be theirs by historic right and from which they are felt to stem." See Smith, *Ethnic Origins of Nations*, 93.

14. Giddens, *Contemporary Critique*, 216. Before the modern epoch, genealogical myths and religious symbols contributed to the normal exclusionary forms of "tribal" group identity. In the modern epoch, nations were formed through processes

in order for a nation to exist, there must be a belief in the existence of a specific territory as "belonging to" only that people.[15]

In the last twenty-five years, the majority of anthropologists concluded that nationality was exclusively a modern phenomenon.[16] Although nationality is a recent conception, OT scholars have noted that a historic homeland was a defining trait for nations in premodern times. According to Thorkild Jacobson, Israel's national identity was tied primarily to their territory with less consideration for the ethnic affiliation or origin of the individuals belonging to the nation.[17] Steven Grosby comments on the significance of land as it pertains to Israel's national identity. He writes, "The existence of the nation, whether ancient Israel or the modern nation-state, is predicated upon the existence of a collective consciousness constituted by a belief that there exists a territory which belongs to only one people, and that there are a people which belongs to only one territory."[18] Speiser concludes that what distinguished a "nation" (גּוֹי) from a "people" (עַם), in the thinking of ancient Israelites, was that a גּוֹי was an עַם with its own *land*.[19]

---

of state centralization and administrative expansion, which fixed the borders of a plurality of nations.

15. Hertz, *Nationality*, 146–51; Grosby, *Biblical Ideas of Nationality*, 23.

16. Grosby, *Biblical Ideas of Nationality*, 13.

17. Jacobson, "Assumed Conflict," 485–95.

18. Grosby, *Biblical Ideas of Nationality*, 27. The territory of ancient Israel was understood to have been delimited as sacred territory; its boundaries were sacred (Josh 22 and 24). The Israelites believed that Yahweh lived in the land of Israel—his land (Josh 22:19; Hos 9:3; Isa 14:2; Jer 2:7)—making the land sacred. They also believed that Yahweh, having entered into covenant with the Israelites, lived among the sons of Israel, thereby making the people of Israel holy (Lev 26:11–13; Deut 7:6; 14:2).

19. Speiser, "People," 157–63. Whether or not Speiser is correct, it is important to note that both עַם and גּוֹי were used in such a way that they were indisputably understood by the Israelites to indicate the existence of a collectivity which embraced within itself the smaller collectivities of the מִשְׁפָּחָה, usually translated as "clan." The use of מִשְׁפָּחָה, while often indicating a "clan," may also refer to an entire people (Jer 10:25; Amos 3:1) or to both the "House of Israel" and the "House of Judah" (Jer 33:24). This imprecision is a consequence of the application of the image of being related by blood to collectivities where factually this is not the case. Passages such as 1 Sam 10:19–24 reveal the existence of a family-clan-tribe distinction and ascending hierarchy within the "people" of ancient Israel. See Pedersen, *Israel*, 46–48; Weber, *Ancient Judaism*, 11–12.

Israel as a Nation

Scholars within the field of OT historical criticism do not dispute whether Israel was a nation, but *when* Israel became a nation.[20] Mario Liverani surmises that Israel became a nation during the Iron Age, since "national" identification was historically possible during this period.[21] Nations linked individuals together based on tribal kinship, common language, common traditions, common territory, and the common worship of a tribal god. Israelite nationality (including land and kingship) was something projected in the past and in the future, even while undergoing a state of crisis.[22] According to Julius Wellhausen, although Israel existed as a nation before its conquest, Israel needed to reestablish their national identity by recapturing their land and kingship, which they had lost in the past.[23] Albrecht Alt believes that Israel viewed themselves as a nation even before the founding of the united monarchy of David and Solomon. He thinks that the territorial unification of the whole of Palestine under David and Solomon represented a change from a national to a territorial state of Israel.[24] Liverani, Wellhausen, and Alt agree that Israel's status as a nation was not in jeopardy during periods when they did not possess a land or king. All three concur that in order for Israel to establish themselves as a nation, they had to possess a land and king at some point in time. In the view of these scholars, the ancient Israelites

---

20. "Nation," *ABD*. Mario Liverani writes, "The application of the term 'nation' to political realities in the old periods of history is possible but is always in need of a specific definition in order to avoid the suspect of anachronism. On the other hand, nationalistic trends in past-century Europe were effective in shaping the institutional history of Israel in terms of a search for national unification." See Liverani, *"Nationality and Political Identity,"* 1031; Sasson, "On Choosing Models," 3–24. For the existence of the nation as a pre-Davidic, tribal unity, see Alt, "Settlement of the Israelites," 161–63. For an analysis regarding the existence of Israel as a nation beginning with the reign of David, see Weber, *Ancient Judaism*, 45.

21. Liverani, *Nationality and Political Identity*, 1033.

22. Liverani, *Nationality and Political Identity*, 1036. Liverani interprets the nationality of Israel as a religious community without political elements in the eschatological state. See also Ahlstrom, *Who Were the Israelites?*, 101–18.

23. For the formation of the nation of ancient Israel before the "conquest of Palestine," see Wellhausen, "Israel," 429–32. Liverani observes that in 1 Sam 8, a people (עַם) of Israel was already at hand. The only feature necessary to transform the people into a nation (גּוֹי), was a kingship. See Liverani, *Nationality and Political Identity*, 1034; Speiser, "People," 157–63.

24. Grosby, *Biblical Ideas of Nationality*, 52.

viewed themselves as a גּוֹי, whether they were living in their land or in exile waiting to return to their historic homeland.

From an anthropological perspective, one way in which Israel maintained their national identity without possession of their land was through religion. Religion is understood to incorporate customs on a national scale and in sanctioning and standardizing laws.[25] In the absence of a state, religious institutions become the guardians as well as the source of common observance of shared customs and laws and created a strong sense of ethnic cohesion.[26] Grosby notes that a nation's collective consciousness of nationality existed because of the "god of the land," even if the nation did not reside in that land. He believes that one observes the ascendancy of Yahweh as the "god of the land," and his concomitant relationship to the land in Num 35:34.[27] It seems reasonable to conclude that Israel considered themselves as the people of Yahweh because of their shared beliefs in the "god of the land," even when they did not dwell in that land (Ezek 36:12, 20; 37:20–28; Dan 2:37–38).

Another defining trait of a nation is an identifiable ethnic core. The issue of race must be addressed when commenting on ethnicity. Some anthropologists commingle the concept of race and ethnicity. Others, however, such as John Stone and Polly Rizova differentiate race from ethnicity. They perceive that while race and ethnicity sometimes are viewed as overlapping, virtually all modern nations are increasingly multiracial in character.[28] Modern Western states have been built on the basis of a dominant ethnic core, which then incorporated surrounding minority populations. Smith discerns that ethnic minorities retained a sense of their cultural distinctiveness and were treated as sociological minorities even when incorporated in the dominant ethnic core.[29] If race and ethnicity were identical, then it would be difficult for a multiracial nation to retain an identifiable ethnic core.[30] Although a nation can be diverse racially, an identifiable ethnic core usually exists. This is the case with

25. Smith, "Chosen Peoples," 436–56.

26. Smith, Ethno-Symbolism and Nationalism, 51.

27. Grosby, Biblical Ideas of Nationality, 58–59.

28. Stone and Rizova, "Ethnic Enigma," 33.

29. Smith, Nation and Nationalism, 61.

30. There are some who argue that race is a recently invented category correlated with the rise of modernity. For an overview on the modern concept of race, particularly from Immanuel Kant's perspective, see Eze, "Color of Reason," 103–4, and Bernasconi, "Concept of Race," 11–36.

ancient Israel where certain Gentile individuals identified with Israel, but the dominant ethnic group remained Israelite.

Conclusion

The purpose of this chapter was to examine whether an anthropological consensus exists on what distinguishes a nation from an ethnic group. Although several factors form a nation (i.e., common language, common economic life, and psychological makeup), two important characteristics of a nation are a common historical homeland and an identifiable ethnic core. In ancient Israel's case, land united successive generations together and became ingrained into their national identity.[31] This is perhaps why during the Babylonian exile Cyrus's recognition of their homeland mattered most to the Judean exiles.[32] Smith remarks how the Jews, even in their exile, are defined as a nation because they were so focused on returning to their historical homeland.[33]

Several OT passages indicate that Israel viewed themselves as a nation because of their land. For example, in Num 34, one can conclude that by this point in history, Israel believed the following: (1) there was a belief in the existence of a trans-clan/tribal people, namely, Israel; and (2) there was a belief in the existence of a trans-local territory. Israel identified as a nation when they believed that they did not and could not exist without the land because the land was essential for their existence as Israel (Hos 9:17). Without the land promised to them by Yahweh, the chosen people of Israel were "incomplete" (Deut 30:19–20) and would be nothing more than a "byword among all the nations" (1 Kgs 9:6–7).[34]

While a nation can be diverse ethnically, an identifiable ethnic core usually exists. Even though nations may be multicultural and multiethnic, the ethnic minorities of a nation do not redefine the dominant ethnic core. Israel was a clear example of a nation with a dominant ethnic core with ethnic minorities. Individual Gentiles integrated into Israel without redefining the dominant ethnic group. Exodus 12:38 mentions a "mixed multitude" that left Egypt to enter the promised land with Israel. The

31. Interestingly, even Israel's concept of heaven alluded to specific traits from their homeland. See Smith, *Nation and Nationalism*, 29.

32. Smith, *Nation and Nationalism*, 94.

33. Smith, *Ethnic Origins of Nations*, 93.

34. Grosby, *Biblical Ideas of Nationality*, 24.

term "mixed multitude" is a clear reference to foreigners as seen in Neh 13:3; Jer 25:20, 24; 50:37. Daniel Hays writes that "there is a strong argument that Cushites were part of the 'mixed crowd' that came out of Egypt as part of Israel."[35] In Exod 2:15–22, Moses meets and marries a Cushite woman. Ethnic Hittites could be assimilated into Israelite society, as shown by Uriah's Yahwistic name and high rank in David's army.[36] Rahab, a Canaanite, was spared and joined Israel because of her confession and demonstrated love for Yahweh (Josh 2:9–13). Ruth, a Moabite widow, exemplified faith in Yahweh and was listed in Christ's genealogy (Matt 1:5). Clearly, Israel was a nation that included ethnic minorities; however, the inclusion of Gentile individuals never redefined the dominant ethnic core of the nation.

The main debate surrounding the topic of Israel is *when* Israel became a nation. For the purposes of this book, it is sufficient to conclude that at some point Israel moved from an ethnic group to a nation when they identified with a specific land. John Armstrong credits the survival of Israel as a nation to their ethnic ties and territorial connection to their homeland.[37] From an anthropological standpoint, a historic homeland and dominant ethnic core are indispensable for any nation. In the following chapter, I will examine the semantic scope of גּוֹי and its relationship with עַם, מִשְׁפָּחָה, אֻמָּה, and ἔθνος in order to establish defining traits of a nation, according to the canon. I will argue that when the biblical text identifies Israelites and Gentiles, as nations, in the eschatological kingdom, then territorial and ethnic distinctions are implied.

35. Hays, *From Every People*, 68, and Brueggemann, "Book of Exodus," 781.

36. White, "Uriah," 1348.

37. Armstrong, *Nations before Nationalism*, 120. Anthony Smith comments that a nation's shared history, which can be built on territorial or ethnic ties, unites successive generations to their national identity. He writes, "*Ethnie* are nothing if not historical communities built up on shared memories. A sense of common history unites successive generations, each with its set of experiences which are added to the common stock, and it also defines a population in terms of experienced temporal sequences, which convey to later generations the historicity of their own experiences." See Smith, *Ethnic Origins*, 25. Kohn observes how a sense of common nationality is ingrained in America and less developed in societies like Poland, Norway, and Ireland. See Kohn, *American Nationalism*.

2

Defining a Nation

Biblical Perspective

THE FIELD OF ANTHROPOLOGY revealed that the two defining traits of a nation are a historic homeland and an identifiable ethnic core. The difficulty of defining a nation, from Scripture, is that a precise definition does not exist. Howe argues that the biblical concept of a nation includes political identification, social interests, and geographical considerations.[1] Andreas Köstenberger includes other traits, such as ethnicity, language, religion, and history.[2] Ronald Clements highlights ethnicity, government, and territory as contributing toward a comprehensive picture of a nation.[3] Undoubtedly, differing opinions exist on which traits are necessary for categorizing a people group as a nation. However, after examining the contextual uses of גּוֹי and its relationship with עַם, מִשְׁפָּחָה, אֻמָּה, and ἔθνος, there are several observations that provide insight on what defines a nation, biblically, and the nature of the eschatological kingdom.

1. Howe, "Nations," 2:1527. Allen Myers adds that "nations" are also bonded by geographical considerations. See Myers, *Eerdmans Bible Dictionary*, 750.

2. Köstenberger, "Nations," 676. Bernhard Anderson adds that religious devotion (more than territory, language, and kinship) is fundamental in binding Israel as a people. See Anderson, *Contours of Old Testament Theology*, 74. All of these different elements show that "nations" are not simply clans or families, but an entity that includes different rudiments such as land and political structure.

3. Clements, "גּוֹי," 428.

Overview of גּוֹי, עַם, מִשְׁפָּחָה, אֻמָּה, and ἔθνος

In the ESV translation, the Hebrew word גּוֹי is most frequently translated as "nation."[4] It appears 570 times and is translated as "nation" 559 of those times. The other 11 times it is translated as "people" or "kind."[5] The word גּוֹי appears 306 times in Psalms, Isaiah, Jeremiah, and Ezekiel with many of those instances referring to nations in the eschatological kingdom.[6]

The word עַם appears 1,860 times in the OT and is often translated as "people" or "clan."[7] There are two instances when עַם and גּוֹי appear together (Exod 33:13; Deut 4:6). In both contexts, Moses is declaring how Israel is God's covenant people and are expected to obey his law. Peter Gentry notes that the term עַם is reserved for Israel which emphasizes God's covenant relationship with them. He writes,

> The word עַם is almost always reserved for Israel. It is a kinship term which expresses effectively the closeness of the family/ marriage relationship between God and Israel established by the covenant made at Sinai (Exod 24). On the other hand, the word גּוֹי is a standard term for the communities or other societies in the world excluding Israel."[8]

When Yahweh highlights his covenant relationship with Israel, he almost exclusively uses the word עַם in contrast to the Gentile גּוֹיִם. Genesis 48:19 displays this contrast: "But his father refused and said, 'I know, my son, I know. He also shall become a people (לְעָם), and he also shall be great. Nevertheless, his younger brother shall be greater than he, and his offspring shall become a multitude of nations'" (מְלֹא־הַגּוֹיִם) (Gen 48:19). Ronald Allen adds that there may be a quantitative difference between גּוֹי

---

4. All further references to translated terms is from the ESV translation, unless otherwise noted.

5. Baumgartner and Richardson, "גּוֹי," 182–83. The OT books where גּוֹי appears the most frequently: Gen (27), Deut (45), Ps (60), Isa (73), Jer (86), and Ezek (87). See Van Groningen, "גּוֹי," 1:153–54; Clements, "גּוֹי," 2:427–28.

6. Peter Gentry writes that "the basic meaning of גּוֹי is an organized community of people having governmental, political, and social structure." Gentry and Wellum, *Kingdom through Covenant*, 243.

7. The primary concentration of the word עַם (singular or plural) is as follows: Exod (175); Jer (165); Isa (130); Ps (119); 2 Chr (112); 1 Sam (110) Deut (107); 2 Sam (102); Num (87); and Josh (70). See Koehler and Baumgartner, "עַם."

8. Gentry and Wellum, *Kingdom through Covenant*, 243.

and עַם. Allen suggest that עַם may refer to a group of people that is larger than a tribe but smaller than a nation and may be translated as "clan."[9]

The word מִשְׁפָּחָה occurs 303 times in the OT and 273 times it is translated as "clan," while 25 times it is translated as "family."[10] In the Table of Nations (Gen 10), גּוֹי and מִשְׁפָּחָה appear together when the sons of Japheth, Ham, and Shem are divided into "clans" (מִשְׁפָּחֹת), "land" (אֶרֶץ), "language" (לָשׁוֹן), and "nations" (גּוֹיִם).[11] Zobel notes that a מִשְׁפָּחָה may denote a portion of a nation but includes more than just the nuclear or extended family.[12]

Several examples within Genesis seem to indicate that מִשְׁפָּחָה emphasizes ethnic ties rather than the territorial aspect of a nation. When God makes a covenant with Abram, in Gen 12:3, he states that through Abram all the families (מִשְׁפָּחֹת) will be blessed. When this promise is re-iterated, in Gen 28:14, God promises that Abraham's offspring will bless all the families (כָּל־מִשְׁפָּחֹת) of the earth. Finally, in Gen 10:32, the clans (מִשְׁפָּחֹת) of the sons of Noah are identified as "nations" (הַגּוֹיִם), who are spread abroad on the earth after the flood, assuming possession of specific territories. These examples seem to indicate that מִשְׁפָּחֹת emphasizes the ethnic characteristic of a nation, while גּוֹי includes a territorial aspect.

The word אֻמָּה appears 7 times throughout the OT with 5 of those occurrences in Psalms.[13] According to Christensen, אֻמָּה describes a smaller unit than מִשְׁפָּחָה, while מִשְׁפָּחָה describes a group of people smaller than a עַם.[14] Also, אֻמָּה seems to emphasize familial/tribal attributes, as seen in Gen 25:16: "These are the sons of Ishmael and these are their names, by their villages and by their encampments, twelve princes according to their tribes (לְאֻמֹּתָם)."

In the NT, the Greek word ἔθνος is translated as "nation."[15] The word ἔθνος appears 163 times within the NT and is translated as "nation" 69 of those times. The other 96 times it is translated as "Gentiles."[16] According

9. Allen, "עַם," 676.

10. The primary concentration of the word מִשְׁפָּחָה (singular or plural) is as follows: Num (159), Josh (47), 1 Chr (19), Gen (12), Zech (11), Jer (9), Judg (8), Exod and 1 Sam (7), and Lev (6). See Baumgartner and Richardson, "מִשְׁפָּחָה," 9:79.

11. Clements, "גּוֹי," 428.

12. Zobel, "מִשְׁפָּחָה," 9:83.

13. Baumgartner and Richardson, "אֻמָּה," 62.

14. Christensen, "אֻמָּה," 1037.

15. Schmidt, "ἔθνος," 2:369; Danker, "λαός," 586; Balz and Schneider, "ἔθνος," 1:382.

16. The primary concentration of ἔθνος is as follows: Matt (15), Luke (13), Acts

to James Scott, ἔθνος can be defined in the following three ways: (1) the nations of the world including Israel; (2) Israel distinguished from the other nations; and (3) individuals of any nation other than Israel.[17] In the Septuagint, ἔθνος appears 1,014 times in the OT. The primary occurrences of the word ἔθνος are in prophetic passages about the eschatological kingdom and in these passages it is used synonymously with גּוֹי.[18]

There seems to be a different emphasis communicated when the words עַם, מִשְׁפָּחָה, or אֻמָּה are employed (i.e., covenant relationship, ethnicity, and tribal).[19] Also, the size of a group may determine which word is used. While עַם, מִשְׁפָּחָה, or אֻמָּה can denote a nation, they usually refer to smaller independent units within a nation. The smallest unit is אֻמָּה, followed by מִשְׁפָּחָה, then עַם. All three words function as subsets to גּוֹי and can include territorial affiliation and ethnic ties. If these two traits can be inferred from the words עַם, מִשְׁפָּחָה, or אֻמָּה, then these traits should also apply to a גּוֹי.[20]

Contextual Uses of גּוֹי

I will categorize the different contextual uses of גּוֹי in order to provide different insights regarding the nature of the eschatological kingdom. First, there are instances when גּוֹי and עַם are used interchangeably when referring to Israel. In Exod 33:13, when Moses speaks to Yahweh, he

---

(43), Rom (29), and Rev (23).

17. Scott, *Paul and the Nations*, 59–60. Of Paul's 45 uses of ἔθνος, 30 percent occur with OT citations.

18. The word ἔθνος (singular or plural) appears in the Septuagint as followed: Gen (37); Exod (16); Lev (12); Num (10); Deut (76); Josh (12); Judg (15); 1 Kgs(2); 2 Kgs (4); 3 Kgs (3); 4 Kgs (18); 1 Chr (11); 2 Chr (14); 1 Esd (22); 2 Esd (10); Esth (29); Jdt (9); Tob (20); 1 Macc (84); 2 Macc (25); 3 Macc (15); 4 Macc (17); Ps (77); Ods (12); Prov (11); Job (5); Wis (9); Sir (25); Song (22); Hos (3); Amos (4); Mic (11); Joel (11); Obad (4); Nah (3); Hab (7); Zeph (5); Hag (4); Zech (17); Mal (6); Isa (73); Jer (86); Bar (7); Lam (7); Lam (3); Ezek (87); Dan (29). For all ἔθνος listed the data were retrieved by performing electronic searches on Rahlf's Septuagint using Logos Bible Software, version 4. λαός occurs only eight times and four of those instances are used synonymously with ἔθνος. Four times the word appears in Revelation within the formula, "nations, tongues, and tribes," reminiscent of Gen 10 and Dan 3:4–7. See Christensen, *ABD*, 1037.

19. The word עַם highlights Yahweh's covenantal relationship with Israel, while מִשְׁפָּחָה stresses ethnic ties and אֻמָּה emphasizes kinship within a nation.

20. Although different ethnicities may exist within a nation and land boundaries may shift over time, nations in both the OT and NT appear to have dominant ethnic cores and particular territorial locations.

refers to Israel as a nation (הַגּוֹי), who is God's people (עַמְּךָ). In Deut 4:6, Moses states that when Israel chooses to obey God's laws, Gentile nations will witness their wisdom and call them a "great nation" (הַגּוֹי) and an "understanding people" (עַם־חָכָם). When David prays to Yahweh, in 2 Sam 7:23, he refers to Israel as "your people" (כְעַמְּךָ) and "nation" (גּוֹי), whom God redeemed from Egypt in order to make a name for himself. Clements notes that although גּוֹי and עַם can be used synonymously, there is a tendency for גּוֹי to "describe a people in terms of its political and territorial affiliation," while עַם retains a "strong emphasis on the element of consanguinity as the basis of union into a people."[21] For Israel, their identity as God's people (עַם) does not negate the fact that they continue to exist as a particular nation (גּוֹי).

Second, every time the Abrahamic covenant is repeated after Gen 12:1–2, Gentiles are identified as גּוֹיִם rather than מִשְׁפָּחוֹת. This seems to reinforce the idea that God intends to build a multinational kingdom through the Abrahamic covenant rather than a kingdom comprised of individuals or multiple "families" (מִשְׁפָּחוֹת). In Gen 18:18, God labels Abraham's offspring as a mighty "nation" (לְגוֹי) and those who will be blessed through him as "nations" (גּוֹיֵי). The Abrahamic covenant blessings will be mediated through Abraham's offspring to the nations. This is repeated, in Gen 22:18 and Gen 26:4, when God reiterates that through Abraham's offspring all the "nations" (גּוֹיֵי) of the earth will be blessed. Finally, in Gen 46:3, God reassures Israel to bring his family to Egypt to meet Joseph by stating the following: "Do not be afraid to go down to Egypt, for there I will make you into a great nation (כִּי־לְגוֹי)." Israel continues to be identified as a "great nation" who will eventually bless the other nations of the world, as God promised repeatedly throughout Genesis after introducing the Abrahamic covenant in Gen 12:3.

Third, there is a connection between the land (אֶרֶץ) God promised Abraham's descendant and their status as a nation (גּוֹי). It accords with the anthropological view that a nation must possess a historic homeland. God promised a specific territory to Israel, in Deut 4:38, by declaring that he will drive out nations (גּוֹיִם) in order to give Israel their land (אֶת־אַרְצָם) as an inheritance. This promise is repeated in Deut 7:1 and Deut 11:23–25 when God promises to bring Israel into the land (אֶל־הָאָרֶץ) by clearing away many nations (גּוֹיִם־רַבִּים), such as the Hittites, the Girgashites, the Amorites, the Canaanites, the Perizzites, the Hivites, and the Jebusites. It

---

21. Clements, "גּוֹי," 427.

was considered typical during the time of ancient Israel for every גּוֹי to possess a territory of its own (Isa 36:18–20; Ps 105:44; 2 Chr 32:13). Israel still considered itself a גּוֹי even before it possessed land (Exod 19:6). Nevertheless, as an עַם or a מִשְׁפָּחָה, Israel could remain the people of Yahweh but hoped to recover once again the status of a גּוֹי with the recovery of its land.[22]

Fourth, king (מֶלֶךְ) or kingdom (מַמְלָכָה) is closely associated with a גּוֹי. Within the OT canon, both Israel and Gentile nations possess a מֶלֶךְ, which would indicate that a political structure is part and parcel to a גּוֹי. When God repeats the conditions of the Abrahamic covenant, in Gen 17:6 and Gen 35:11, he promises that "nations" (לְגוֹיִם) and "kings" (וּמְלָכִים) will come from Abraham. In Exod 19:6, God declares to Moses that if Israel keeps his covenant, he will make them into a kingdom (מַמְלֶכֶת) of priests and a holy nation (וְגוֹי), highlighting an association between the concept of a "kingdom" and "nation." Later in Deut 17:14–15, Moses explains that when Israel enters their land (אֶל־הָאָרֶץ) and desires to have a king (מֶלֶךְ), God will choose one for them.

Fifth, God identifies Israel as a גּוֹי when delineating blessings or curses for them according to his covenant stipulations. In Deut 28:1, God informs Israel that if they obey his commandments, he will set them "high above all the nations (כָּל־גּוֹיֵי) of the earth." However, if Israel disobeys God's covenant, Lev 26:33 states that God will scatter Israel among the nations (בַגּוֹיִם) and cause their land (אַרְצְכֶם) to become a desolation. Interestingly, even when Israel becomes exiled from their land, God continually identifies them as a nation because of his promise that they will eventually repossess their land.

Sixth, prophecies about the eschatological kingdom identify both Israel and Gentiles as גּוֹיִם, as opposed to מִשְׁפָּחֹת. Regarding future judgment on nations, God identifies both Israelites and Gentiles as "nations." In Zech 14:16–19, God declares that he will punish all families (מִשְׁפָּחֹת) (who are later called גּוֹיִם in v. 19) who do not go to Jerusalem to observe the Feast of Booths. In Jer 9:25–26, God declares that he will punish all nations (כָּל־הַגּוֹיִם) who are circumcised merely in the flesh, which includes Egypt, Judah, Edom, Ammon, Moab, and Israel.

Regarding Israel's future restoration in the eschatological kingdom, Isa 11:12 depicts the Davidic king as the agent who will gather the "banished of Israel" and the "dispersed of Judah" to Jerusalem by raising a signal to the nations (לַגּוֹיִם). Later in Isa 49:22, Yahweh declares that he will

---

22. Clements, "גּוֹי," 433.

lift up his hand "to the nations" (אֶל־גּוֹיִם) as a signal in order to bring the "sons and daughters" of Israel to Zion. Jeremiah 31:10 repeats this promise by describing the Lord telling the nations (גּוֹיִם) that he will gather Israel as a "shepherd keeps his flock." When Jer 31 introduces the New covenant, God compares the certainty of his promise to restore Israel as a nation, in Jer 31:36, to the fixed order of creation: "If this fixed order departs from before me, declares the Lord, then shall the offspring of Israel cease from being a nation (גּוֹי) before me forever." Undoubtedly, God promises a future restoration of Israel such that they would be identified as a nation (גּוֹי) in his eschatological kingdom.

Regarding Gentiles in the eschatological kingdom, they are identified as nations who will receive blessings via the Davidic king. The Davidic king will function as a light for the nations (גּוֹיִם), according to Isa 42:6. God promises to make Jerusalem "known among the nations" (בַּגּוֹיִם), in Isa 61:9, which affirms God's earlier promise that Jerusalem will "eat the wealth of the nations" (גּוֹיִם), which is seen with foreigners serving as shepherds, plowmen, and vinedressers in Jerusalem. It is the nations (בַּגּוֹיִם) who will see Jerusalem's righteousness and glory, according to Isa 62:2, which echoes the picture from Isa 2:2, where "all the nations" (כָּל־הַגּוֹיִם) will travel to Jerusalem in order to worship Yahweh. The reason why Jerusalem is featured prominently in the eschatological kingdom is because this city will function as the "throne of the Lord," where all nations (כָּל־הַגּוֹיִם) will see the Davidic king, as Jer 3:17 states. It is this city that will be a source of joy, praise, and glory to all the nations (גּוֹיֵי) of the earth because of what God will do through the Davidic king from there for them, according to Jer 33:9. In sum, if the language describing the eschatological kingdom identifies both Israelites and Gentiles as גּוֹיִם, then it seems that a multinational kingdom is envisioned.

Conclusion

The purpose of this chapter was to present observations about the biblical conception of a nation by examining the contextual uses of גּוֹי and its relationship with עַם, מִשְׁפָּחָה, אֻמָּה and ἔθνος. First, גּוֹי and עַם can be used interchangeably. When both words appear together, they may be emphasizing different attributes of a nation. As Clements notes, גּוֹי usually highlights political and territorial attributes of a people and עַם the common ancestry.[23] However, the use of עַם, particularly when referring to Israel, does not preclude Israel's status as a גּוֹי. Second, when the Abrahamic covenant is repeated after Gen 12:1–2, Gentiles are described as גּוֹיִם rather than מִשְׁפָּחוֹת. This seems to indicate that the kingdom predicted in the Abrahamic covenant will be fulfilled in a multinational paradigm. Third, God's promise of a future land (אֶרֶץ) for Israel is so certain that he refers to Israel as a גּוֹי, even before they occupied it. Also, the Gentile nations who dwell in the promised land are called גּוֹיִם, which highlights the importance of land (אֶרֶץ) to the identity of a nation. Fourth, מֶלֶךְ or מַמְלָכָה frequently appear with גּוֹי. The fact that Israel continually sought to legitimize their standing as a גּוֹי by seeking both a land and king (1 Sam 8) lends credibility to this observation. Fifth, God refers to Israel as a גּוֹי when delineating his covenant stipulations for them, regardless if he promises blessings or curses. Sixth, on a consistent basis, the word גּוֹיִם is used to describe both Israelites and Gentiles in the eschatological kingdom. This seems to indicate that the eschatological kingdom, as promised in the Abrahamic covenant, will consummate with a multinational kingdom rather than one comprised simply of individuals or "families" (מִשְׁפָּחוֹת). In the following chapter, I will examine Gen 10–12 in order to elucidate the intended relationship God promised, in the Abrahamic covenant, between Israel and Gentiles nations in the eschatological kingdom.

---

23. Clements, "גּוֹי," 427.

3

Foundation for a Multinational Kingdom

Genesis 10–12

NATIONS ARE FIRST INTRODUCED, canonically, in Gen 10–12. These three chapters provide a biblical foundation for a multinational kingdom, specifically with the introduction of the Abrahamic covenant. I will explore three important topics from Gen 10–12: (1) The Table of Nations in Gen 10; (2) God's positive purpose for the Tower of Babel; and (3) Role of nations in the Abrahamic covenant. Informed by these three theological perspectives, this chapter will seek to demonstrate that God promises to build a multinational kingdom from Gen 10–12.

Genesis 10: Definition of a Nation

Immediately following the Table of Nations, Babel explains how different nations were formed. Following the narrative of Babel, Abraham becomes the primary focus regarding God's redemptive plan for all nations. God's interaction with nations throughout the OT happened as a result of God's dealing with Abraham and his offspring. Thus, it becomes important to interpret Gen 10–12 in order to formulate a foundation for a multinational kingdom within the canonical narrative.

The genealogies in Gen 10 are listed according to the three sons of Noah. They may also be categorized into three different spheres: domestic, political, and religious.[1] Hays uses this paradigm to support the notion

---

1. Hays, *From Every People*, 57–58. Hays defines "domestic" as encompassing the

that Gen 10 functions not only to provide a list of genealogies, but also to present the defining characteristics of a nation. He highlights four of them in Gen 10: מִשְׁפָּחָה (family), לָשׁוֹן (language), אֶרֶץ (land), and גּוֹי (nation). These four elements are echoed in the Abrahamic covenant when Abraham is commanded to leave his land (אֶרֶץ) to become a great nation (גּוֹי) in order to bless all the families (מִשְׁפָּחָה) of the earth. Hays posits that Rev 5–7 also echoes these four elements with "families" appearing in 5:9 and "nations" in 7:9.[2] These four elements (family, language, land, nation) may also reveal how a "family" develops into a "nation" through a common language and land.

Within Gen 10, there appears to be a connection between land and government structure. The Table of Nations ends all three genealogies with גּוֹי (Gen 10:20, 31) to indicate the political and national affiliations as the primary emphasis.[3] Von Rad states that the "Table of Nations is not according to race or language [alone], but politically and historically structured as distinct from one another."[4] He seems to support the interpretation that a nation is more than simply a people with common ethnicity or language, but also includes a political structure. Jeffrey Rogers takes it a step further by arguing that the political and national affiliations are linked together primarily with the concept of land.[5] This would be consistent with anthropological studies on nations, which affirm that a historic homeland is part and parcel to any nation. In Rogers's words, Gen 10 engages in "ethnography by political geography rather than by

---

biological, economic, and geographical aspects. Hays is responding to two other interpretations of Gen 10: (1) three sons of Noah as heading three major races of mankind; and (2) widespread influence of black people in ANE. Westermann argues that Gen 10:5 shows that a nation is more than a "mere conglomeration of persons." He includes ethnicity, language, land, and political structure as basic characteristics of a nation. See Westermann, *Genesis 1–11*, 509.

2. Hays, *From Every People*, 198–99.

3. James Scott argues that Gen 10 divides descendants according to their "tongues in their countries and in their nations" (Gen 10:5, 20, 31). He connects Gen 10 with the Abrahamic covenant showing that the importance of the land for Israel is intricately connected with the definition of a nation from Gen 10. See Scott, *Paul and the Nations*, 61–62.

4. Rad, *Genesis*, 140.

5. Jeffrey Rogers states that an important clue to the nature of Gen 10 is the connection between land and nations. See Rogers, "Table of Nations," 1271.

ethnic origins."[6] The Table of Nations does not simply list ethnic groups, but nations defined by common territory and possibly political structure.

Canonical Uses of Genesis 10

The theological question in Gen 10 centers on whether the Table of Nations functions as the backdrop to Israel's history or to primeval world history. Claus Westermann highlights this important issue:

> Basic to the theological understanding of the Table of Nations is the question of whether its real thrust is in the line of salvation history [i.e., Israel's history] or of a universal history seen in a theological context.[7]

There are two interpretations for the Table of Nations. Either it serves as context for the salvation history of Israel (in Gen 12), or it provides the world salvation history (Israel and Gentile nations). Andreas Köstenberger writes, "Contrary to Israel's perception of Abraham as their [exclusive] ancestor, the Table of Nations places [Abraham's] call within the context of world history."[8] He prefers the latter option and this interpretation seems to better synthesize the canonical uses of Gen 10.

Genesis 10 exerts a strong influence on the rest of the canon. There are three primary applications of Gen 10. First, Gen 10 provides the

6. Rogers, "Table of Nations," 1271.

7. Westermann, *Genesis 1–11*, 528. Von Rad views Gen 10 as the extremely complex reality in which Israel found itself as representative of God's creation. Von Rad interprets Gen 10 as simply the context providing the salvation history for Israel, meaning that the emphasis on OT narrative is on Israel's salvation history. Baker categorizes von Rad as the "one salvation history" view. This means that von Rad views the one salvation history as the "canonical" saving history presented and developed in Israel's history. See Rad, *Genesis*, 148; Baker, *Two Testaments*, 140.

8. Abraham will be a father to many nations (Gen 17:4–6) and a blessing to "all families on the earth" (Gen 12:3; 18:18; 22:18; 26:4; 28:14). God's treatment of Israel served as a public display to the nations of his character. His laws revealed his wisdom (Deut 4:6); the exodus displays his power (Lev 26:45); Israel's election displays his faithful love (Deut 7:7–9); his discipline of Israel displays his holiness (Deut 8:20); and his universal offer of salvation displays his righteousness to the nations (Ps 98:2; Isa 62:2). Köstenberger notes how the nations are an important factor in Israel's history and should not be neglected. See Köstenberger, "Nations," 676–77. Scott argues that the Table of Nations serve to show that God's plan with Abraham, in Gen 12, has all the nations in mind. He notes that the Table of Nations is not only a description of the past (Gen 10), but of the present (1 Chr 1:1—2:2) and eschatological future (Ezek 38–39). See Scott, *Paul and the Nations*, 9–11.

geographical organization of nations. Scott notes how the genealogies in Gen 10 are repeated in 1 Chronicles and lists the nations of the world "in a circle."[9] The nations move counterclockwise from the north, to the west, to the south, to the east, with Israel in the center. This concept seems to be alluded to in Ezek 5:5 when Jerusalem is seen as the "center of the earth." Acts describes Paul's missionary route coinciding with this organization, which places Jerusalem at the center of the world. Also, in Rom 15:19, the result of Paul's Spirit-empowered ministry to the nations is given. Paul's progress in the process of stimulating the full number of nations begins from "Jerusalem to Illyricum," showing the same geographical pattern of Jerusalem in the center followed by a counterclockwise movement to the East.[10]

Second, the number of nations listed from Gen 10 seems to represent the totality of mankind. The seventy-two nations listed in the Table of Nations are referred to in the NT. In Luke 10, when Jesus appoints seventy-two workers to preach the gospel, some have argued that the number refers to the seventy-two nations listed in Gen 10.[11] In Rom 11:25 when Paul refers to the "full number of the nations," this expectation is probably based on the nations from Deut 32:8, which echoes the nations listed in Gen 10.

Third, the four attributes listed in Gen 10 (families, language, land, and nation) is alluded to in the NT. In Acts 2, James Scott contends that the Jews in Acts 2:5–11 are listed similarly to the nations in Isa 66 and Gen 10 (according to families, language, land, and nations).[12] The canonical uses of Gen 10 seem to indicate that the Table of Nations serves as a backdrop to the salvation history of all nations rather than Israel's alone.

9. Scott writes that the Table of Nations influenced the geographical view of the world in other Jewish literature. For example, *Jubilee* alludes to the same break up of geography as the Table of Nations. The Jubilee world map from *Jubilee* 8–9 is an exposition of Gen 10. *Jubilee* further emphasizes the position of Zion as the God-ordained center of the world, as seen in 1 Chr 1, where there is an "Israel-centric" makeup. Scott, *Paul and the Nations*, 192.

10. Scott, *Paul and the Nations*, 136.

11. Scott, *Paul and the Nations*, 168. Scott also observes how Luke foreshadows the mission for the church to the nations that unfolds in Acts (Acts 1:26; 2:5) with Jesus' seventy-two workers.

12. Hays argues that the overall theme of Gen 10–12 (blessing for the nations) affects the interpretation of Acts 2:5–11. Instead of the reading of Acts 2 as the "reversal" of Babel, Hays prefers the argument that the theme of God's blessing for all the nations is reiterated from Gen 10–12. See Hays, *From Every People*, 165.

Genesis 11: Positive Purpose for Nations

The Tower of Babel is intricately connected with the Table of Nations and explains the purpose of nations. Von Rad writes:

> The story of mankind's dispersion into many nations actually begins once again where the Table of Nations began and is to some extent parallel with it; for it too seeks to explain humanity's division into many nations. The chapters must be read together, because they are intentionally placed next to each other in spite of their antagonism. The multitude of nations indicates not only the manifold quality of God's creative power but also a judgment. The disorder in the international world was not willed by God but is punishment for the sinful rebellion against God.[13]

There is tension between Gen 10 and 11 in explaining the reason for different nations. On the one hand, Gen 11 gives a picture of man's hubris and rebellion with God's response of judgment. On the other hand, Gen 10 gives a neutral account that seems to contradict the Babel narrative. Gordan Wenham argues that Gen 10 and 11 may appear contradictory but are united under the same תּוֹלְדוֹת. In other words, they are to be read together to understand the purpose of nations.[14] When God chooses Abraham to become the vehicle of blessing to all the *other* nations, this discloses the purpose of the judgment that resulted from Babel. One must carefully examine the Babel narrative to resolve the tension between Gen 10 and 11.

Overview of Genesis 11:1–9

The proper interpretation of Babel begins with a proper understanding of God's desire for Adam and Eve. After he creates mankind, God gives his first command in Gen 1:28: "Be fruitful and multiply and fill the earth." The mandate that God gives is reiterated after God destroyed the world with the flood. After God gave his covenant to Noah, he commands him to "be fruitful and multiply" in Gen 9:1. This shows that God's plan for mankind to fill the earth still needed to be fulfilled at the time of Babel and it is with this understanding that the narrative of Babel comes into focus.

---

13. Rad, *Genesis*, 152.
14. Wenham, *Exploring the Old Testament*, 32.

Genesis 11:1–9 is the final narrative of the primeval events that prepare the way for the introduction of Abraham by means of Shem's genealogy (Gen 11:10–26). This narrative must be seen within the primeval events collectively in the backdrop. The Table of Nations, in Gen 10, paints a basically positive, or at least neutral, picture of the relationships between the nations. However, the shorter narrative of the Tower of Babel, in Gen 11, sheds light to Gen 10 in showing the event that brought forth the Table of Nations. Just as Gen 2 explains in detail the creation account from Gen 1, Gen 11 describes in detail the creation of the nations listed in Gen 10.

Grüneberg states that the placement of Gen 10 before the Tower of Babel suggests that nations are not intrinsically sinful.[15] David Clines supports this assertion by stating the following:

> If the material of Gen 10 had followed the Babel story, the whole Table of Nations would have had to be read under the sign of judgment; but where it stands it functions as the fulfillment of the divine command of Gen 9:1 . . . which looks back in its turn to Gen 1:28.[16]

Bernhard Anderson also observes that the theme of Babel is the blessing of national diversity given at creation (Gen 1:28) and renewed in the new creation after the flood (Gen 9:1, 7). Anderson views Babel not as simply "a failure and punishment, but of God's intended will for the diversity of nations from creation."[17]

Although Gen 11:1–9 gives a picture of God's judgment on human pride, it does not mean that the result of different nations is intrinsically sinful. The attempt of the Babelites to transgress human limits is reminiscent of Eve's ambition in Gen 3. As in the tower story, the divine plural also appears in the garden account (Gen 3:22), and both indicate the divine distress over the potential havoc that the new knowledge achieved by mankind may bring (Gen 3:22; 11:6).[18] Before Babel the human race was united, but after Babel it became divided. This so-called unity is to be seen, first of all, in the use of the adjective "one" for modifying three different nouns: "one (same)" speech, "one (same)" word, and "one

15. Grüneberg, *Abraham, Blessing and the Nations*, 129.

16. Clines, *Theme of the Pentateuch*, 74; Clines, "Genesis 1–11," 499–502.

17. Anderson, *From Creation to New Creation*, 167–76.

18. Mathews, *Genesis 1–11:26*, 467; Reyburn and Fry, *Handbook on Genesis*, 248–59.

(whole)" people (Gen 11:1).[19] This desire for unity is an act of mankind arrogating to himself divine prerogatives: building a tower to make a *name* for themselves. And it is in Babel that the Lord confuses human speech, so that all the descendants of Noah can no longer live together and are forced to fulfill God's intention to "scatter" and "fill" the earth.[20]

Hermeneutical Observations from Genesis 11:1–9

There are several hermeneutical observations that clarify the relationship between God's judgment and providence in this narrative. First, Gen 11 shows how the Table of Nations resulted from God's intervention. Previously, God had commanded Noah and his family in Gen 9:1 to "be fruitful and multiply, and fill the earth," but in Gen 11 the people have "settled" in the land. This is not incidental since "settled" is an antonym of the narrative's key idea of "scattering" and opposes the divine command directed to Noah and his offspring to "fill the earth" (Gen 9:1).[21] The disobedience of men to scatter brings God's intervention to fulfill his command and purpose of "filling the earth."

Second, God's intervening act was punitive. Mankind built the tower to "make a name," which shows the builders' ambition for autonomy from God. Instead of submitting to the "name" of God, they desire to make their own "name."[22] Von Rad writes, "[Babel] arises as a sign of

19. Grieve, "Origin of Languages," 16. Genesis 11:1 clearly lays out the idea that all of civilization is united with one language and one people. The phrase "the whole earth," or literally "all the earth," points to all the inhabitants of the earth collectively. This phrase forms an inclusio with the end of this narrative, which has the same phrase in Gen 11:9. This nuance of inclusiveness dominates the narrative as shown by the comparable phrase "over the face of the whole earth" in vv. 4, 8–9. See Wenham, *Genesis 1–15*, 238; Mathews, *Genesis*, 477.

20. Wenham, *Genesis 1–15*, 242. Westermann's commentary overviews the purpose of Babel as the diversity of nations. See Westermann, *Genesis 1–11*, 531–57.

21. Wenham, *Genesis 1–15*, 239. The word "settled" shows that the Noahic descendants had taken up permanent residence. This same phrase occurs once more in Genesis where Abram's family makes its home in Haran after migrating from Ur (Gen 11:31). There is also a connection between Gen 11 and 12 where Abraham's obedience to God's command to "leave" his family residence and to "go" to an undesignated land sharply contrasts with the Babelites' resolution to "settle." It was thereby Abraham's willingness to depart the "land of Shinar" that resulted in the salvation of the stubborn people who had earlier refused to "scatter."

22. Baze, "Dispensational Model," 248. Wenham points out that the Babelites' motive, to "make a name," was in direct violation of God's will expressed to Noah and his

their valiant self-reliance, the tower as a sign of their will to fame. Their joy in their inventiveness."[23] To erect a citadel was not in itself so great a crime, but to raise an eternal monument showed headstrong pride as well as contempt for God. In Gen 11:6, God interprets the Babelites' action of building as being a logical outgrowth of the unanimity of sin.[24] God confuses or "confounds together" their language with a purpose: "so that one could not understand another" (Gen 11:7).[25] God's ultimate goal was to disperse rebellious humanity. What human beings were trying to achieve in their arrogance was doomed ultimately to frustration and failure.[26]

Third, God's intervening act was also preventative. The themes previously found in Gen 1–11 illustrate the punitive/preventative pattern. For example, the expulsion from the garden, in Gen 3:22–23, and the limitation of life spans in Gen 6:3 may be preventative as much as punitive. God intervened to prevent the continued spread of the corruption of mankind. Likewise, the confusion of language in Gen 11:7 is necessary to prevent humans from uniting to rival God and their dispersal may be more an enforced fulfillment of the divine mandate than a punishment.[27] Von Rad notes that "God resolves upon a punitive, but at the same time preventive act so that he will not have to punish man more severely as his

---

family after the flood: "Be fruitful and multiply and fill the earth." God's response to human pride in this narrative again echoes the narrative from the garden. Since Adam and Eve ate from the tree of knowledge, the next natural step would have been for them to eat from the tree of life. Since the Babelites were building the tower, an egotistical undertaking in itself, this could also lead to further trespass on the divine prerogatives: "nothing they plot" will "be beyond them" (v. 6). The Hebrew phrase for "be beyond them" is used in only one other passage in the Old Testament, Job 42:2. That verse is about Job confessing before God about his character, and more specifically about his providence. Wenham suggests that this parallel shows that the Babelites are attempting to emulate their creator in his sovereignty. See Wenham, *Genesis 1–15*, 240.

23. Rad, *Genesis*, 148.

24. "Behold, they are one people, and they have all the same language. And this is what they began to do, and now nothing which they purpose to do will be impossible for them" (v. 6). See Grieve, "Origin of Languages," 16.

25. Gesenius, "בָּלַל," 123. Westermann argues that the motif of confusing languages in the narrative is amalgamated with the dispersion of humanity. See Westermann, *Genesis*, 535.

26. There is irony when God says to Abraham, "*I* will make *your* name great" (Gen 12:2). The interplay between Gen 11 and 12 shows that it is only by God's providence that one's "name" can become great. God granted to Abraham the very thing that the Babelites were trying to achieve: a great name.

27. Grüneberg, *Abraham, Blessing and the Nations*, 133.

degeneration surely progresses."[28] Christopher Wright displays how Gen 12 resulted from God's gracious intervention in Gen 11:

> What can God do next after Babel? Something that only God could have thought of. He sees an elderly, childless couple in the land of Babel and decides to make them the fountainhead, the launch pad of his whole mission of cosmic redemption.[29]

Theological Implications from Genesis 11:1–9

How one interprets Babel affects one's understanding on the purpose of nations. Dumbrell writes: "The effects of Babel include all the tensions which affect our modern world, the ethnic, linguistic, social and cultural are erected as a divine reaction to man's search for the center of his world within himself and his society."[30] Some have interpreted nations as a product of sin, and von Rad even argues that culture is "rebellion against God."[31] Based on this assumption there is a need to "reverse" the effects of Babel by uniting all nations into one people through the Abrahamic covenant.[32] However, the reconciliation between God's providence over Babel and man's responsibility in his sin will correct this misconception.

There are two implications that harmonizes the tension between God's providence and judgment in Babel. The first implication is that God's

---

28. Rad, *Genesis*, 149.

29. Wright, *Mission of God*, 199.

30. Dumbrell, *End of the Beginning*, 129–31. Dumbrell writes that modern day frustration to unity is attributed to Babel. "Thus [Babel] begin the social, linguistic, ethnic, and cultural distinctions that have frustrated all efforts at human cooperation since Babel." See Dumbrell, *Faith of Israel*, 27.

31. Rad, *Genesis*, 149.

32. Dumbrell argues that Isa 40–55 shows a renewed city that is a "reversal" of Babel. He writes, "The Jerusalem goal set forth in Isa 40 is to proceed by way of a New Exodus and re-establishing His covenant. . . . Isaiah's notion of Jerusalem is that God will establish a city as a unified political community. The Babel concept of Gen 11 has been reversed." See Dumbrell, *End of the Beginning*, 18–19. Hays claims that the OT prophets picture all peoples worshipping God as a reversal of Gen 10–11 and fulfillment of Gen 12. Hays views Acts 2 as a reversal of Babel which is fully consummated in Revelation when people from every tribe, language, and nation are united. God's redemptive plan, according to Hays, is *to save individuals from all people groups and to reunite them as the people of God.* Hays implies that God's plan is primarily for a redeemed humanity consisting of individuals, rather than national entities, based on his interpretation of Babel. See Hays, *From Every People*, 62–63.

providence included his intervention to scatter the Babelites. The narrative of Babel is reminiscent of the garden episode. In the garden, the issue was the newly acquired knowledge, whereas in Babel, the issue is the desire for power. In both cases, God did not tremble in fear in response to mankind's advances because his providence was never thwarted. Instead it is better understood that God was grieved over the consequences that would fall upon mankind without his merciful intervention. Although God was judging the pride of the Babelites, the results of different nations, languages, and cultures were not a by-product of sin. Ken Davis writes,

> Some have inferred from [Babel] that different nations, language, and culture are purely the result of sin and God's subsequent judgment. A better way of interpreting the Babel incident is to see the people of the earth attempting to *counteract* what they correctly understood to be God's purpose in diversifying and scattering the human race. From the beginning God had been in the process of separating people from one another in order to implement his desire that man should "be fruitful, and multiply, and fill the earth" (Gen 1:28).[33]

The Babel narrative should be viewed as the beginning steps of God's plan to create a multitude of nations for a positive purpose.[34] God's providence does not negate human responsibility of sin, but it allows that the scattering of nations is a part of his intended purpose.[35]

33. Davis, "Biblical Theology of Ethnicity," 102.

34. Westermann traces the motif of languages in Zeph 3:5–11, where the speech of all peoples will be changed to serve Yahweh in one accord. Acts 2:11 bursts the language barriers as well. However, Westermann observes how these verses do not in any way alter the plurality and difference of languages. It corresponds to Babel in that the barriers set to understanding by the variety of languages have also a positive aspect, which serves humanity. See Westermann, *Genesis*, 557.

35. Bruce Ware has tried to explain the tension between God's providence and human responsibility with a form of "compatibilist middle knowledge," meaning that human actions were just "one" of many options that could have happened. According to compatibilist middle knowledge, Babel was one of the many scenarios that could have happened in order for God to accomplish his will. However, compatibilist middle knowledge does not seem like a viable option for Babel. Passages such as Gen 45:4–8, Isa 10:5–19, and Acts 2:23 demonstrate that God's sovereign control must be compatible with the choices and actions that human beings perform, and this must occur in such a way that humans fully carry out their actions and are fully responsible for their sin. It seems better to understand Babel as humankind's sinful action and God's sovereign act to spread humankind across the face of the earth in order to establish nations (cf. Acts 17:26). For an explanation of compatibilist middle knowledge, see Ware, *God's Greater Glory*, 111–19.

The second implication is that God providentially brought about positive results from a negative situation. In the Babelites' eyes, God's intervention in preventing the building of the tower would have been a punishment, but in the larger scheme of God's purposes it was an act of gracious intervention to ensure that humanity would eventually attain the blessing given in the Noahic covenant. Ken Mathews notes that the same "irony" occurs in the scattering of the church (Acts 8), where persecution propelled the church into the Diaspora to accomplish the charge of Jesus from Acts 1:8.[36] Furthermore, Acts 17:26 seems to indicate that God intended to create a diversity of nations, even though it came through a negative event: "And he made from one man every nation of mankind to live on all the face of the earth, having determined allotted periods and the boundaries of their dwelling place." These two theological implications help interpret Gen 10 and 11. The Babel event ultimately resulted in God creating a multitude of nations (as defined in Gen 10) to be blessed through Abraham (Gen 12).

Genesis 12: Abrahamic Covenant as a Multinational Paradigm

Some scholars think that the Abrahamic covenant functions as the solution to address the problem from Babel. For example, Dumbrell states that the Abrahamic covenant is the "Exodus in response to the curses of Babel."[37] He sees the call of Abraham as "[undoing] the punishment from Babel," which causes barriers to human unity.[38] According to Dumbrell, the results from Babel are divisions within the framework of human culture and impossibility of complete human cooperation. Based on his reading of Gen 11, Dumbrell asserts that גוי, in Gen 12, refers to a future world government established by God's kingdom instead of national Israel. He writes: "The focus of גוי in the Abrahamic Covenant is pointing forward to a future governed world seen in Rev 21–22. Babel attempted to establish a world government and its failure led to Abram as the real alternative. From Abram a 'great nation' or new world system will come into being which Israel is simply anticipation."[39] Patriarchal history,

36. Mathews, *Genesis*, 474.

37. Dumbrell, *Covenant and Creation*, 58.

38. Dumbrell, *Covenant and Creation*, 59–63.

39. Dumbrell, *Covenant and Creation*, 66–67.

though, should not be viewed in complete discontinuity with primeval history such that the Abrahamic covenant supposedly reverses the result from Babel. Grüneberg properly responds to Dumbrell's interpretation:

> Unless the Babel episode has altered God's desire to preserve and bless all humanity, [Gen] 12:1–3 can hardly imply a limitation of God's purposes to Abraham and his descendants: it must rather function as a reaffirmation of God's original intentions, even if their outworking is now somewhat altered by the particular place given to this one family (Abraham).[40]

Genesis 12 begins the motion of the redemptive narrative after Babel. The focus shifts from one individual (Abram), then to his מִשְׁפָּחָה, then to a עַם, and finally a גּוֹי. This process shows the development of the concept of nations first recalled from Gen 10.[41] This process of a single family eventually becoming a nation begins with the introduction of the Abrahamic covenant. The Abrahamic covenant can be deconstructed into three primary strands: land, descendants, and blessings for Gentile nations.[42] Anderson also proposes a similar paradigm: perpetual holding of a particular land, numerous descendants, and a special relationship.[43] These three motifs will be analyzed in order to show the intended relationship between Israel and Gentile nations.

Land

The Abrahamic covenant begins with the land motif, which God has prepared for Abraham: "Go forth . . . to the land which I will show you" (Gen 12:1). The land is connected with God's promise, in v. 2, to establish Abraham's offspring as a גּוֹי. Rolf Rendtorff remarks how the land motif is connected with the descendants motif.[44] This promise shows that

---

40. Grüneberg, *Abraham, Blessing and the Nations*, 141.

41. Westermann writes, "The time when a people were coming into being and a state was being formed, the perspective was based on the memory of origin from families and ancestors." See Westermann, *Genesis 12–36*, 23.

42. Wisdom, *Blessing for the Nations*, 18. Genesis 26:4 shows the promise of blessing for the nations confirmed in Isaac. The three strands are present. The land (Gen 26:3–4), descendants (Gen 26:4), and blessing for the nations (Gen 26:4).

43. Anderson, *Contours of Old Testament Theology*, 98.

44. Rolf Rendtorff notes how the covenant (בְּרִית) first appears in Gen 15 and includes God's promise to give Abraham an offspring and land. The same promise is given in Gen 17 where the word בְּרִית appears thirteen times. In Gen 17:1–8, the same twofold

God's plan for Israel will include their occupation of a land in becoming a national entity.[45] The significance of land in the Abrahamic covenant is a reoccurring theme throughout Genesis.[46] The Abrahamic covenant is reiterated to Jacob and includes a promise of land (Gen 28:13), God's protection (Gen 28:15), and a safe return to the land (Gen 28:15).[47] Grüneberg also observes how God's explicit promise of Canaan with its borders, in Gen 13:15, reveal that a *specific* land is promised to Abraham.[48] Both anthropological and biblical concepts of a nation include a homeland, which supports the view that God has a particular land in mind when speaking to Abraham about his future offsprings.

---

content of בְּרִית is explicated from Gen 15: God will make Abraham "the father of a multitude of nations" (vv. 4–6)—and in addition to that will be the God of Abraham and his descendants (vv. 7, 8b); and he will give them the land (v. 8a). See Rendtorff, "Covenant," 391; Rendtorff, *Covenant Formula*. Speiser writes, "Unlike עַם, גּוֹי requires a territorial base, since the concept is a political one." See Speiser, *Genesis*, 86.

45. Merrill argues that land is essential to any meaningful definition of dominion and nationhood. The definition of the land, "from the river of Egypt to the great river, the Euphrates" (15:18), further specifies both its historical and geographical reality and its extent. Canaan thus became the focus of God's redemptive and reigning activity on the earth. This explains why the patriarchs and their Israelite descendants hallowed the land and valued it as a theological *sine qua non*. Testimony to this is the erection of altars at significant sites, places that Yahweh particularly invested with his presence (Gen 12:7; 13:18; 26:25; 33:20; 35:1, 7) See Merrill and Zuck, *Biblical Theology*, 26–30.

46. Jeffrey Wisdom writes: "In [Gen] 13:14–17 the land is to be an eternal gift and is conjoined with the first explicit reference to the image of Abraham's descendants multiplied like the dust of the earth. Again, in Genesis 15 the promise of land is repeated twice (15:7, 8) and is prominent in [Gen] 17:8." See Wisdom, *Blessing for the Nations*, 25.

47. Wisdom, *Blessing for the Nations*, 35.

48. Grüneberg, *Abraham, Blessing and the Nations*, 164. Dumbrell, on the other hand, views the boundaries of the land only as "the ideal" border of the promised land. He argues that Gen 13:15 suggests that Israel is to become the dominant power in the region, and does not specify a specific land to Abraham. He supports his argument with Gen 15:5 and suggests that the promises were not to be exhausted in the fortunes of political Israel. See Dumbrell, *Covenant and Creation*, 50–53. This view is problematic because of the specific dimensions repeated about the land throughout Genesis and the necessary connection a specific homeland has with the definition of a גּוֹי.

Descendants

The descendants motif confirms the Table of Nations' definition of a nation. It is noteworthy that God foretells that Abraham's offspring will become a nation (גּוֹי) rather than simply a people (עַם). Hamilton writes:

> God does not promise to make of Abraham a great people (עַם) Israel will be a (גּוֹי) among the (גּוֹיִם). Abraham is already an עַם simply because he has his nephew Lot. The use of the word גּוֹי in this context adds the special elements of the status and stability of nationhood in a land designated for that purpose. Whereas עַם refers to people or nations in terms of centripetal unity and cohesiveness, גּוֹי is linked with government and territory.[49]

There are political and territorial traits implied in God's promise to make Abraham's offspring into a nation. Abraham's family is to become a political entity, not just an important family.[50] Westermann also believes that גּוֹי is a political concept whereas עַם designates kinship.[51] This seems to indicate that גּוֹי, in this context, shows continuity with the concept of a גּוֹי from Gen 10.

Since this promise is placed in the future, there may be application for both Abraham and national Israel.[52] Mark Carroll observes that both material and spiritual blessings are applied to Abraham and his offsprings throughout the patriarchal narratives. He concludes that the blessings for Israel cannot be dichotomized as either physical or spiritual.[53] Both physical and spiritual blessings are endowed on Abraham and his descendants to show the progression of this second strand.

---

49. Hamilton, *Genesis 1–17*, 371–72.

50. Grüneberg indicates how the word גּוֹי "designates an entity linked together by race, government, and territory while עַם denotes more a gentilic unit." See Grüneberg, *Abraham, Blessing and the Nations*, 163.

51. Westermann, *Genesis*, 149.

52. Williamson notes that a kin's reputation is typically connected to his subjects' greatness. If Abraham is depicted after the model of a king, then the promise of blessing to him could imply Israel's success as well. See Williamson, *Variations on a Theme*, 122–23. Westermann argues that the reason why the sentence "I will bless you" does not stand at the beginning of the covenant is probably due to the overarching function of Gen 12:1–3. The promise is directed to Israel and shows that it goes beyond Abraham. The emphasis is not on God's blessing of Abraham, but to make his descendants a great nation. See Westermann, *Genesis 12–36*, 147.

53. Carroll, "Blessing the Nations," 30.

This pattern is unpacked throughout Genesis to illustrate how Israel becomes a "great nation."[54]

Blessing for all Nations

The third and final strand is the "blessing for all the nations." God's purpose of making Abraham's offspring a "nation" is seen in this strand (v. 3): "And in you all the families (מִשְׁפָּחֹת) of the earth will be blessed." There are two important observations to investigate in this verse. First, it is important to discuss whether the use of מִשְׁפָּחֹת, as opposed to גּוֹיִם, changes the interpretation of this covenant. Dumbrell believes that גּוֹי is attributed to "Israel," referring to a future order uniting mankind under the kingdom of God, in contrast to the מִשְׁפָּחֹת of the world.[55] According to Dumbrell, the heavenly Jerusalem, in Rev 21–22, functions as an image of final political unity to be expressed through a redeemed גּוֹי. He writes, "Though Israel is certainly the nation which the Abrahamic promises have immediately in view, Israel as a nation, as a symbol of divine rule manifested within a political framework, was intended itself to be an image of the shape of final world government, a symbol pointing beyond itself to the reality yet to be."[56] "Israel," for Dumbrell, does not refer to national Israel but to a future final world government. He builds his argument on the assumption that the use of מִשְׁפָּחֹת, in Gen 12:3, contrasts the nations of the world with the "great nation" (גּוֹי) that will come from Abraham.

There are three usages of מִשְׁפָּחָה throughout the canon: (1) denotes a family unit (2 Sam 16:5); (2) denotes a tribal unit (i.e., tribe of Dan in Judg 13:2); or (3) denotes a nation (Jer 33:24; Amos 3:1–2). מִשְׁפָּחֹת is used in Gen 10:5, 18, 20, 31, 32 and clearly denotes large units and perhaps nations. Therefore, מִשְׁפָּחֹת does not inherently exclude the concept of "nations."[57] It is problematic to impose the first definition of מִשְׁפָּחֹת

---

54. Dumbrell interprets the "great nation" eschatologically, meaning that the nation is the company of the redeemed who will fulfill the call to Abram (Rev 5:11). Dumbrell looks to the NT to fulfill his concept of "Israel," which failed to be realized in the OT. See Dumbrell, *Faith of Israel*, 28.

55. Dumbrell, *End of the Beginning*, 125.

56. Dumbrell, *Covenant and Creation*, 66–67.

57. Grüneberg, *Abraham, Blessing and the Nations*, 185. מִשְׁפָּחָה was previously seen in the Table of Nations. "From these the coastlands of the nations were separated into their lands, every one according to his language, according to their families (מִשְׁפָּחָה) into their nations (גּוֹיִם)" (Gen 10:5). This shows that מִשְׁפָּחָה is intricately

in Gen 12:2 without synthesizing the other definitions of מִשְׁפָּחוֹת within Genesis. In fact, Gen 18:18 alludes to the Abrahamic covenant and uses the word גּוֹיִם in place of מִשְׁפָּחוֹת when commenting on the recipients of the Abrahamic covenant blessings from Gen 12:3. Also, the term גּוֹי never refers to a worldwide kingdom throughout the OT canon. A גּוֹי refers to a group of people who are a subset of the world's population but not to the entire human population of the world within the canon of Scripture. Dumbrell makes an unfounded argument by proposing that גּוֹי refers to a worldwide kingdom since his definition is disconnected in meaning from its standard usage within the canon.

Second, it is important to appropriately interpret the phrase "will be blessed." The two main interpretations of this verse are "will be blessed" or "will bless themselves." Either this verb should be understood in the middle or in the passive sense. It seems that the passive sense should be adopted because of the use of the niphal.[58] This means that Abraham will be privileged to become a source of blessing to all peoples of the world.[59] How this blessing translates for Gentiles in the NT is debated. For the purpose of this book, it is sufficient to note that Abraham will be the instrument of blessing for the nations.

---

connected with the understanding of a nation. Abraham's national offspring would bless all the "families" of the world, which shows that all nations will ultimately be blessed through Israel. Hays also speaks to this connection in his paradigm in understanding Gen 10. See Hays, *From Every People*, 57–58.

58. There are three factors to consider: (1) comparison with the hithpael used in Gen 22:18; 26:4; (2) grammatical arguments concerning the proper force of the niphal; and (3) arguments from context. See Grüneberg, *Abraham, Blessing and the Nations*, 176. The dominant meaning of the niphal has been debated in recent work on linguistic issues in Biblical Hebrew. See Benton, "Biblical Hebrew Niphal and Hitpael"; Benton, "Verbal and Contextual Information," 385–99; Boyd, "Synchronic Analysis"; Creason, "Semantic Classes"; Dobbs-Allsopp, "Biblical Hebrew Statives," 21–53; Gzella, "Voice in Classical Hebrew," 292–325; Jenni, *Studien Zur Sprachwelt Des Alten Testaments*; and Noonan, "Abraham, Blessing," 73–93.

59. For further support of the passive interpretation, see Hamilton, *Book of Genesis*, 374–76; Speiser, *Genesis*, 86; Cassuto, *Genesis*, 2:315. E. W. Hengstenbergy and J. C. K. von Hoffman adhered to the passive tense. F. Delitzsch, A. Dillman, H. Gunkel, H. Holzinger, J. Skinner translate the verb reflexively as "bless themselves." O. Procksch diverges and translates the verb in a receptive (middle) sense: "are to find blessing in you." Von Rad goes further in this direction and understands it passively. H. W. Wolff, G. Wehmeier, and A. de Pury translate it as "win a blessing." Westermann prefers the reflexive translation because it is philologically more probable and concrete. See Westermann, *Genesis*, 152.

Abrahamic Covenant as a Paradigm

Regarding the blessing to Abraham, Cassuto writes: "We have here the first allusion to the concept of universalism inherent in Israel's faith, which would subsequently be developed in the teaching of the prophets."[60] Cassuto notes that the seven expressions of blessing God gives in Gen 12:1–3 is recalled in Gen 26:3–4 and Gen 27:28–29. This shows a pattern of blessing following the Abrahamic covenant. When God blessed Isaac in Gen 26:3–4, the blessing is ascribed to "nations" and not "families," showing the progression of communities that are forming from the family unit: "I will be with you and bless you, for to you and to your descendants I will give all these lands, and I will establish the oath, which I swore to your father Abraham. I will multiply your descendants as the stars of heaven and will give your descendants all these lands; and by your descendants all the nations of the earth shall be blessed." When God blessed Jacob in Gen 27:28–29, Cassuto rightly notes how the Abrahamic covenant becomes the foundation for future blessings for Israel. He writes, "This is no coincidence, but a preconceived scheme."[61] God's blessing to Abraham in Gen 12:1–3 establishes God's future plan for Israel and Gentile nations in his eschatological kingdom.

There are three theological conclusions from the Abrahamic covenant. The first conclusion is that *God will make Abraham into a nation.* He already possessed a family (i.e., Sarah and Lot), but God would further propagate his offspring to have territorial and political dimensions. This is fundamental in the future expectation for Israel to be restored to their land in order to gather all nations to worship in Jerusalem.

The second conclusion is that *God's covenant with Abraham served a purpose for all nations.* All the nations of the world would be blessed as a result of their interaction with Israel, Abraham's offspring. This covenant manifests itself throughout the historical narrative of Israel. Stephen Barton writes: "Israel's role as kingdom of priests and a holy nation is a particular role and a privileged role. It is also a representative role set against a universal horizon. Israel's identity is always being negotiated in the context of both its relationship with God and other nations."[62]

---

60. Cassuto, *Genesis*, 2:312–13.

61. Cassuto, *Genesis*, 2:213.

62. Barton, "Unity of Humankind," 241. Barton states that the oneness of Israel is not a contradiction to the unity of humankind. He views Israel and the nations as two separate entities seen side by side and as a metaphor for the church.

God's choice of Abraham, though initially exclusive, was for the sake of a maximally inclusive end. Election was to serve all the nations created from Babel.[63] Wright comments how Gen 12:1–3 is the great promise of God to be "totally, covenantally, and eternally committed to the mission of blessing the nations through the agency of the people of Abraham."[64] Israel's election was not a rejection of other nations, but was explicitly for the sake of all nations.

The final conclusion is that *the Abrahamic Covenant becomes the paradigm for future blessings.* God's blessing to Isaac and Jacob shows similar language that recalls the Abrahamic covenant. From this lens, the future prophecies about Israel and Gentile nations will be an outworking of the initial framework presented in the Abrahamic covenant.

Conclusion

The purpose of this chapter was to develop a foundation for a multinational kingdom. By exploring Gen 10–12, several issues were highlighted. First, Gen 10 reveals that the progression of a family becoming a nation is highlighted in the four elements highlighted from Gen 10: מִשְׁפָּחָה (family), לָשׁוֹן (language), אֶרֶץ (land), and גּוֹי (nation). Genesis 10 discloses how territorial and political distinctions are essential in defining a people as a nation.

Second, Gen 11 is a pivotal passage in how one understands the role of nations throughout the canon. When properly placed in its context, Gen 11 seems to indicate that nations are a result of God's original mandate from creation and not a result of sin. As Paul indicated in Acts 17:26, a multitude of nations was predetermined by God. The placement of the Table of Nations before Babel seems to communicate that although Babel

---

63. Davis, "Building a Biblical Theology," 104. Christianne Noisette writes, "Il nous semble important de souligner que ce thème de l'élection d'Abraham et, en lui, de la bénédiction offerte par Dieu aux nations, par quoi commence l'histoire sainte d'Israël, met clairement en évidence ce qu'on pourrait appeler la pédagogie de Dieu: le choix d'un homme singulier, puis d'un peuple particulier, appelés à porter son projet de salut à tous les hommes appelés à porter son projet de salut à tous les hommes" (*It seems important to us to note that this theme of the election of Abraham and, in him, of the blessing given by God to the nations, for what begins the sacred history of Israel, makes clearly in evidence that which could be called the pedagogy of God: the choice of a singular man, then a peculiar people, called to carry his plan of salvation to all men*). See Noisette, "Abraham," 156.

64. Wright, "Mission as a Matrix," 133–34.

was a sinful event, God's providentially brought about a positive result of a diversity of nations from this act of rebellion.

Third, the Abrahamic covenant foretells Israel becoming a great nation in order to bless the nations of the world. This paradigm of God blessing Israel in order to bless the nations will be further developed, particularly in Genesis. Also, the Abrahamic covenant provides a backdrop for a multinational kingdom theme to develop within the OT. The Abrahamic covenant will become the framework by which future blessings will be administered to Gentile nations through Israel.

Although several theologians have concluded that the new covenant community (church) replaces the multinational kingdom foreshadowed in the Abrahamic covenant, Gen 10–12 presents Israel as the primary recipient of the blessings from the Abrahamic covenant for the sake of Gentile nations.[65] The question is if this multinational paradigm introduced in the Abrahamic covenant continues in the OT canon.

65. Some have suggested that the Abrahamic covenant blessings for the nations was entirely fulfilled with the church's mission to the nations (Matt 28:19). Dumbrell characterizes this view when he sees Gal 3:28 as the reversal of Babel and Gal 6:16 referring to "Israel of God" as the church. There are three senses to Abraham's seed, from Rom 4, that undermines Dumbrell's argument: (1) Abraham's seed refers to ethnic Israel. Paul quotes Gen 15:5 and Gen 17:4 to show that Abraham's faith was characterized by having a firm trust that God will give him an offspring and make him the father of nations. OT prophecies also affirm this expectation by giving pictures of redeemed Israel bringing redeemed nations to Jerusalem in the eschatological kingdom; (2) Abraham's seed can also refer to Christians. In Rom 4, Paul presents the salvific unity that exists between Jew and Gentiles. However, salvific unity does not replace the functional distinctions between Christ, Israel, and Gentile nations; and (3) Abraham's seed can also refer to Jesus. Jesus is Abraham's seed because he blesses the nations with salvation. Christ is the one who administers the Abrahamic covenant to believers now and in the eschatological kingdom. See Dunn, *Romans 1–8*; Hendrickson, *Romans*; Moo, *Romans*; and Schreiner, *Romans*. Paul's quotation of the Abrahamic covenant in Gal 3 signifies that individual justification is included in God's blessing for Israel and the nations. Whether individual justification in the church reinterprets OT blessings promised for Israel is debated. For analysis of this issue, see George, *Galatians*; Bruce, *Galatians*; Longenecker, *Galatians*. Romans 11 is another passage that Dumbrell views "all Israel," in Rom 11:26, as referring to the manner in which the remnant will be saved. He synthesizes Rom 11:25–26 with Eph 2:12–20, suggesting Christians now enjoy the privileges that was exclusive to Israel. See Dumbrell, *End of the Beginning*, 158. Michael Vlach argues to the contrary that Rom 11:12 seems to indicate that a progression of blessing will occur for Gentiles. The "riches" Gentiles are experiencing while Israel is "stumbling" will escalate when national Israel is saved. There seems to be greater blessings to come for Gentiles when national Israel is saved and restored. Vlach contends that Rom 11:25–26 refer to national Israel because of her relationship to Gentile nations from the OT being fulfilled in the eschaton. See Vlach, *Has the Church Replaced Israel?*, 172.

4

Nations in OT

IN THIS CHAPTER, I will present both a cogent and comprehensive argument for a multinational eschatological kingdom from the OT canon. Although I will not be able to examine the canon exhaustively, I will survey several passages that comment on the relationship between Israel and Gentile nations, particularly in an eschatological or idealized setting. I will divide the passages in three sections: (1) nations in OT narrative; (2) nations in OT prophets; and (3) nations in OT poetic and wisdom writings. I will argue that a multinational kingdom, as predicted in the Abrahamic covenant, is a consistent theme in the OT that does not become altered or reimagined with the introduction of the New covenant.

OT Narrative

Role of Israel

Kaiser explains that the Abrahamic covenant provides "the formative theology" for "a divine program to glorify himself by bringing salvation to all [nations]."[1] John McIntosh defines the Abrahamic covenant as "God's mission to communicate salvation to the world."[2] When God delivered Israel from Egypt into the wilderness, he gave them his law and his expectation for them as his "chosen" nation. In Exod 19:4–6, God declares Israel's purpose as his nation:

1. Kaiser, *Mission in the Old Testament*, 13.
2. McIntosh, "Missio Dei," 631–32.

You yourselves have seen what I did to the Egyptians, and how I bore you on eagles' wings, and brought you to Myself. "Now then, if you will indeed obey My voice and keep My covenant, then you shall be My own possession among all the peoples, for all the earth is Mine; and you shall be to Me a kingdom of priests and a holy nation." These are the words that you shall speak to the sons of Israel.

John Durham notes how the phrases "own possession," "kingdom of priests," and "holy people" are closely related yet not synonymous. Each term adds nuance to Israel's mediatory role between Yahweh and Gentile nations.[3] God distinguishes Israel from Gentile nations in order to fulfill his mission of extending his kingdom presence on earth. As Douglas Stuart notes, "[Israel] represents the separation of his chosen people from the general world population, or, stated in terms of the overall biblical plan of redemption, the beginning of the outworking of his intention to bring close to himself a people that will join him for all eternity as adopted members of his family."[4]

God's kingdom plan for Israel does not exclude Gentile nations. As Walt Kaiser writes, "Election was not a call to privilege but a choosing for service to God. As such, the priestly character of the nation of Israel came into view almost from the very beginning of its existence as a nation. The people were to be God's ministers, his preachers, and his prophets to their own nation as well as to the other nations."[5] Yahweh's call for Israel to be "a kingdom of priests and a holy nation" pictured the responsibility inherent in the Abrahamic covenant: in *you* all the families of the earth will be blessed.[6]

---

3. Durham, *Exodus*, 263.

4. Stuart, *Exodus*, 422.

5. Kaiser, *Mission in the Old Testament*, 14.

6. Stuart details the four different ways Israel would function as a priest to the nations: (1) Israel would be an example to the people of other nations, who would see its holy beliefs and actions and be impressed enough to want to know personally the same God the Israelites knew. (2) Israel would proclaim the truth of God and invite people from other nations to accept him in faith as shown by confession of belief in him and acceptance of his covenant. (3) Israel would intercede for the rest of the world by offering acceptable offerings to God. (4) Israel would keep the promises of God, preserving his word already spoken and recording his word as it was revealed to them so that once the fullness of time had come, anyone in the whole world could promptly benefit from that great body of divinely revealed truth. See Stuart, *Exodus*, 423.

In the book of Deuteronomy, God separated Israel from Gentile nations by giving them his law. Deuteronomy 4:34 describes Israel as a nation (גּוֹי) from the midst of the nations (גּוֹיִם), emphasizing the unique nature and function of Israel. In Deut 28, Moses promised alternative blessings (Deut 28:1–14) or curses (Deut 28:15–68), depending on how Israel fulfilled God's covenant stipulations. Duane Christensen sees a connection between Israel's call "to be a holy people," in Deut 28:9, and Exod 19:6, where Israel is labeled "a kingdom of priests."[7] Israel's faithfulness should have caused Gentile nations to look upon Yahweh with amazement and fear, for they would see that Israel was "called by the name of the Lord."[8] Even when Israel disobeyed God's covenant, other nations would continue to come to Yahweh because of his promises for Israel (Deut 28:46).[9] Eugene Merrill comments on this promise: "The inevitable calamities that befall the disobedient nation would be indelibly engraved in their memories and forever after would witness to the truth that the Lord and his covenant cannot be flaunted."[10] Even in a state of judgment, Israel would continue to be a witness to the nations.[11]

After God established Israel's mediatory role to the nations, he also promised them land to occupy. In the book of Joshua, Israel desired their land because they believed that Israel transcended the boundaries of clan and tribe.[12] God would begin to administer the land promised from the Abrahamic covenant (Gen 12:7). Israel achieved great status in the community of nations as they defeated other nations and established their national identity.[13] Daniel Block comments on the conditions of Israel's new status among the nations:

---

7. Christensen, *Deuteronomy*, 673. Driver affirms Christensen's observation that God confirmed Israel's "honorable position" in Exod 19:5 with material blessings. See Driver, *Deuteronomy*, 305–6.

8. Merrill, *Deuteronomy*, 354. God's provision for Israel should cause fear in other nations since they would understand Yahweh's protection and ownership of Israel. The concept of ownership also appears in an appeal from a Canaanite vassal to Pharaoh. Thus, Deut 28:9–10 functioned as a legal act by which ownership was claimed and established by Yahweh. See Christensen, *Deuteronomy*, 673.

9. Driver, *Deuteronomy*, 314.

10. Merrill, *Deuteronomy*, 364.

11. Kaiser, *Mission in the Old Testament*, 18. Kaiser notes how the priestly role of Israel is similar to the priesthood of believers in the NT (1 Pet 2:9; Rev 1:5; 5:10).

12. Grosby, *Biblical Ideas of Nationality*, 16.

13. Davis, "Building a Biblical Theology," 102.

With the goal of setting Israel above all other nations, God granted to Israel extraordinary prosperity and economic as well as political hegemony over other nations. However, as God himself expressed so forcefully in [Exod] 19:5, this status and role would be contingent on their fidelity to Him, demonstrated in obedience to the covenant stipulations (Deut 28:1).[14]

Role of Nations

Gentile nations were the context from which the Lord chose Israel and established them as his people. The nations would witness the covenant between God and Israel and function as the audience from which they were to be drawn to Yahweh. In OT narratives, Gentile nations were not attracted to Yahweh because of Israel's poor example of fidelity to God's law. Whether Yahweh would continue building his multinational kingdom program, as promised in the Abrahamic covenant, or usher in a different kingdom consummation because of Israel's disobedience remained unclear.

There are some who assume that the relationship between Gentiles and Israelites was only hostile in the OT.[15] According to this assumption, the election of Israel implied the reprobation of Gentile nations. Ronald Clements challenges this assumption by analyzing the semantic range of גּוֹי when applied to Gentile nations. He writes:

> Even with this increasing tendency for the non-Israelite גּוֹיִם to be identified as "heathen nations," at no point in the OT is the semantic development reaching in which גּוֹי in itself means "heathen nation." Israel fully retained the recognition that it had itself constituted a גּוֹי, and it preserved the hope and expectation that it would again do so. Existence as a גּוֹי was a goal to be desired, and the term did not itself imply any adverse religious connotation.[16]

Charlie Trimm has explored the supposed mutually antagonistic categories of the election of Israel and the judgment of Gentile nations

14. Block, "Privilege of Calling," 403.

15. Clements describes the assumption as such: "Although Israel was to have its own place among the גּוֹיִם, there is an implied hostility toward these other nations on the grounds that their religion is not pleasing to Yahweh and represents a temptation to Israel." See Clements, "גּוֹי," 2:432.

16. Clements, "גּוֹי," 2:432.

by looking at Yahweh's relationship with different Gentile nations.[17] In his study, Trimm analyzes Yahweh's relationship with Gentile nations and challenges the categories typically used to describe Israel versus Gentile nations: elect versus non-elect. Trimm argues that Gentiles should not be categorized as "non-elect" but on a spectrum of "pro-Yahweh" to "anti-Yahweh."[18] In other words, Israel's election did not automatically entail the condemnation of Gentile nations. Instead, Israel's election was supposed to include Gentile nations depending on their response to Yahweh.[19]

Merrill summarizes Israel's mission to the nations: "[Israel's] mission was to be a kingdom of priests and a holy nation thereby representing the Lord among the nations and attracting them to him for redemption and restoration of fellowship."[20] Instead, Israel disobeyed the Mosaic covenant and joined with other nations in their sin. It would seem that based on Israel's response to God's covenant that a different kingdom paradigm that excluded Israel would be introduced. Stephen Dempster argues, however, that God's kingdom agenda did not change because of Israel's disobedience. He writes, "Significantly, a key concept in the last narrative section of the Tanakh that begins with Daniel and ends with Chronicles is the term 'kingdom' [of God]. The Tanakh ends on a note of hope, pointing to the future."[21] God's kingdom agenda, as initiated from the Abrahamic covenant, continued in the OT even when Israel and Gentile nations responded to Yahweh negatively.

After surveying God's purpose for Israel and Gentile nations in OT narratives, I will analyze prophetic passages about the eschatological kingdom. I will look at prophetic passages outside of Isaiah, since Isaiah will be examined in the following chapter. By focusing on passages about the eschatological kingdom, I hope to highlight that despite Israel's

17. Trimm, "Nations," 521. Trimm looks at Yahweh's relationship with Sodom and Gomorrah, the Amalekites, the Egyptians, the Midianites, and the Canaanites to show that God's disposition toward Gentile nations depended on their response to Yahweh and not on the fact that they were Gentile nations.

18. Trimm, "Nations," 534.

19. T. J. Ramsdell points to Isa 25:6–8 as indicating that both Jews and Gentiles are recipients of God's salvation as he prepares a feast for them. Ramsdell writes, "We have then in one of the chief enemies of Israel's prophetic books a plain and emphatic setting forth of the truth that the Gentiles are called to the same salvation as Israel. It is to be a salvation mediated through Israel." See Ramsdell, "Missionary Future," 197.

20. Merrill, *Everlasting Dominion*, 494, 521–46.

21. Dempster, *Dominion and Dynasty*, 49.

historical disobedience, the eschatological kingdom continues to project a multinational picture, which includes both Israel and Gentile nations.

Nations in OT Prophets

During the time of the prophet Micah, Israel substituted religious practice for genuine worship. Although God repeatedly commanded Israel to live according to his commandments, they brought sacrifices devoid of devotion which inevitably demanded God's discipline. Despite God's harsh discipline on Israel, there are pictures of a future restoration for Israel depicted in Micah. Micah 4 prophesies of a future Jerusalem and temple that will be restored since they were destroyed during his time. Instead of being the center for Israel alone, Jerusalem will become the worship center for all nations. Ralph Smith comments on the significance of Mic 4 for Gentile nations: "It looks forward to the day when the enmity that separated the nations at Babel (Gen 11) will be put aside and all peoples of the world will worship the one true God. They will be taught Yahweh's law and not the ways of war. A universal reign of peace will prevail, and each individual will participate in it (v. 4)."[22] The type of peace and prosperity that will exist in God's eschatological kingdom is pictured with the restoration of Zion and its former dominion (v. 8). For God to promise that he would gather the lame and the outcasts represented a change in Israel's present situation.[23] Micah already prophesied that Israel would be delivered back to their land (Mic 2:12–13), but in Mic 4 the Lord will reign from his temple with many Gentile nations following his ways.

Jeremiah described Israel's idolatry as "breaking the yoke" of God's covenant (Jer 2:20).[24] They were engaged in paganism and reflecting the immorality of Sodom and Gomorrah (Jer 11:13–14), which required God's punishment. Interestingly, Gentile nations were also accountable to God, as evidenced by the number of oracles of judgment prophesied against them in Jer 46–51 (i.e., Egypt, Philistines, Moab, Ammon, Edom, Elam, and Babylon).[25] Merrill points out the purpose of God's judgment on nations: "God brings nations down in severe discipline in order to raise them up purified and equipped to serve him with the integrity and

22. Smith, *Micah–Malachi*, 37.

23. Smith, *Micah–Malachi*, 39.

24. Holladay, *Jeremiah*, 97.

25. Huey, *Jeremiah, Lamentations*, 813–14.

righteousness intended at the initiation of his kingdom design."[26] According to Jeremiah, God's kingdom standard applies to other nations, besides Israel, since all nations were subjected to God.

One prophecy that speaks about God's future restoration of Israel and Gentile nations is found in Jer 3:11–18. Jeremiah indicates that Israel had turned away from God with the following metaphor in v. 13: scattered your favors among foreigners. Peter Craigie notes how this metaphor explains the manner in which Israel had turned away from God. They have "scattered" their favors among foreigners by worshipping foreign deities.[27] In vv. 14–15, God indicates that repentance would be followed by a restoration of government in Zion, which in turn will be recognized by all nations.[28] The ark of the covenant, mentioned in v. 16, had symbolized God's presence for Israel historically. In the eschatological kingdom, however, Jerusalem would symbolize God's presence for all nations. This prophecy paints a picture that goes beyond national Israel and includes Gentile nations. Israel will live up to their role as a nation of priests, as promised in Exod 19:5–6. Craigie correctly remarks that these verses "clearly speak of a future eschatological kingdom."[29]

In Ezekiel, God condemns both Israel and Gentile nations. In Ezek 16 and 23, God depicts Israel as an unfaithful wife whom the Lord had brought into covenant with himself. God castigated several Gentile nations, such as Ammon (Ezek 25), Moab (Ezek 8–11), Philistia (Ezek 35), Phoenicia (Ezek 26–28), and Edom (Ezek 12–14; 35) for their pride. Despite negative descriptions of both Israel and Gentile nations, God promises a new era in his relationship with them. As Robert Saucy writes, "The restoration of Israel is not only a display of God's love and power in behalf of his people, but also 'an event necessary to the preservation of the honor of the true God.'"[30] Saucy observes that Israel's election was to be a witness to the Gentile nations and that the prophecies from Ezek 39:21–29 speak of a future awakening.[31] This eschatological reality is also affirmed in Dan 2 where the kingdom of God becomes a great mountain which fills the whole earth (Dan 2:34–35). God's kingdom will "never be

26. Merrill, *Everlasting Dominion*, 529.

27. Craigie, *Jeremiah 1–25*, 57–58.

28. Craigie, *Jeremiah 1–25*, 60.

29. Craigie, *Jeremiah 1–25*, 61.

30. Saucy, *Progressive Dispensationalism*, 297–323.

31. Saucy, *Progressive Dispensationalism*, 313.

destroyed, nor shall its sovereignty be left to another people" (Dan 2:44). In another vision, a Son of Man is "given dominion and glory and kingdom, that all peoples, nations, and languages should serve him" (Dan 7:13–14). Both Ezekiel and Daniel predict a time where all nations will live under the authority of the Son of Man. In this kingdom, both Israel and Gentile nations will live faithfully to God's commandments and his blessings will be administered to them by the Son of Man.

Zechariah 8 builds on the theme of God's covenant faithfulness to Israel. Judah no longer served as an object of cursing but instead God promises to bless them for the sake of the nations. The restoration of Israel and Judah entails leaders to be appointed and God establishing his sovereign rule over Judah and Gentile nations.[32] In Zech 8:21, people from various cities will come to Jerusalem to seek Yahweh. McComiskey comments on this scene:

> Verse 21 expands the promise that Judah and Israel will be a blessing to the nations in language that is less prosaic than that of verse 20, containing a strong emotional undercurrent. We see Gentiles in great numbers streaming from one city to another, encouraging others to join them in seeking the Lord. . . . [Isaiah] (2:2–4) and [Micah] (4:1–4) contain a common prophetic oracle reflecting the same mutual encouragement of the nations to seek the Lord.[33]

Zechariah then concludes his prophecy in Zech 8:20–23 by highlighting Gentile worship. The Gentiles coming to worship in Jerusalem recalls the Abrahamic covenant when God promised that all families on the earth would be blessed through Abraham's offspring. Israel can only fulfill their commission from Gen 12:3 when they first worship Yahweh with undivided loyalty and uprightness of life. Zech 8: 23 depicts foreigners apprehending the garment of one Jew in order to worship the Lord since he is with Israel.[34] This prophecy promises a future reality where all nations will come under the sovereign rule of Christ after Israel has been elevated as the vessel of blessings for the nations. The gathering of the Gentiles was an expected feature of the final age. It was associated with the presentation of the one like a "son of man," who according to

32. Klein, *Zechariah*, 245.

33. McComiskey, "Zechariah," 1156.

34. The number "ten" may symbolize the totality of humanity showing the complete unity that will be practiced during that time.

Dan 7:13–14, received rule over "all peoples, nations, and languages" in a kingdom that will not be destroyed.[35] Hans Wolff connects Zech 8 to the Tower of Babel. Wolff writes:

> The mission to humanity is now illustrated in a single scene: one Israelite will draw ten foreigners. In this the universal extent is not abandoned but rather clarified in a new way. The ten foreigners come from the nations of every tongue, as if the confusion of tongues at the end of the Babel narrative were standing in the background [as in Gen 12:3].[36]

As Merrill concludes, "Yahweh has promised that Jerusalem will be restored, repopulated, and reconfirmed at the center of His covenant interests."[37]

Zechariah 14:1–5 stresses Yahweh's power over history and the peoples of the world.[38] Zechariah 14:16–19 describes nations going to Jerusalem to observe the Feast of Tabernacles. Duane Lindsey argues that the "survivors" in this prophesy are not the Jewish remnant that had been scattered among the nations. Instead, they are the survivors from the nations whose armies were destroyed by the Messiah (vv. 1–5).[39]

The final pericope in Zech 14 is made up of two parts: the pilgrimage of Gentile nations to Jerusalem to observe the Feast of Tabernacles (vv 16–19) and the sanctification of all things in the eschatological kingdom (vv 20–21).[40] Gentiles traveling to Jerusalem does not necessitate that they are Jewish proselytes (Isa 2:2; 14:1; 66:23; Zech 8:23). Instead, this picture of worship is "a newly instituted religious order embracing both Jews and Gentiles," as Lindsey writes.[41] The Feast of Tabernacles was normally reserved for Israel.[42] Thomas McComisky elaborates on this point about the Feast of Tabernacles:

35. Scott, "Gentiles and the Ministry of Jesus," 167.

36. Wolff, "Kerygma of the Yahwist," 157.

37. Merrill, *Haggai, Zechariah, Malachi*, 224.

38. Smith, *Micah-Malachi*, 286.

39. Lindsey, "Zechariah," 1:1571.

40. Smith, *Micah-Malachi*, 292.

41. Lindsey, "Zechariah," 1571.

42. This feast was the third and most important of the three annual festivals that all Jewish adult males were supposed to observe. According to Deut 16:14, foreigners were also allowed to join in this festival, so this idea is not new in Zechariah. See Clark and Hatton, *Zechariah*, 363.

[This feast], which recalls the wilderness experience, functions as a motif for the childlike obedience that sometimes marked the Israelites' response to God in their earliest history . . . in the new heavens and the new earth, all the people of God will live in obedience to him. Nothing external (the nations) or internal will threaten the integrity of the kingdom of God.[43]

In Zech 14:19, Yahweh singles out Egypt as an example of the consequences for those who neglect to observe Feast of Tabernacles. Egypt was often described as the enemy of God's people within OT narratives. By highlighting Egypt, God promises that all nations, including Israel's political enemies, will worship him in the eschatological kingdom. Nations previously excluded from worshipping Yahweh are now expected to worship him.[44] Zechariah's prophetic book that began with a call to repentance (Zech 1:2–6) now concludes with an affirmation that all will be "holy to the Lord," including Israel and Gentile nations (Zech 14:20–21).[45]

When examining prophetic passages, Christensen asserts that the language of both nationalism and universalism exists in tension. In other words, God's focus on Israel was never at the exclusion of the salvation of Gentile nations. Christensen writes, "Even wicked Assyria is the work of Yahweh's hands (Isa 19:24), and as such she enjoys the same potential relationship to Yahweh as did Israel of old. As a light to the nations, Israel has a mission to the nations."[46] A multinational kingdom is consistently portrayed in OT prophecies about the eschatological kingdom. God does not speak simply of individuals from Gentile nations participating in his kingdom, but of individuals who continue to be identified with national and territorial distinctions (i.e., "Egypt," "Assyria").

Nations in Poetic and Wisdom Writings

The role of the future Davidic king in God's eschatological kingdom appears repeatedly in the Writings. God intended to give Israel a king, as written in Deut 17:14–20. A king was always a part of the divine plan for Israel.[47] The Davidic covenant, as it appears in 2 Sam 7, speaks about an

---

43. McComiskey, "Zechariah," 1242.

44. Butterworth, "Zechariah," 881.

45. Lindsey, "Zechariah," 157.

46. Christensen, "אֻמָּה," 1038.

47. Kaiser, "Blessing of David," 22.

offspring from David's body who will link this covenant with the Abrahamic covenant.[48] Ronald Youngblood writes that 2 Sam 7 is the "focus of . . . the Deuteronomic history itself."[49] Walter Brueggemann regards the Davidic covenant as the "dramatic and theological center of the entire Samuel corpus" and as "the most crucial theological statement in the Old Testament."[50] The Davidic covenant promises a king who will mediate the blessings from the Abrahamic covenant to the nations in the eschatological kingdom. Michael Grisanti connects the Davidic covenant with the Abrahamic covenant. He writes:

> As with Abraham (Gen 12:1–3), Yahweh promised David an eternal progeny and possession of land. Loyal sons, i.e., those who lived in accordance with the stipulations of the Mosaic Covenant, would fully enjoy the provisions offered them. . . . He affirms that the Davidic house and throne will endure forever, giving the hope that Yahweh would one day raise up a loyal son who would satisfy Yahweh's demands for covenant conformity.[51]

Kaiser also believes that the Davidic covenant builds upon the Abrahamic covenant by stating that David "was fully cognizant of the fact that he was participating in both the progress and organic unity of revelation. The 'blessing' of Abraham is continued in this 'blessing' of David."[52]

Psalms is the main portion of the Writings that provides detail about the future Davidic king, especially concerning his relationship with Israel and Gentile nations. Psalm 2 is cited multiple times by NT writers as a messianic psalm and Rev 19:15 portrays Jesus as ruling over the nations: "From his mouth comes a sharp sword with which to strike down the nations, and he will rule them with a rod of iron." In its historical context, Ps 2 is considered a royal psalm and is seen in light of Hebrew monarchy.[53] Fausset remarks that this prophecy cannot be attributed to David's reign

---

48. Bergen, 1, 2 Samuel, 340.

49. Youngblood, "1, 2 Samuel," 3:880.

50. Brueggemann, First and Second Samuel, 253; 259.

51. Grisanti, "Davidic Covenant," 233.

52. Kaiser, "Blessing of David," 310.

53. Craigie summarizes Ps 2 into four sections: (1) Foreign nations and their rulers express rebellion against God and his king (Ps 2:1–3); (2) God mocks the kings by announcing a king of his own choosing in Zion (2:4–6); (3) The Davidic king speaks and declares the words of God (Ps 2:7–9); and (4) A warning is given to the nations and their kings of God's wrath and the consequences of his anger (Ps 2:10–12). See Craigie, Psalms 1–50, 64–65.

but to a future reign: "Though the warlike events of David's reign may have suggested its imagery, the scenes depicted and the subjects presented can only find a fulfillment in the history and character of Jesus Christ, to which, [in Heb 1:5; 5:5] the New Testament writers most distinctly testify."[54] In Ps 2:6, God declares that he has set his "anointed one" on his holy hill, Jerusalem. This language recalls the Davidic covenant because at the heart of the covenant was the understanding of sonship between Yahweh and the appointed king (Ps 2:7).

New Testament citations of Ps 2 indicate that this prophecy describes the inauguration of Christ as King. In Acts 13:33, Paul's quotation implies an application to Jesus' divine nature to be the Son of God.[55] Hebrews 5:5 cites Ps 2:6 to show that Jesus is the ideal high priest because he is the only perfect priest who represents mankind. These words spoken by Yahweh in Ps 2:6 reveals that this psalm predicts that Christ will one day reign over all nations in his kingdom.

Psalms 67 and 72 also depict a picture of nations under the rule of the Davidic king. When one remembers that it was at the Feast of Pentecost that God was to pour out his Spirit on all people, just as the prophet Joel had predicted, the connection of Ps 67 with the Feast of Pentecost is apparent. Kaiser explains this connection: "[The] psalmist sees the ingathering of the crops as a [down payment] and a symbol of the spiritual harvest that God desired for every tribe, tongue, and nation."[56] In Ps 72, God promised to give his anointed king dominion over the entire earth (vv. 8–11). Although this psalm may have been written at the beginning of Solomon's reign, it envisions ideals never fully realized in Israel's history.

Psalm 98 describes Yahweh ruling as king.[57] Like Ps 95, Ps 98 speaks in the language of Isa 40–55, which emphasize Yahweh's right hand and holy arm as the means of deliverance (Isa 41:10; 52:10).[58] Psalm 98 is similar to Ps 96 in extolling Yahweh for his victories in the past and

---

54. Fausset, "Psalms," 1:347.

55. Fausset, "Psalms," 1:347.

56. Kaiser, "Blessing of David," 29.

57. Boice, *Psalms 42–106*, 2:799.

58. Goldingay, *Psalms 90–150*, 121. Psalm 98 is considered a "Divine Warrior" victory song, which celebrates the return of Yahweh as the commander of the heavenly hosts. Divine Warrior language is evident within this psalm and the style is that of a hymn of triumph, similar to those who follow the successful completion of Yahweh's action in war (Judg 5:4–5; Deut 33:2–5, 26–29). See Tate, *Psalms 51–100*, 524.

foretelling his return to reestablish the universal reign of justice.[59] Each of the three stanzas of this psalm calls on one part of creation to praise God, and in the first stanza this is Israel (vv 1–3). Through the salvation accomplished for Israel, all the earth will see their salvation as well. John Goldingay connects "wonderful things," from v. 1, with "before the eyes of the nations," from v. 2, because he sees language from Isa 40–55 in Ps 98. He suggests that this psalm is pointing forward to the final historical deliverance: Yahweh's righteous reign in the messianic kingdom.[60]

What is important to note is that the word "nations," in Ps 98:2, is in the third person while Ps 98:3 labels Yahweh as "our God." This shows that the psalmist is primarily writing to Israel, but Gentile nations are also part of this prophecy.[61] All the finite verbs of vv 1–3, excluding the imperative verb, are *qatal*, while v. 9 speaks of what Yahweh has come to do but has not completed yet with the *yiqtol* verb form. Yahweh's acts of deliverance for Israel (vv 1–3), in the past, will give a preview of what he will do for both Israel and Gentile nations (vv 4–9), in the future. As Ronald Allen states, the salvation depicted in Ps 98 is "made possible by Christ's death and resurrection" but is realized at his return as king over all nations.[62]

Conclusion

After surveying the theme of nations from OT narrative, prophecies, and writings, there are several conclusions. First, God's multinational kingdom agenda continues for both Israel and Gentile nations, even when God disciplines them. Even though Israel resembled pagan nations during different periods in its history, God remained faithful to his covenant with Abraham. Also, the picture of Gentile nations streaming to Jerusalem was not realized in OT narratives. This was not a failure on God's part to fulfill his kingdom agenda, but a reflection of how incompetent Israel fulfilled their mission as a light to the nations.

59. Dahood, *Psalms 51–100*, 365.

60. Goldingay, *Psalms 90–150*, 121. Most commentators interpret Ps 98 as depicting the millennial kingdom. The reason is that Ps 98 is within the royal psalms, which are primarily referring to Yahweh's future righteous reign that is portrayed through the millennial kingdom.

61. Goldingay, *Psalms 90–150*, 119.

62. Allen, *When Song Is New*, 43.

Second, OT prophecies predict a time when both Israel and Gentile nations will worship Yahweh in his eschatological kingdom. Egypt participating in the Feast of Tabernacles and Assyria labeled as the "work of Yahweh's hands" clearly envision a future scene where Gentile nations will be a part of the eschatological kingdom. Gentiles are identified with national and territorial distinctions, as evidenced in Zech 8:20–23, when Gentiles travel to Jerusalem from cities outside of Jerusalem in order to meet with God. The Gentiles coming to worship in Jerusalem fulfills the Abrahamic covenant when God promised that all families on the earth would be blessed through Abraham's offspring, namely the Davidic king.

Third, the Writings explain the role of the Davidic king in the eschatological kingdom. Even during periods of exile or judgment, God continually promises a future where Israel and Gentile nations will live under the rule of this Davidic king. With undoubtedly deliberate intent, Rev 21 comes to its climax with the picture of the nations purged of all their sin and walking in the light of God, bringing their wealth and splendor into the city of God, and contributing glory and honor to the Lamb of God.[63] This provides an almost chiastic structure in understanding the purpose for nations when looking at the beginning and the end as the "book ends." Richard Middleton describes this eschatological multinational kingdom:

> The reference to kings and nations in the new creation is a telling signal that cultural, even national, diversity is not abrogated by redemption. Salvation does not erase cultural differences, rather, the human race, still distinguished by nationality, now walks by the glory or light of the holy city, which is itself illuminated by the Lamb (Rev 21:24).[64]

---

63. Wright, *Mission of God*, 454.
64. Middleton, *New Heaven and a New Earth*, 212.

5

Isaiah's Eschatological Kingdom

As demonstrated in the previous pages, a multinational eschatological kingdom is a consistent theme presented throughout the OT canon. Several theologians argue, however, that the kingdom of God becomes reconceptualized with the introduction of the new covenant by the OT prophets (i.e., Isaiah). One example is Peter Gentry and his work, *Kingdom through Covenant*. He writes, "Isaiah announces that the people of the new Zion will be far more numerous than those of the old because the nations will be drawn in to the new Zion . . . more land will be required than just the real estate entailed in historical Israel."[1] Gentry claims that Isaiah predicts an increase in the people of Zion through the inclusion of Gentile individuals. This also involves an expansion of Zion's borders to the ends of the earth, thereby resulting in a unification of Israelites and Gentiles to form a new "Israel." Accordingly, Gentry believes Isaiah portrays an eschatological kingdom which is a worldwide singular nation, comprised of Jews and Gentiles. This "new" Israel is an "expansion" of the old Israel in terms of both composition and territory.

There are several scholars, along with Gentry, who utilize Isaiah as evidence for a mono-national, multiethnic eschatological kingdom.[2]

---

1. Gentry and Wellum, *Kingdom through Covenant*, 468.

2. Theologians who affirm Gentry's interpretation of "Israel" as a type of the eschatological kingdom include: Berkhof, *Systematic Theology*, 571; Woudstra, "Israel and the Church," 221–38; and Clowney, *Church*, 42–44. Horton states that the "New Testament church is complete only as it grows out of the Old Testament church. The Israel of God attains its eschatological form only with the inclusion of the nations." See Horton, *Christian Faith*, 730. James Muilenberg writes, "With the admission of

However, for the purposes of this book, I will use Gentry as a case study for those who interpret Israel as type of the eschatological kingdom in Isaiah. I will analyze Gentry's arguments, from *Kingdom through Covenant* (1st and 2nd editions), because he offers extensive textual details for his claims. I will follow the same textual order Gentry presents in his chapter on Isaiah and argue that a consistent reading of these passages will support the view that the kingdom consummation in Isaianic theology is better read as a multinational, multiethnic reality in which Israel retains its national integrity rather than a single-nation, multiethnic kingdom which redefines national Israel.

Gentry's Interpretation of the Abrahamic Covenant

Gentry's understanding of the Abrahamic covenant affects how he interprets portrayals of the eschatological kingdom in Isaiah. Gentry argues that the term גוי in the OT refers to a group of people with both a homeland and political structure.[3] Both territorial and political elements are implied in God's promise that Abraham would become a nation in Gen 12:2. Gentry writes, "You cannot have a great nation without land, without territory, without a place for a large number of people to live and call home. So, the idea of land is implied in [the Abrahamic covenant], and the Lord makes this explicit in [Gen 12:7]."[4] According to Gentry, the use

---

foreigners to the community of the covenant people, the meaning of 'Israel' acquires wider range and inclusiveness: not those who are Israel according to the flesh, but those who confess the God of Israel as Lord belong to the covenant community." See Muilenburg, *Interpreter's Bible*, 5:504. William Dumbrell builds his argument for a mono-national kingdom from the Abrahamic covenant, which is reiterated in Isa 40–66. See Dumbrell, *End of the Beginning*, 119–20. Hays affirms a multinational kingdom from the Abrahamic covenant but sees Isaiah as a turning point in which national distinctions are erased in God's eschatological kingdom with the new covenant. See Hays, *From Every People*, 106. Moo comments on the expansion of Israel's promised land from Isaiah. He writes that "in his familiar prophecies about a 'new heavens and new earth,' Isaiah envisages an ultimate salvation that extends beyond the people of Israel or even the land of Israel to include the entire cosmos: a 'new heavens and new earth' (Isa 65:17–22; cf. 66:22–24)." See Moo, "Creation and New Creation," 45.

3. Gentry writes, "The basic meaning of גוי is an organized community of people having governmental, political, and social structure." See Gentry and Wellum, *Kingdom through Covenant*, 243.

4. Gentry and Wellum, *Kingdom through Covenant*, 235. Clines notes that in Genesis it is the "promise of progeny" and the "promise of the land" that has predominated, in Exodus, Leviticus, Numbers, and Deuteronomy. See Clines, *Theme*

of גּוֹי (nation), as opposed to עַם (people), signifies that God will create a future political government through Abraham. He comments:

> The background of [Gen] 12 is chapters 10 and 11. There we have the history of Babel (Gen 11), where we see a complete confidence and naïve optimism about human achievement and effort. Man is at the centre of his world, and he can achieve any-thing. This philosophy comes under divine judgment in [Gen] 11 and results in the nations being lost and scattered over the face of the earth (Gen 11:9 and chapter 10). By contrast, [Gen] 12 presents a political structure brought into being by the word of God, with God at the centre and God as the governmental head and rule of that community. In other words, we have the kingdom of God brought into being by means of the covenant (i.e., the covenant between God and Abram).[5]

Gentry assumes that Gen 12 "brings into existence a new order" out of the chaos of Babel.[6] Based on his reading of Gen 11, the Abraha-mic covenant reverses the effects of Babel by uniting all nations into one people in a new kingdom. Gentry's view assumes that the result of the diversity of nations must be reversed with a future kingdom promised to Abraham in Gen 12. However, God's purpose in the Abrahamic covenant was not to build a kingdom as a response to the problem of Babel but to create a "great nation" (with a homeland and political structure) in order to bless all the nations of the world that came from Babel.[7] Rather

---

of the Pentateuch, 64–65. By the close of the Pentateuch, not only is the promise of land prominent, the necessity of obedience in relation to the land is solidified as a significant theme in Deuteronomy. Nelson provides a list of passages in Deuteronomy that deal with the land and the conditions for Israel to inhabit said land. See Nelson, *Deuteronomy*, 11.

5. Gentry and Wellum, *Kingdom through Covenant*, 244.

6. Gentry and Wellum, *Kingdom through Covenant* (2nd ed.), 261. Gentry later adds, "Out of the post-Babel chaos portrayed by the nations and peoples of the world lost and scattered in the earth, and by the deadness and infertility of Abram and Sarai's bodies, the word of God to Abram is a powerful word bringing something out of noth-ing." See Gentry and Wellum, *Kingdom through Covenant* (2nd ed.), 295. Gentry in-terprets Babel as a purely negative event that must be counteracted by God's kingdom promised through Abraham. Although Babel was a negative event, the Abrahamic covenant was not simply a response to the Babel event but a continuation of the prom-ised Seed of the Woman (Gen 3:15) in order to bring about God's plan of redemption through Abraham and his seed.

7. Goldingay and Oswalt see the Abrahamic covenant as the backdrop to the Ser-vant's mission as a "light to the nations," in Isa 42. Oswalt comments, "Through his obedient service to God, Israel will be enabled to perform the service of blessing the

than viewing the "great nation" as a reference to national Israel, Gentry believes that this "nation" will function as a type of Adam which will find ultimate fulfillment in the new creation.[8] Based on his view of typology (which I will address later in this chapter), this nation serves a number of purposes in God's plan: first, as a physical nation by which God brings about his promises to the world; second, as a type of a greater Son, Jesus Christ; finally, as a type of the true people of God, which, in his view, is the church.[9]

The assertion that Israel functions as an OT type of the church underlines Gentry's interpretation of the Abrahamic covenant.[10] Gentry views

---

nations that had been prophesied in Gen 12:3 and elsewhere." Goldingay adds, "As Abraham was to be a blessing to the world so Israel is to be a covenant for people and a light for nations." See Oswalt, *Book of Isaiah*, 108, and Goldingay, *Book of Isaiah*, 242. Although Israel was to serve as a blessing in the midst of nations (Gen 12:1; Isa 19:24), it is debated whether they will also function as the Servant of the Lord. The servant Israel is depicted as "blind" (Isa 42:18) within the same context of Isa 42:7. It seems that the Servant, in 42:7 and 49:6, refers to an individual since this person will also restore national Israel ("raise up the tribes of Jacob"; "bring back the preserved of Israel"). The writer opts to view the servant as the messianic king, mentioned in Isa 11 and 53. However, this does not preclude Israel's role as a blessing in the "midst of the earth" (Isa 19:24; Zech 8:13), which God predicted they would become in Gen 12:1–3.

8. Wellum writes, "Israel as a nation serves as 'another Adam' and fulfills that role to the nations. Given the placement of the covenant with Israel in Scripture, this can only mean that it is through Israel that God will fulfill his promise began in [Gen] 3:15, namely, to bring about a resolution of the sin and death caused by the first Adam, ultimately culminating in the dawning of a new creation." See Gentry and Wellum, *Kingdom through Covenant*, 636–37. Wellum's argument that Israel functions as a type of Adam connects with his assertion that Israel will occupy the whole world. However, one must question whether Israel functions as a type of Adam, especially since Wellum fails to provide clear textual support for his view. If Israel does not function as a type of Adam, then it brings into question whether Israel functions as an OT type of the eschatological kingdom since these concepts are closely connected in Wellum's argumentation.

9. Gentry and Wellum, *Kingdom through Covenant*, 646.

10. Gentry's interpretation of the Abrahamic covenant builds upon yet modifies previous Reformed interpretations of the Abrahamic covenant. In his study of the Abrahamic covenant, William Dumbrell finds connections to the creation theme via "new creation" language. He sees the Abrahamic covenant as the "framework" for all subsequent concepts of relationships, including the Sinai covenant, which is a partial fulfillment of the Abrahamic covenant. Dumbrell follows Reformed theology in his view of a covenant related to creation. He argues that Gen 1–3 implicitly reveals a foundational covenant that was made when God's act of creation necessarily placed him in a covenant relationship with humanity and the created world. See Dumbrell, *Covenant and Creation*, 33–61. Williamson does not see exegetical evidence for a creation covenant, as per Dumbrell, but he does see in the Noahic covenant a divine commitment to creation and affirms that any theological study of the covenants must place

the church as a single community comprised of individuals of different ethnicities and extends as such worldwide. According to Gentry, Israel will expand to include individuals from all nations. He references Gen 17 as evidence that Israel will function this way.[11] He writes: "In [Gen] 17 the royal ideology of the promises in [Gen] 12:1–3 comes to the fore and it seems that not only will Abraham be a blessing to the nations, but he will become more than one nation, in fact, a *multitude* of nations . . . he would inherit more than the land of Canaan; he would inherit the world."[12]

---

the covenant within the context of creation since the restoration of creation must be a major telos of salvation history. See Williamson, *Sealed with an Oath*, 69–76. In terms of covenant typology, Gentry and Wellum tend to eschew traditional classifications of suzerain-vassal and grant-type covenants, opting instead to see unconditional and conditional elements in each covenant (i.e., Williamson). The fact that they see a covenant with creation as a biblical covenant suggests a strong biblical-theological affinity for covenant theology. For Gentry, the Abrahamic covenant is seen as a foundational covenant for all human-divine relationships and the "backbone" to the metanarrative plot and his conclusion that Israel functions as an OT type of Christ and the church leads to a certain reading of Isaiah's eschatological kingdom. See Gentry and Wellum, *Kingdom through Covenant*, 120, 135, 177–221, 291–95.

11. There is a debate whether Gen 15 and 17 depict two separate covenants or comment on the same covenant. Williamson's literary theological study of the Abrahamic covenant led him to conclude that there are two distinct covenants represented in Gen 15 and 17. Williamson sees Gen 15 as an unconditional unilateral covenant while the covenant in Gen 17 as conditional. See Williamson, *Sealed with an Oath*, 69–76. Those who see only one covenant view the differences between Gen 15 and 17 as indicative of multiple stages in the development of the Abrahamic covenant. See Chisholm, "Evidence from Genesis," 35–54. Chisholm acknowledges that the covenant in Gen 15 is technically distinct from the one in Gen 17 but argues that Gen 17 serves as an expansion of Gen 15 once Yahweh's ratifies all the promises as a single covenant in Gen 22. Chisholm, "Evidence from Genesis," 44n30. As Chisolm notes, beginning with Abraham's obedient move to Canaan in Gen 12 and culminating with Abraham's offering of Isaac in Gen 22, Abraham's obedience over the course of several years results in the ratification of the covenantal promises (Gen 26:3–5). See Chisholm, "Evidence from Genesis," 38n9. Both the "two-covenant" and "one covenant" view agree that there are textual markers in Gen 15 and 17 that signifies them as distinct from one another. Both views also agree that the divine oath, in Gen 22, functions as the defining moment in the Abrahamic covenant narrative resulting in the ratification of the previous covenantal promises given to Abraham.

12. Gentry and Wellum, *Kingdom through Covenant*, 266. Hahn observes a framework in which each of the three main promises of Gen 12:1–3 (great nation, a great name, and blessing for all nations) is addressed in Gen 15, 17, and 22. See Hahn, *Kinship by Covenant*, 103–11. In Gen 17, the promise of nationhood is confirmed (Gen 17:6–8), but the promise of a "great name" comes to the fore as Yahweh builds upon the covenant content revealed in Gen 15. The promise of kings from Abraham's line (Gen 17:6, 16) adds royal lineage to the covenant promises, which is also related to a

Gentry assumes, on the basis of this prophecy, that Israel will expand to include a multitude of nations resulting in the expansion of the promised land to encompass the world.[13] However, the promise that Abraham will become "the father of a multitude of nations" (Gen 17:4) does not state that his descendants through Isaac will become such.[14] Instead, this promise begins to unfold with Ishmael, a physical son of Abraham, who would also become a "great nation" (Gen 17:20). Later, when Rebekah is pregnant with Jacob and Esau, God describes them as "two nations" in her womb (Gen 25:23). Indeed, Abraham does become a "father of a multitude of nations" (i.e., Ishmaelites, Midianites, Edomites, and Amalekites).

Gentry acknowledges that one can "reasonably" argue that the promise of Gen 17:5 may be fulfilled by the descendants of Ishmael (Gen 25:12–18), Abraham's second wife, Keturah (Gen 25:1–5), Esau (Gen 30:1–19, 31–43), Moab (Gen 19:37), and Ammon (Gen 19:38).[15] Yet, Gentry claims that Gen 35:11 does not allow this interpretation.[16] For Gentry, since Gen 35:11 says that a "company of nations" will come from Jacob, he concludes that the descendants of Abraham will expand to

---

"great name." Gentry and Wellum, *Kingdom through Covenant*, 105–6.

13. Gentry and Wellum, *Kingdom through Covenant*, 105–6. Hahn notes that the promised land in Gen 17 is smaller than the land in Gen 15, which may reflect that Canaan is for Isaac and his descendants and refers specifically to Israel's homeland. See Hahn, *Kinship by Covenant*, 107.

14. Williamson argues that only the Israelites and Edomites can literally trace their ancestry to Abraham. Thus, God's promise of many nations encompasses more than biological ancestry. See Williamson, "Covenant," 147. Hahn also views the status of "father of many nations" as a metaphorical expression based on the concept of kinship that was used in ANE international treaties. Hahn posits that "father" is used metaphorically of Abraham as a suzerain since his royal descendants, David and Solomon, later rule as "suzerains" over all nations from Egypt to the Euphrates (2 Sam 8 and 1 Kgs 4:21; cf. Ps 2:7–12; 72:8–11; 89:25–27). See Hahn, *Kinship by Covenant*, 106–7. Even if one were to affirm a metaphorical reading of "father of many nations," this does not demand an expansion of national Israel and its land. Instead, as Hahn notes, Gen 17:5–6 promises to make Abraham the father of many nations (Gen 17:5–6, 16) and the progenitor of a great multitude of descendants (Gen 17:2), adding a dimension of "international significance" to Abraham's covenantal legacy. Also, the Lord promises that kings will be among his descendants (Gen 17:6, 16), which serves as an important backdrop for later revelation regarding David's royal line in the Davidic covenant, which predicts a multinational kingdom under the rule of a future Davidic king.

15. Gentry and Wellum, *Kingdom through Covenant*, 292–93.

16. And God said to him, "I am God Almighty: be fruitful and multiply. A nation and a company of nations shall come from you, and kings shall come from your own body" (ESV).

include Gentiles from a multitude of nations in order to form a new covenant community.[17] He states that a pattern occurs in God's dealing with the patriarchs where "the human perception of God's promises" fall short of what God really has in mind. Thus, their conception of the promised land and their identity as a nation does not envision the final fulfillment of the Abrahamic covenant, which for Gentry, is realized with a mononation, multiethnic kingdom.[18]

Gentry's interpretation of Gen 35:11, however, appears inconsistent with the language of Gen 28:3–4 and 48:3–4. Previously in Gen 28:3–4, Isaac promises Jacob what is later echoed by God in Gen 35:11–12: "God Almighty (אֵל שַׁדַּי)[19] bless you and make you fruitful and multiply you, that you may become a company of peoples (לִקְהַל עַמִּים). May he give the blessing of Abraham to you and to your offspring with you, that you may take possession of the land of your sojournings that God gave to Abraham!" Isaac uses the phrase "company of peoples" (לִקְהַל עַמִּים), which is the same phrase Jacob utilizes in Gen 48:3–4 when he recalls the episode at Bethel (Gen 35:11–12) to Joseph: "And Jacob said to Joseph, 'God Almighty (אֵל שַׁדַּי) appeared to me at Luz in the land of Canaan and blessed me, and said to me, "Behold, I will make you fruitful and multiply you, and I will make of you a company of peoples (לִקְהַל עַמִּים) and will give this land to your offspring after you for an everlasting possession."'" All three promises (Gen 28:3–4; 35:11–12; 48:3–4) are dealing with physical descendants of Jacob. No textual details in these three promises envision a redefinition of national Israel as a reference to a mono-national, multiethnic universal kingdom. Instead, God depicts internal distinctions within Jacob's physical

17. Gentry and Wellum, *Kingdom through Covenant* (2nd ed.), 330.

18. Gentry cites Chee-Chiew Lee as support for his interpretation. Lee writes, "While Abraham becoming 'the father of many nations' may still be fulfilled through other physical descendants of Abraham, Jacob becoming 'a nation and a company of nations' can only be fulfilled beyond his physical descendants." See Lee, "גּוֹיִם," 473–74.

19. There has been debate over the meaning of אֵל שַׁדַּי ("God Almighty"). See Albright, "*Shaddai and Abram*," 173–210; Gordis, "Biblical Root," 34–43; Mettinger, *In Search of God*, 69–72. The name אֵל שַׁדַּי is used in contexts where God appears as the source of fertility and life, especially in Genesis, when God appears to the patriarchs. In Gen 17:1–8, God appeared to Abram as *El Shaddai* (אֵל שַׁדַּי) and announced his intention to make the patriarch fruitful. In Gen 28:3, Isaac pronounced a blessing on Jacob and calls on God as אֵל שַׁדַּי. God repeated the words, from Gen 17, to Jacob in Gen 35:11 and later Jacob prayed that his sons would be treated with mercy when they returned to Egypt with Benjamin, in Gen 43:14. In Gen 48:3, Jacob, prior to blessing Joseph's sons, recounts how אֵל שַׁדַּי appeared to him at Bethel and promised to make him fruitful.

lineage, which are labeled a "company of nations" or a "company of peoples." In Gen 35:11, when God mentions that both a nation and a company of nations will come from Jacob, "a company of nations" fits conceptually within a notion of a physical lineage with distinctions. If this is so, then the phrase "a company of nations" cannot be taken as a universal reference to all humanity, as Gentry proposes.

Furthermore, there is no basis for Gentry's assumption that all the covenant promises of Gen 12:1–3 are universally applied to "a company of nations."[20] Although Ishmael will be blessed and become a "great nation," God reiterates that he will establish his covenant with Isaac (Gen 17:21).[21] When the covenant is reiterated throughout Genesis, it is restricted to a particular branch of Abraham's descendants. Ishmael would not share in Isaac's inheritance (Gen 21:10), neither does Esau in Jacob's (Gen 27:37). The election of Isaac over Ishmael (Gen 17:21), and Jacob over Esau (Gen 25:23) assumes a distinction between a specific nation (descendants of Jacob) from the other nations (i.e., descendants of Ishmael or Esau) that come from Abraham. A particular strand of the covenant promise is the land promise, which God expresses in covenantal terms with Jacob (Gen 28:3–4; 48:4). Genesis reveals that although many nations (i.e., Ishmael and Esau) will be blessed in Abraham, only the offspring (singular) of Jacob will inherit the promised land as an everlasting possession (Gen 17:8; 26:4; 28:13–14; 35:11–12; 48:3–4). In Gen 28:13–14, when God speaks to Jacob, he promises to give the promised land to Jacob's offspring and through his offspring "all the families of the earth" will be blessed.[22] A distinction exists between Jacob's offspring, who will possess the promised land, and the families of the earth, who will be blessed through Jacob's offspring. Gentry makes a logical jump in argument when he argues that "Israel" will expand to include a multitude of nations requiring their land to encompass the entire earth. This logical jump is most evident in Gentry's discussion of the use of מִשְׁפְּחֹת in Gen 12:3.

---

20. Gen 12:1–3 delineates God's choice of Abraham to father a people to function as God's representative/mediators. Abraham's descendants are God's chosen vehicle to bring blessing to all peoples on the earth. Eventually, it is only those descendants of Abraham through Isaac and Jacob who function as God's chosen representatives.

21. When Abraham proposes that Ishmael would be the heir of the covenant (Gen 17:18), God responds that he will establish his covenant with Isaac, who was yet to be born (Gen 17:19).

22. When God says that he is "the God of your father Abraham and the God of Isaac," the Hebrew word for "father" can be used in a broader sense and can apply to Jacob's grandfather, Abraham.

According to Gentry, when God speaks of מִשְׁפָּחֹת in Gen 12:3, that is "families," to be blessed in Abraham, he is drawing a contrast between Abraham's future kingdom (גּוֹי) and the multiple kingdoms of the world at the time (מִשְׁפָּחֹת). Gentry states:

> The promise in [Gen] 12:3 is cited or quoted several times in later texts of the Old Testament. In [Gen] 28:14 the nations of the world are also called *mispahot* to form an *inclusio* with [Gen] 12:3 and mark off a literary section. In [Gen] 18:18, 22:18, 26:4, [Jer] 4:2, and [Ps] 72:17, however, the five other texts that directly refer to [Gen] 12:3, the nations of the world are called by the more common and normal term, *goyim*. This shows that the author has a real purpose in [Gen] 12:3 in using the term *mispahot*: *he wants to indicate that the kingdoms of this world will never amount to anything; only the kingdom of God will last forever.*[23]

The last sentence is important to examine. Gentry claims that the author purposefully chose מִשְׁפָּחֹת, as opposed to גּוֹיִם, in Gen 12:3, when identifying the nations of the world in order to indicate that the גּוֹי that will come through Abraham will become the "kingdom of God." William Dumbrell makes a similar argument by stating, "from Abram a 'great nation' or new world system will come into being which Israel is simply anticipation."[24]

Gentry claims that גּוֹי, from Gen 12:3, refers to a worldwide mononational, multiethnic eschatological kingdom since the word מִשְׁפָּחָה is no longer employed when the Abrahamic covenant is repeated after Gen 12:3. Thus, Gentry argues that the author highlights that the "great nation" (גּוֹי) refers to something conceptually greater than a nation since it stands in contrast to the מִשְׁפָּחֹת of the world. A drawback to this conclusion is that the term גּוֹי never refers to a worldwide kingdom throughout the OT canon. A גּוֹי refers to a group of people who are a subset of the world's population but not to the entire human population of the world. Gentry makes an unfounded argument by proposing that גּוֹי refers to a worldwide kingdom since his definition is disconnected in meaning from its standard usage within the canon.

By means of his interpretation of גּוֹי, in Gen 12:3, Gentry postulates that the מִשְׁפָּחֹת will be blessed in Abraham by becoming a part of the "great nation" (גּוֹי) that will come from Abraham. In so doing, Gentry

---

23. Gentry and Wellum, *Kingdom through Covenant*, 244 (emphasis mine).

24. Dumbrell, *Covenant and Creation*, 66–67.

conflates two lines of promise from the Abrahamic covenant ("I will make you a great nation"; "in you all the families of the earth shall be blessed") into one. The promise does not state that the "families of the earth" will become the "great nation" that will come from Abraham. Instead, God promises to bless both this great nation and the other families of the earth through Abraham.

There is textual evidence that challenges Gentry's interpretation that the families of the world will become the "great nation." In Gen 22:17–18, after Abraham obeyed God's command to sacrifice Isaac, God distinguishes between Abraham's offspring and all the "nations of the earth" who would be blessed by Abraham's offspring: "I will surely bless you, and I will surely multiply your offspring as the stars of heaven and as the sand that is on the seashore. And your offspring shall possess the gate of his enemies, and in your offspring (בְזַרְעֲךָ) shall all the nations (גּוֹיֵי) of the earth be blessed, because you have obeyed my voice."[25] There is a distinction between Abraham's offspring who will "possess the gate of his enemies"[26] and the "nations of the earth" who will be blessed through Abraham's offspring. God reiterates this same promise to Isaac, in Gen 26:4–5, and continues to describe a distinction between Isaac's offspring from the nations of the earth: "I will multiply your offspring as the stars of heaven and will give to your offspring all these lands. And in your offspring (בְזַרְעֲךָ) all the nations (גּוֹיֵי) of the earth shall be blessed, because Abraham obeyed my voice and kept my charge, my commandments, my statutes, and my laws."[27] A distinction exists between Isaac's offspring, who will possess "these lands," and the "nations of the earth," who will be blessed through Isaac's offspring. In Acts 3:25–26, when the Apostle Peter appropriates the promise of universal blessing found in Gen 22:18

25. The use of the infinitive absolute before the finite verbal form ("bless"; "multiply") emphasizes the certainty of the blessing. The Hebrew term זֶרַע ("offspring") may mean "seed" (for planting), "offspring," or "descendants" depending on the context. In this context, זֶרַע refers to "offspring." The phrase "because you have obeyed my voice" is a causal clause and comes at the end of the sentence. Abraham's obedience brought God's ratification of the earlier conditional promise. In the Abraham narrative, the promises of the covenant seem conditional (Gen 17; 18:19; 26:5) until Yahweh swears a solemn oath that seals the promises and renders them irrevocable in Gen 22:15–18. See Williamson, *Abraham, Israel, and the Nations*, 134; Chisholm, "Evidence from Genesis," 38n9.

26. The word "gate" stands for a walled city and to break through the gate would be to conquer the city, for the gate complex was the main area of defense.

27. The verb "shall be blessed" is taken as passive to indicate that Abraham's descendants were going to be a channel or source of blessing to the nations.

and 26:4, Peter urges his fellow Jews to repent since Jesus was sent first
to the Jews in order to bless them: "You are the sons of the prophets and
of the covenant that God made with your fathers, saying to Abraham,
'And in your offspring shall all the families of the earth be blessed.' God,
having raised up his servant, sent him to you first, to bless you by turning every one of you from wickedness." Interestingly, Peter identifies the
Jews as "sons" of the Abrahamic covenant and does not indicate that the
Gentiles have replaced or integrated with national Israel, during his time,
affirming the distinction between Abraham's physical offspring, Israel,
and the nations of the world. Finally, in Gen 28:13–14, when God speaks
to Jacob, he reiterates the distinction between Jacob's offspring, who will
possess the promised land, and the families of the earth, who will be
blessed through Jacob's offspring:

> And behold, the Lord stood above it and said, "I am the Lord,
> the God of Abraham your father and the God of Isaac. The land
> on which you lie I will give to you and to your offspring. Your
> offspring (זַרְעֶךָ) shall be like the dust of the earth, and you shall
> spread abroad to the west and to the east and to the north and
> to the south, and in you and your offspring shall all the families
> (מִשְׁפְּחֹת) of the earth be blessed."[28]

The language construction of the Abrahamic promise—you will be
a blessing—occurs in two other passages that clearly distinguish Israel
from other nations: Isa 19:24 and Zech 8:13.[29] In both passages, Israel
is neither portrayed as integrating with Gentile nations nor depicted as
synonymous with Gentiles. Instead, Israel is described as a distinct nation among other nations. This is the same distinction that is found in
the narratives of the patriarchal promise. Genesis 18:17–18 affirms this

---

28. The niphal stem, "bless," can be translated either as passive or reflexive. The
niphal form of "bless" is only used in formulations of the Abrahamic covenant (Gen
12:2; 18:18; 28:14). Traditionally the verb is taken as passive, but in other formulations
of the Abrahamic covenant (Gen 22:18; 26:4), the hitpael replaces the niphal form,
suggesting a translation of nations "blessing one another." Gen 28:14 recalls Gen 12:2
and 18:18, which all communicate that Jacob's offspring will be the medium of blessing
for the nations, thus rendering the niphal stem, in this context, as a passive verb.

29. "In that day Israel will be the third with Egypt and Assyria, a blessing in the
midst of the earth" (Isa 19:24); "And as you have been a byword of cursing among the
nations, O house of Judah and house of Israel, so will I save you, and you shall be a
blessing. Fear not, but let your hands be strong" (Zech 8:13). Wenham notes that "be
a blessing" is an unusual construction (היה בברכה) and occurs in only Isa 19:24 and
Zech 8:13. See Wenham, *Genesis 1–15*, 276.

portrayal of Israel by alluding to the language of the Abrahamic covenant and differentiating between Abraham's offspring (לְגוֹי גָּדוֹל) and the other nations (גּוֹיֵי) of the world: "The Lord said, 'shall I hide from Abraham what I am about to do, seeing that Abraham shall surely become a great and mighty nation (לְגוֹי גָּדוֹל), and all the nations (גּוֹיֵי) of the earth shall be blessed in him?'"[30]

It is consistent (1) grammatically, (2) contextually in the patriarchal narratives, and (3) contextually canonically that Gen 12:3 promises that God will bless both the "great nation" that will descend from Abraham through Jacob and all the "families of the earth," rather than signifying that the "families of the earth" will become the "great nation." The unwarranted conflation of these two separate aspects of the Abrahamic covenant seems to be the basis for a proposed typology in which Israel is seen as an OT type of a worldwide mono-national, multiethnic eschatological kingdom. Gentry utilizes this hermeneutical assumption when he reads passages about Isaiah's eschatological visions.

Gentry's Interpretation of Isaiah's Eschatological Kingdom

Isaiah 54

Gentry's interpretation of Isa 54 depends on his view of the Servant of Yahweh from Isa 40–55. The identity of this servant has been highly contested.[31] The servant has been seen as either an individual or as national

---

30. In Gen 18:17–19, Yahweh makes a statement that affirms his intentions to make Abraham the progenitor of a great nation and the agent of international blessings. The accumulation of covenant language describing an eternal covenant and a sworn promise of land indicates that the Abrahamic covenant's land oath to be an irrevocable promise upheld unilaterally by Yahweh. See Williamson, *Abraham, Israel, and the Nations*, 134.

31. For a survey of the proposed identity of Yahweh's servant, see Blenkinsopp, "Servant," 1:155–75. The phrase "light to the nations" appears in Isa 42:6 and Isa 49:6. In Isa 42:6 and 49:6, אוֹר גּוֹיִם appears, while Isa 51:4 has אוֹר עַמִּים. This change does not seem to change the overall meaning since גּוֹי and עַם function as synonyms within the same context. In Isa 42:6 and 49:6, the phrase "light to the nations" (אוֹר גּוֹיִם) is associated by way of elaboration with the expression "covenant to the people" (בְּרִית עָם). It is debated whether Gentile nations or dispersed Israelites are the intended audiences of the servant. De Boer suggests that the servant (redeemed Israelites) will serve as a "light respected by the nations." See de Boer, *Second Isaiah's Message*, 93. Snaith argues that the expression connotes a "worldwide light to guide all scattered Israelites home,"

Israel.[32] Those who see the servant as an individual point to the prediction that this one will also restore Israel ("raise up the tribes of Jacob"; Isa 49:6).[33] Gentry believes that the servant, in Isa 42, originally referred to national Israel, but now, in Isa 49, refers to the future Davidic king.[34] The reason for the change, he believes, is because Israel failed in their mission. He writes:

---

connecting Isa 49 with Isa 66. See Snaith, "Isaiah 40–66," 235–64. Lohfink concludes that the Hebrew Bible is occupied with the end time pilgrimage of Gentile nations to Mt. Zion. This pilgrimage will include the observance of the torah and Gentile nations will become part of God's covenant with Israel, connecting Isa 42 and 49 with the vision from Isa 2. See Lohfink, *God of Israel and the Nations*, 47. Clearly, depending on how one interprets the intended audience of the servant and whether the servant replaces national Israel affects how one sees the fulfillment of the servant's function as a "light to the nations."

32. If one were to assume an individualistic interpretation of the servant, there are five options theologians have proposed: 1. Messianic/christological figure; 2. Historical personality; 3. Ambiguous individual; 4. Prophet himself; and 5. Cyrus. Jean Steinmann argues that the servant is either an exclusively future figure or a historical person who anticipates the coming Messiah. See Steinmann, *Le livre*. Although Dumbrell asserts that the servant "is Israel in some form," he refers to the "striking" parallels between the appointment of the servant and the royal Messiah and delineates the servant's mission with terms commensurate with a messianic figure. See Dumbrell, "Role of the Servant," 105, 108. Concerning the historical personality view, Julian Morgenstern links the Servant Songs with a Davidic descendant named Menahem. Gillis Gerleman sees David in all four servant songs. G. R. Driver identifies the servant as an unknown Jewish preacher or prophet. See Driver, "Isaiah 52:13—53:12," 105; Morgenstern, "Suffering Servant," 406–31; Gerleman, "Der Gottesknecht bei Deuterojesaja," 38–60. Westermann believes the servant refers to an ambiguous individual. He writes, "The cryptic, veiled language used is deliberate. This is true of every one of the servant songs alike. From the very outset, there must be no idea that exegesis can clear up all their problems. The veiled manner of speaking is intentional, and to our knowledge, much in them was meant to remain hidden even from their original hearers." See Westermann, *Isaiah 40–66*, 93. Artur Weiser identifies the Servant as Second Isaiah. He argues that in view of his certain death by execution, his faith rose up to a daring hope and his suffering and death were representative for the conversion of Israel and served the nations. See Weiser, *Introduction to the Old Testament*, 201–5. Watts views the servant to be Cyrus. Previously, Cyrus was "called" and "appointed" to be a servant of Yahweh, who promises to "strengthen" and "keep" him. See Watts, *Isaiah 34–66*, 661.

33. Out of the twenty occurrences of the singular עֶבֶד in Isa 40–55, twelve refer to the nation (41:8–9; 42:19; 43:10; 44:1–2; 44:21; 44:25; 45:4; 48:29) and the remaining eight concern the servant figure (42:1; 49:3, 5–7; 50:10; 52:13; 53:11). Every reference to this figure depicts the servant figure as an individual.

34. In Isa 42:6, the word בְּרִית ("covenant") probably functions as a metonym, indicating a covenant mediator. The identity of עָם in the phrase "a covenant for the people (בְּרִית עָם)" seems to refer to the "nations" in v. 6. In Isa 42:5, עָם referred to mankind, which corresponds with the concept of "nations (גּוֹיִם)" in 42:6.

Israel as a servant is in dire need herself, not just of rescue from exile and all that entails, but also of a full resolution of the problem of a broken covenant relationship (e.g., 43:22–28) . . . how can God keep his promises to Abraham when Israel has completely failed as the servant of the Lord . . . how can the servant be both the nation and the deliverer of the nation? There is only one possible solution that resolves this conundrum fairly, and Isaiah has prepared us for this in the first part of his work: the servant must be the future king described earlier (e.g., 11:1–10).[35]

Gentry claims that the only way to understand Isaiah's prophecy regarding the deliverance of Israel is by means of a definitional change whereby Israel ceases to be a national reality but is rather redefined first as the individual, messianic king and then second as a multiethnic community in the person of the king. However, this fails to account for the positive predictions in Isaiah's prophecies of a future restoration of national Israel alongside the predictions of a future individual king. Isaiah 11:10–12 specifically mentions that a Davidic king ("root of Jesse")[36] will stand as a "signal" to the nations in order to recover Israelites from all over the world, portraying both a Davidic king and national Israel in the same passage:

> In that day the root of Jesse (שֹׁרֶשׁ יִשַׁי), who shall stand as a signal for the peoples—of him shall the nations (גּוֹיִם) enquire, and his resting place shall be glorious. In that day the Lord will extend his hand yet a second time to recover the remnant that remains of his people, from Assyria, from Egypt, from Pathros, from Cush, from Elam, from Shinar, from Hamath, and from the coastlands of the sea. He will raise a signal for the nations and will assemble the banished of Israel (יִשְׂרָאֵל) and gather the dispersed of Judah (יְהוּדָה) from the four corners of the earth.

The promise to gather national Israel in Isa 11:11 is reiterated in Isa 43:5–7: "Fear not, for I am with you; I will bring your offspring (זַרְעֶךָ) from the east, and from the west I will gather you. I will say to the north, Give up, and to the south, Do not withhold; bring my sons from afar and my daughters from the end of the earth, everyone who is called by my

---

35. Gentry and Wellum, *Kingdom through Covenant*, 439–40.

36. The text mentions David's father Jesse, instead of David himself. Perhaps this is done for rhetorical reasons to suggest that a new David, not just another Davidic descendant, will arise. Other prophets call the coming ideal Davidic king, "David," or picture him as the second coming of David. See Jer 30:9; Ezek 34:23–24; 37:24–25; Hos 3:5; and Mic 5:2.

name, whom I created for my glory, whom I formed and made." These passages reveal that a Davidic king functioning as a servant of Yahweh does not entail a replacement or redefinition of Israel's national identity nor does Isa 49:6 require such a replacement.[37]

According to Isa 49:6, there is a twofold task of the servant. First, he is to "raise up the tribes of Jacob" and second, he is to become a "light to the nations."[38] Gentry claims that the Davidic king will restore "Israel" by drawing nations to Yahweh, resulting in a reconstituted "Israel," comprised of Jews and Gentiles.[39] In other words, he interprets the two tasks of the Servant as synonymous.[40] However, a more likely interpretation of the twofold task of the servant is to view them as distinct, but related.[41]

37. Various scholars have suggested at least four alternatives to how the servant Israel carries out a ministry to national Israel in Isa 49:6: (1) leave the issue unresolved. See Melugin, *Isaiah 40–55*, 146; (2) regard "Israel" as a gloss. See Lohfink, "Israel," 217–29; (3) interpret "Israel" as a reference to all, some part, or an ideal form of Israel. See North, *Isaiah 40–55*, 189; or (4) view "Israel" as a designation for the servant individual. See Williamson, "Concept of Israel," 146. The fourth option seems the most likely interpretation based on the twofold task of the servant to "raise up the tribes of Jacob" and function as a "light to the nations." However, by affirming "Israel" as a designation for an individual does not indicate that Israel's national identity becomes redefined or replaced by said individual.

38. Goldingay notes, "The task to bring Jacob back was not primarily to bring the Babylonian community back to Palestine, but to bring them back to Yahweh. Being a light to the nations has been the task of Yahweh's servant since Isa 42:6. Yahweh commanded Jacob/Israel only a few verses previously to proclaim to the ends of the earth that Yahweh has redeemed servant Jacob (48:20)." See Goldingay, *Isaiah*, 283.

39. Gentry and Wellum, *Kingdom through Covenant*, 442.

40. Edward Young also views the twofold task of the Servant as synonymous. He writes, "The raising up and restoring of the people is essentially the same work as becoming light and salvation. It is in his being light and salvation to Israel (apart from the fact that he is also that to the Gentiles) that the servant raises up and restores Israel . . . that the reference is to spiritual Israel or the elect is clear from the whole context. Nowhere does the Bible teach that the entire physical Israel will be saved." See Young, *Book of Isaiah*, 275. Like Gentry, Young interprets the two tasks of the Servant as synonymous because he assumes that there is no future salvation for national Israel.

41. John Goldingay notes that the Servant's task "to raise" the tribe of Jacob "imply a restoration of Jacob-Israel that is both religious-spiritual-inward and political-national-material." He adds that the servant's task to serve as a "light to the nations" does not "replace" the servant's ministry to Israel, denoting two separate tasks. Goldingay, *Message of Isaiah 40–55*, 372–73. In Isa 49:8–12, the Lord assures the Servant that he will make him "to be a covenant for the people" (49:8). His mission objectives (to restore the land and bring the Israelites back from exile) suggest that he serves in this "covenant" role with regard to Israel. The prophet's placement of these two phrases in his delineation of the servant figure affirms a twofold ministry for the servant, to Israel and to the nations.

The task to "raise up the tribes of Jacob" recalls the commission given to Cyrus in Isa 45:13: "'I have stirred him up in righteousness, and I will make all his ways level; he shall build my city and set my exiles free, not for price or reward,' says the Lord of hosts." Implicit in the task to rebuild Jerusalem, Cyrus will also stabilize the economic and social structures of surrounding nations in Palestine.[42] The Servant, in Isa 49:6, will accomplish a task similar to Cyrus's but to a greater degree.[43] This Servant will restore national Israel and will also stabilize the social structures of surrounding nations by functioning as a "light to the nations" and by bringing God's salvation to the "ends of the earth" (Isa 49:6). Even if the Servant refers to the Davidic king, which I affirm, his twofold task does not result in the redefinition of national Israel. Instead, the Servant's twofold task can be seen as what he will accomplish for national Israel and surrounding nations of the world.

Based on his view of the servant of Yahweh, Gentry argues that a reconstructed Israel is described in Isa 54:1–3. In this text, a "married woman" is contrasted with a "desolate woman," whose offspring will inherit the nations and supposedly enlarge their family "tent":

> "Sing, O barren one, who did not bear; break forth into singing and cry aloud, you who have not been in labor! For the children of the desolate one will be more than the children of her who is married," says the Lord. "Enlarge the place of your tent and let the curtains of your habitations be stretched out; do not hold back; lengthen your cords and strengthen your stakes. For you will spread abroad to the right and the to left, and your offspring (זַרְעֶךָ) will possess the nations (גּוֹיִם) and will people the desolate cities."

42. John Watts notes that chaos and disorder reigned until Persia established control under Cyrus. He views "salvation" in political and economic terms and argues that Isa 49:6 promises a future servant, who will function like Cyrus, by bringing stability to the nations by restoring their economies and social order. In other words, the task of restoring Israel will lead to the stability of the surrounding nations. See Watts, *Isaiah 34–66*, 737.

43. Just as Cyrus (a representative/ ruling figure) brings to pass Israel's return from the Babylonian exile as an initial fulfillment of this, even so will the servant figure accomplish the great and final return of God's children from the four corners of the world. Yahweh's use of Cyrus as his instrument prepares the way for Israel's comprehension of the function and identity of the servant figure in the final sense. Ulrich E. Simon regards Cyrus as a type of the servant figure. See Simon, "Konig Cyrus," 83–89.

For Gentry, the "married woman" refers to Israel before the exile and the "desolate woman" refers to a reconstituted Israel after the exile. Since the children of the desolate woman will "be more" than those of the married woman, Gentry concludes that from the point of view of the NT, "Israel inherits the nations because they become part of the family."[44] Gentry argues that when the "offspring" of the "desolate woman" inherits the nations, both Gentiles from a multitude of nations will join Israel to form a new covenant community, otherwise known as the NT church.[45] As Motyer states, the barren woman refers to the church, comprised of Jews and Gentiles, who will be born by "supernatural birth."[46]

It seems that Gentry conflates Israel and the city of Zion in Isa 54. In Isa 49:14, it is Zion who views itself as "forsaken" and "forgotten" by Yahweh. Later in Isa 62:13, Yahweh promises to reverse Zion's condition and calls them a "city not forsaken," alluding back to Isa 49:14. In this setting, the desolate woman, in Isa 54:3, is most naturally read as the city of Zion, not Israel per se. Gentry even acknowledges that the verses of Isa 54:11–17 "speak of the woman as a city, the city of Zion."[47] Yet, Gentry concludes that the language of expansion, in Isa 54:1–3, refers to the inclusion of Gentiles into a new multiethnic "Israel." However, there is a problem with this interpretation. Understanding that the term "children

---

44. Gentry and Wellum, *Kingdom through Covenant*, 442.

45. One reason why some have interpreted the offspring of the barren woman as a reference to the NT church is because of Paul's use of Isa 54:1 in Gal 4:27. Those who view Gal 4:21–31 in terms of typology include Ellis, "New Testament," 51–53; Silva, "Galatians," 808; Roehers, "Use of the Old Testament," 210–12. Others who view Paul's use of Isa 54:1 as an allegorical interpretation include Longenecker, *Galatians*, 199–10; Hays, *Echoes of Scripture*, 116; Hanson, *Allegory and Event*, 89; Meyer, *End of the Law*, 116–19. There are others who view both elements of allegory and typology: Schreiner, *Galatians*, 293–300. Moo, *Galatians*, 294–96; De Boer, "Paul's Quotation," 370–89; Cosgrove, "Sarah," 221; Barker, "Allegory and Typology," 193–209; Harmon, "Allegory," 154–58. Whether Paul uses Isa 54:1 in Gal 4:27 as a form of typology is highly disputed. Some, such as Brent Parker, assume that two of the Abrahamic promises are read as one in their reading of Isa 54:1. Parker writes, "The inextricable link between the promise of being a great nation and the global promise of all the families of the earth being blessed is further established in how the prophets portray the nations becoming part of end-time Israel." See Parker, "Israel-Christ-Church," 218–20. The drawback with Parker's reading of Isa 54:1 is that Paul states in Gal 4:26 that the "mother" refers to the "Jerusalem above," and not to Israel. If Paul is reading the "barren woman," from Isa 54:1, typologically, then it seems better to interpret the "mother," from Gal 4:25, as referring to the future Zion rather than to a future multiethnic Israel.

46. Motyer, *Prophecy of Isaiah*, 447.

47. Gentry and Wellum, *Kingdom through Covenant*, 443.

of the desolate woman" refers to Zion's citizens, clearly an expansion of the city has nothing to do with a redefinition of national Israel. Instead, it most naturally means that the city of Zion will become much larger, including more citizens than it previously had before the Babylonian exile.

Particularly problematic with Gentry's reading of Isa 54 is his interpretation of v. 3: "for you will spread abroad to the right and to the left, and your offspring (זַרְעֶךָ) will possess the nations and will people the desolate cities." The phrase "possess the nations" may be an allusion to Ps 2:8, where God promises that his "son" (Ps 2:7), who will reign from Zion, will inherit the nations: "Ask of me, and I will make the nations your heritage, and the ends of the earth your possession."[48] Gentry, however, views the phrase "possess the nations" from Isa 54:3, as denoting something more than "simply bringing the exiles back to the land."[49] He believes that Israel will "inherit the nations" not as a "destructive military conquest" but by bringing Gentiles into their family, which refers to the

---

48. Ps 2 belongs to the royal psalms, clearly designated a special group, which have as their common theme the term "king." As Herman Gunkel notes, these psalms include 18, 20, 21, 45, 72, 89, 101, 110, 132, and 144. See Gunkel, *Introduction to Psalms*, 99–120. Walford, Jacobson, and Tanner note that most commentators agree that Ps 2 was most likely performed as part of the coronation ceremony of a new king in Jerusalem. On the other hand, Kraus argues that it may have formed part of some sort of annual enthronement festival. See DeClaissé-Walford et al., *Psalms*, 66–68; Kraus, *Psalms 1–59*, 125–26. Some, such as Noth, assert that the sonship of the Jerusalem king is based on a process of adoption, which highlights his legal standing rather than comment on his nature. See Noth, "Gott," 222. However, as Kidner indicates, there is no textual basis for understanding "begotten" as adoption. He notes that Ps 2 enlarges the pledge of adoption given to David's heir in 2 Sam 7:14. See Kidner, *Psalm 1–72*, 51. When Paul cites Ps 2:7, in Acts 13:33, in regards to Jesus' resurrection and identity as the son of God, this confirms that the Davidic king depicted in Ps 2 is identified as God's son because of his divine nature confirmed through his resurrection. Furthermore, NT passages emphasize Christ's royal and divine authority: to Christ has been given all authority in heaven and on earth (Matt 28:18); he is the son and heir (Matt 21:38); he is the true son of the Father (Heb 1:5; 5:5). Acts 4:25; 13:33; Rev 2:26–27; and 19:15 all cite Ps 2 in the context between Christ the exalted king with the hostile Gentile nations. What is relevant for this work is that Ps 2:8 declares that this king in Jerusalem will inherit the nations as his heritage. As Goldingay and Dahood observe, Yahweh's commitment to the king in Jerusalem is closely related to his concern with Jerusalem itself because the king is to be a means of Yahweh's authority over the entire world. See Goldingay, *Psalms 1–41*, 72; Dahood, *Psalms 1–50*, 12–13. Isaiah 54:3 correlates with the depiction of Jesus as the king in Jerusalem, according to Ps 2:7–8, instead of portraying Israel "inheriting" Gentiles in order to form a new multiethnic community.

49. Gentry and Wellum, *Kingdom through Covenant*, 442.

NT church.[50] Motyer also argues that the Servant's work in Isa 54 fulfills the promise that Abraham's offspring will possess other nations by integrating Gentiles with Israel (Gen 22:17; Exod 34:24; Deut 9:1; 11:23; Josh 23:9).[51] Both Motyer and Gentry's interpretation of Isa 54:3, however, seem to dismiss the textual details within Isaiah that promise the Davidic king's future rule over Israel and Gentile nations within a multinational kingdom paradigm.

Isaiah 11:1 describes a future Davidic ruler who is a "shoot from the stump of Jesse" and will spring forth after God will "cut down" the forest of Assyria (Isa 10:33–34). This new ruler from Jesse's line will fear the Lord (Isa 11:2), judge righteously (Isa 11:4), signal the nations (Isa 11:10, 12), and restore Israel and Judah from the "four corners of the earth" (Isa 11:12). Not only will this king gather Israel from the "coastlands" (Isa 11:11), but also will reconcile the two divided kingdoms ("Ephraim shall not be jealous of Judah, and Judah shall not harass Ephraim"; Isa 11:13). In Isa 11:14, the restored kingdom of Israel will advance eastward through the inhabited regions into the wilderness of Syria and Arabia to seize the nations' wealth, implying the subjugation of Gentile nations to this Davidic king ("but they shall swoop down on the shoulder of the Philistines in the west, and tougher they shall plunder the people of the east"). This Davidic king will establish a type of peace that removes the original curse between man and creation, alluding to the conditions of Eden (Isa 11:6–9; cf. Gen 3:14–19).

In Isa 62:8, God swears by "his right hand"—which may refer to him taking an oath or to the use of his military might—to no longer allow Gentile nations to take Zion's grain or wine: "The Lord has sworn by his right hand and by his mighty arm: 'I will not again give your grain to be food for your enemies, and foreigners shall not drink your wine for which you have labored.'" Isaiah 60:16 adds that Zion will "suck the milk of nations" and receive their "wealth" (Isa 60:5), which predicts the subjugation of Gentile nations to Zion because of their submission to the Davidic king.[52] These texts seem to indicate that Isa 54:3 refers to the

---

50. Gentry and Wellum, *Kingdom through Covenant*, 442.

51. Motyer, *Isaiah*, 384.

52. Charles Cruise states that the same line of thought is revealed in Isa 18:7 and 45:14. So, "wealth of the nations" and its associated nationalistic aspects cannot be dismissed as artificial or even accidental in Isaiah. See Cruise, "Wealth of the Nations," 296.

Davidic king's future rule, from Zion, over the nations in his kingdom rather than a reference to the NT church.[53]

Putting aside Gentry's conflation of Israel and Zion, Gentry's interpretation of Isa 54:13 assumes that God never intends to redeem national Israel. According to Gentry, the community described in Isa 54:13 portrays a new multiethnic people, distinct from national Israel, since it depicts a believing community ("All your children shall be taught by the Lord, and great shall be the peace of your children"). As Gentry's coauthor, Wellum, explains, "The most distinguishing difference between [Israel and the church] is that Israel is a mixed community (i.e., comprised of believers and unbelievers) while the church is a regenerate community (i.e., comprised of believers who have been born of the Spirit and have professed faith in Christ)."[54] Wellum presents a false dichotomy where there are only two types of people: Israel (comprised of believers and unbelievers) and the church (comprised of believers). According to this dichotomy, any description of a believing community in Isaiah must refer to the NT church, rather than national Israel. Gentry's conclusion that the "children," in Isa 54:13, is "perfectly coextensive" with the NT church seems to be based on this false dichotomy.[55]

Contrary to Gentry and Wellum's reading of Isa 54:13, Isaiah consistently predicts the future restoration of national Israel in the eschatological kingdom. In Isa 10:20–25, God promises that a future "remnant" from Israel will return to Zion and this remnant will no longer "rely on" Gentile nations but will trust in the "Holy One of Israel" (Isa 10:20).[56]

---

53. Gentry appeals to the NT as evidence that the desolate woman, from Isa 54:1–3, refers to the NT church. There is a shortcoming to Gentry's interpretation because there is an absence of any NT appropriation of Isa 54:1–3. As Oswalt notes, there must be "clear markers in the text" that specifies that Isa 54 describes the NT church otherwise one should avoid such an interpretation. See Oswalt, *Book of Isaiah*, 418n30. Gentry fails to point out any "clear" textual markers in the NT that references Isa 54:1–3 as portraying the NT church.

54. Gentry and Wellum, *Kingdom through Covenant*, 646. Based on his assumption that Isa 54:13 anticipates the church, Gentry sees 1 Pet 2:14 as a parallel passage to Isa 54:12 since the metaphor of the church as "living stones" is reminiscent of the restored city built with beautiful and lasting materials, referring to the new covenant community. Gentry's reading, however, does not consider Isa 60:10, which states that foreigners will build up the city walls of Jerusalem, which seems to correlate with Isa 54:12 more than 1 Pet 2:14.

55. Gentry and Wellum, *Kingdom through Covenant*, 444.

56. The referent of אֵל גִּבּוֹר ("mighty God") in Isa 10:21 is uncertain. The title appears only here and in Isa 9:6, where it is one of the royal titles of the coming Davidic

Although, historically, Israel's possession of their land was conditioned on their holiness (Lev 18:28), God reaffirms his election of Israel by promising that he will "set" them back in their land in the future in Isa 14:1 ("For the Lord will have compassion on Jacob and will again choose Israel, and will set them in their own land, and sojourners will join them and will attach themselves to the house of Jacob"). Previously in Isa 5:26, God signaled the nations to use their military might to "devour" Israel (Isa 5:5), but in Isa 11:12 and 49:22, God will signal the nations in order to gather Israelites from the "four corners of the earth" in Zion. These texts reveal that God intends to gather and redeem national Israel along with restoring their city, Zion. The reason why God will never abandon Zion like a "nursing mother" never forgets her child (Isa 49:15) or a person forgets about a "cut in his hands" (Isa 49:16), is because there is a close correlation between Zion's restoration and that of Israel as a whole. Implicit in God's promise to restore Zion is his promise to gather and restore national Israel to their land.

Gentry argues that the "covenant of peace" (new covenant) functions as a replacement of the Israelite/Mosaic covenant, thus resulting in a new covenant community that replaces national Israel.[57] He writes, "The new covenant renews and restores the broken old covenant. But it is more than that. It is a new covenant, different from the old one and superior to it, because it depends not on God's people but instead on the everlasting kindness of God."[58] However, Isaiah does not introduce this "covenant of peace" as a replacement of the Mosaic covenant but instead links it conceptually to the Noahic flood. He specifically mentions that God's compassion will be like the "days of Noah" when "the waters of Noah should no more go over the earth" (Isa 54:9).[59] Gentry acknowledges this connection by stating:

> This new exhibition of love and mercy is illustrated by a comparison between the new covenant and the covenant that God made with Noah. Just as he promised there that never again

---

king. Similar titles appear in Deut 10:17, Neh 9:32, and Jer 32:18. The preceding verse, however, mentions Israel relying on the Lord, so it is likely that the title refers to Yahweh instead of the Davidic king.

57. Isaiah never utilizes the term "new covenant," but "covenant of peace" or "eternal covenant" (Isa 54:10; 55:3).

58. Gentry and Wellum, *Kingdom through Covenant* (2nd ed.), 498.

59. The Hebrew text reads literally, "For the waters of Noah [is] this to me." כִּי־מֵי ("for the waters of") should be emended to כִּימֵי ("like the days of").

would he judge the entire world by a flood, so here he is promising never again to be angry with his people. The mountains will
give way and the hills will totter, but his *hesed*, his covenant
faithfulness, and love will never be taken away in the new covenant. That is why it is called a covenant of peace.[60]

Gentry suggests that the connection between the new covenant and
the Noahic flood is with the parallel display of God's love and mercy.
However, Isaiah seems to be connecting the Noahic flood with the covenant of peace in a different manner. Several scholars have argued that
Isaiah utilizes water imagery in order to tell how Yahweh will deliver his
people by restoring "order from chaos."[61] Three events that display God's
restorative power include the creation, flood, and exodus, and several
passages within Isaiah allude to these events. The flood, in particular,
seems to serve as a paradigm to show the *order of events* in God's deliverance of Israel from exile.[62]

In Isa 44, God reveals that he will appoint Cyrus to deliver Israel from
Babylonian exile. In Isa 44:24–28, God confirms his promise by recalling
his power in creation ("who made all things, who alone stretched out the

---

60. Gentry and Wellum, *Kingdom through Covenant* (2nd ed.), 498. Lohfink also
connects the language of the new covenant with the Noahic covenant. He writes, "The
passage, which employs Noah terminology, is framed and defined through the root
רָחֶם, 'to have compassion' (Isa 54:7, 8, 10). When readers of the Bible later come to
Jeremiah, they will meet the word again in Jer 31:20, in an emphatic form and in
a very similar context, and it will impart its tone to the word 'forgive' (סָלַח) in Jer
31:34, which ends the prophecy about the new covenant." See Lohfink, "Covenant and
Torah," 51.

61. McCarthy writes how water imagery, in Isaiah, either communicates how Yahweh will restore "order" by means of waters or save his people from "waters," which
symbolize evil. See McCarthy, "'Creation' Motifs," 401. Bernard Anderson references
Isa 51:9–11 as an example of Yahweh's kingship over the rebellious waters of chaos. He
argues that the exodus story serves as a "typological anticipation" of the new creation
when Yahweh would make a path through the chaotic waters so that his people could
pass into the promised land. See Anderson, *Creation versus Chaos*, 108–9. Anderson
adds that Isa 54:9–10 affirms that Yahweh's purpose is to reverse the "threat of chaos"
with his everlasting love by binding himself to Israel with a covenant, as he did in
the days of Noah when he reverses the chaotic waters. See Anderson, *Creation versus
Chaos*, 127.

62. David Gunn notes how creation is a theme of order from chaos, which is
echoed in the flood account and later depicted in Isaiah when God delivers Israel
from the "chaos of exile into a new order, a new creation." See Gunn, "Deutero-
Isaiah," 493, 497.

heavens"; Isa 44:24) and the flood ("dry up your rivers"; Isa 44:27).[63] In Isa 50:2, God reiterates his intention to deliver Israel by recounting his mighty acts from the flood and exodus episodes: "Why, when I came, was there no man; why, when I called, was there no one to answer? Is my hand shortened, that it cannot redeem? Or have I no power to deliver? Behold, by my rebuke *I dry up the sea*, *I make the rivers a desert*; their fish stink for lack of water and die of thirst."[64] In Isa 51, God alludes to his power in creation, the flood, and exodus as confirmation that he has the power to restore Zion. Specifically, in Isa 51:10, there are allusions to both the flood and exodus accounts, with the phrase "the waters of the great deep" closely resembling the language from the flood (cf. Gen 7:11; 8:2), and the phrase "pass over" recalling the exodus ("Was it not you who dried up the sea, the *waters of the great deep*, who made the depths of the sea a way for the redeemed to *pass over*?"). The exodus, in particular, illustrates the climatic event of redemption in Israel's history and serves as a prelude to the "new" exodus[65] promised in Isa 51:11 ("And the ransomed of the Lord shall return and come to Zion with singing; everlasting joy shall be upon their heads; they shall obtain gladness and joy, and sorrow and sighing

63. The verb "dry up" is the same verb used twice in the flood accounts (Gen 8:7, 13) and "rivers" is a closely related concept to the "fountains of the deep" from Gen 7:11 and 8:2. See Westermann, *Isaiah 40–66*, 157.

64. The phrase "their fish stink for lack of water" may allude to the flood since rotting fish suggests a longer period of "drying up" than associated with the crossing of the Red Sea. See Gunn, "Deutero-Isaiah," 500–501.

65. Isa 11:10–16; 40:3–11; 49:8–12; and 51:1—52:15 seem to indicate that the exodus of Israel from Egypt typologically points to a greater new exodus, an eschatological event whereby Israel's sin and rebellion are dealt with, Zion is restored, and salvation is extended to the ends of the earth. See Watts, "Exodus," 478–87. The exodus event is the act of creation that brings Israel into being as a nation so that they may serve God as God's "son." See Atlas, "Creation of Israel," 30–59. Robin Routledge writes that the exodus functions as a paradigm for God's future deliverance and restoration of his people. He writes, "The use of exodus traditions in the later prophetic writings points to a typological correspondence between the people of God in Egypt and those languishing in exile in Babylon—and their respective deliverances. This is not simply calling to mind an example of God's redemptive power in the past in order to give reassurance for the future. It is that; but it also points beyond it to the ongoing purpose of God for his people. The God who redeemed and created them in the exodus events continues his work of redemption, renewal, and (re-) creation—in order that the people should be what they were called to be." See Routledge, "The Exodus and Biblical Theology," 204–5. Isaiah's allusion to the exodus event as prefiguring a "new exodus" points to the eschatological reality when God will reverse the "chaos" of Israel's exile in order to establish a multinational kingdom because of the Davidic king who will restore Israel and function as a light to the nations, according to Isa 49:6.

shall flee away"). Finally, in Isa 55:10–11, God reverses the imagery of water since he connects the certainty of his word with the imagery of water that brings a harvest on the earth:

> For as the rain and the snow come down from heaven and do not return there but water the earth, making it bring forth and sprout, giving seed to the sower and bread to the eater, so shall my word be that goes out from my mouth; it shall not return to me empty, but it shall accomplish that which I purpose, and shall succeed in the thing for which I sent it.

Just as Noah's dove served as a messenger that returned with an "olive leaf" as a sign of a restored new world (Gen 7:12), so too will God's word return with an "everlasting sign" of a restored new creation, namely the covenant of peace ("Instead of the thorn shall come up the cypress; instead of the brier shall come up the myrtle; and it shall make a name for the Lord, an *everlasting sign* that shall not be cut off"; Isa 55:13).[66]

In sum, the "days of Noah," from Isa 54:9, functions as an allusion to the flood when God reversed the "chaos" of the flood and confirmed his peace on earth with an everlasting sign. In the same way, the "covenant of peace" will serve as an everlasting sign and confirmation that God will reverse the "chaos" from the exile and establish peace between Israel and Gentile nations in his multinational kingdom (Isa 2:4; 19:24–25; 27:4–5; 61:5–6; 62:2–3). Gentry's argument that the covenant of peace functions as a replacement of the Israelite/Mosaic covenant, thus resulting in a new covenant community that replaces national Israel, does not correlate to Isaiah's other allusions to the flood. It seems that Isaiah does not connect the covenant of peace with the mercy displayed in the Noahic covenant but alludes to the flood as a pattern of how God will bring "order from chaos" after the exile.

Gentry concludes his treatment of Isa 54 by arguing that the "servants" in Isa 54:17 connects with the "suffering servant" of Isa 53. Motyer comments that the saving work of the Servant creates servants, which

---

66. David Gunn writes, "Yahweh's promise (covenant) to Noah was guaranteed by a sign, the rainbow, a natural concomitant of the cosmic disaster which had befallen man, an adjunct of the rains which had destroyed but which could also bring new life, so now he gives to his people in the new situation of deliverance from national disaster an appropriate sign, the prophetic word, uttered and recorded before the event and available to all following generations as a reminder and guarantee of his 'covenant of peace' with them." Gunn, "Deutero-Isaiah," 508.

results in the Servant's blessing being shared with his servants.[67] Gentry concurs with Motyer's argument:

> Subtly and quietly, but also unmistakably, Isaiah links [the servants] to the greatest servant of all. As he was a disciple, taught by the Lord (50:4), so are they (54:13). They have suffered affliction (54:11), as did he (53:4). And as he will surely be vindicated (50:8), so will they be (54:17). They are called servants of the Lord because they follow in the footsteps of the perfect servant.[68]

Gentry also states that Isa 56:6 reveals that the servants, from Isa 54:17, are foreigners:

> We were shocked to discover in 54:17 that those who are included in the new covenant community are called the servants of the Lord. The sins of many have been born by the servant, and the victory of the one servant is shared by the many and in the end, they become servants too. Now, we are further shocked because it is foreigners who are called the servants of the Lord.[69]

By connecting the "servants," in Isa 54, with the suffering servant, from Isa 53, Gentry utilizes a "one in many" paradigm where the blessings ascribed to the Servant apply to the many who identify with him, including

---

67. Motyer, *Prophecy of Isaiah*, 451–52.

68. Gentry and Wellum, *Kingdom through Covenant* (2nd ed.), 498–99. Parker also sees a "one in many" paradigm between the suffering Servant, in Isa 53, with the servants in Isa 54. He comments that the atoning sacrificial death of the suffering Servant entails an "escalation" in the people of God. He writes, "The covenant community under his headship and representation is greater than national Israel in the sense that it is an international community that enjoys the complete forgiveness of sins through Christ's once and for all death, and is characterized by a Spirit-filled, faithful, regenerate people who have circumcised, torah-inscribed hearts (Rom 2:29; 2 Cor 3:3, 16–18; Col 2:11; Phil 3:3). In sum, Jesus fulfills the Servant-Israel's mission by his atoning death (Isa 53; cf. Rom 4:23–25; 8:32; Gal 1:4), a work that brings about the cleansing and restoration of Israel, a restoration that pointed to a renewed eschatological Israel made up of true and faithful servants." See Parker, "Israel-Christ-Church," 263.

69. Gentry and Wellum, *Kingdom through Covenant*, 448. Fantuzzo concurs with Gentry's interpretation of "servants" in Isaiah. He writes, "Only those disciples whose turning from transgression demonstrates their solidarity with the righteous Servant are true servants of Yahweh ([Isa] 59:20; cf. 49:23; 57:13; 64:3; 65:16). Only they are the 'Redeemed of the LORD' (62:12)." Fantuzzo, "True Israel's 'Mother and Brothers,'" 116. Fantuzzo also observes that in the final chapters of Isaiah "there is narrowing: Yahweh will restrict the Israel of God to the offspring of the Servant. Only those whose servanthood indicates their solidarity with the Servant can inhabit holy Zion." See Fantuzzo, "True Israel's 'Mother and Brothers,'" 119.

foreigners. Based on this paradigm, the Abrahamic and Davidic blessings previously promised to national Israel are redefined by a future Davidic king to the new covenant community since they become connected to him as "servants of the Lord."[70]

Applying a "one in many" paradigm to the "servants" in Isa 54 and 56 such that national Israel becomes redefined by a future Davidic king is problematic. There are no textual indicators in Isaiah's eschatological visions that shifts the meaning of Israel and their land or erases ethnic and territorial distinctions between Israelites and Gentiles. The Davidic king will restore Israel (Isa 11:12; 49:6), purify them (Isa 4:4), and "plant" them in their land as "oaks of righteousness" (Isa 61:3). In passages such as Isa 11:12 and 49:22, distinctions remain between the Gentile nations and the Israelites they will gather from the "four corners of the earth" to Zion. In Isa 49:6, the Servant will perform separate acts regarding Israel ("raise up the tribes of Jacob") and Gentile nations ("I will make you as a light for the nations, that my salvation may reach to the end of the earth"). Isaiah does not portray the Davidic king administering covenant blessings to a multiethnic Israel, thus indicating that every "servant of the Lord" receive all of the Abrahamic and Davidic covenant blessings. Instead, Isaiah portrays national distinctions between Israelites and Gentiles in regard to their relationship to the Davidic king. Gentry continues to apply this tenuous "one in many" paradigm in his interpretation of Isa 55:3.

Isaiah 55

In Isa 55:3, God initiates an everlasting covenant that promises a life filled with satisfaction, as opposed to one marked by hunger and thirst ("Incline your ear, and come to me; hear, that your soul may live; and I will make with you an everlasting covenant, my steadfast, sure love for David"). If "David" functions as an objective genitive, then he is the recipient of the covenantal promises (בְּרִית), which means that the "everlasting covenant" anticipates kingdom blessings that are analogous to the one given to David so that Zion will become a city of blessings as a witness

---

70. Gentry explains what he sees the covenant of peace accomplishes in Isa 54: "(1) it brings the numerous seed promised in the Abrahamic covenant, (2) it brings the righteousness between God and humans and among humans aimed at in the Israelite covenant, and (3) it establishes the city of God ruled by the Davidic King." Gentry's conclusion assumes that Israel functions as an OT type of the church where individuals are linked to Christ. See Gentry and Wellum, *Kingdom through Covenant*, 445.

to the nations (Isa 55:5).[71] Gentry, however, claims that "David," should be interpreted as a subjective genitive, which means that the "steadfast, sure love" are performed *by* David and not promised *for* David.[72] According to his interpretation of Isa 55:3, Gentry believes that Isaiah joins the Davidic covenant with the new covenant, as he has defined it, and that the "steadfast, sure love" performed by David serves as the basis for the promise of the "everlasting covenant."[73] Gentry adds that Isa 55:3 points to "the antitype of David" who "will inaugurate a new covenant," thus serving as a "rubric for the future king."[74] Regarding Isa 55:4–5, Gentry notes, "The blessings do come to the nations, not because Yahweh's promises to David are democratized in the way some think but because a new David who is an obedient son succeeds in bringing Yahweh's Torah to all humans."[75] For Gentry, the way the "new" David brings blessings

71. Michael Grisanti writes, "Israel's exalted position is a benefit they enjoy by means of Yahweh's fulfillment of His promises to David. In his call for covenant renewal, Yahweh promises Israel the benefits of His covenant with David. Like David, the nation will hold a position of leadership over the nations of the world (the result of God's intervention on their behalf)." See Grisanti, *Israel and the Nations*, 76. The syntactical relationship of חַסְדֵי ("steadfast, sure love") to the preceding line is unclear. If the term is appositional to בְּרִית ("covenant"), then the Lord transfers the promises of the Davidic covenant to national Israel. If חַסְדֵי functions as an adverbial accusative, then the בְּרִית is viewed as an extension or perhaps fulfillment of the Davidic promises. If taken as a comparative, then the new covenant is analogous to the Davidic covenant. Verses 4–5 compare David's international prominence to what Israel will experience and seems to favor the view that the "everlasting covenant" given to Israel is analogous to the covenant given to David. Acts 13:34 references Isa 55:3 to show that the permanent dominion of David's "throne" (2 Sam 7:16), in Zion, as a witness among the nations, is possible only if the Davidic king lives forever and never sees "corruption" (Acts 13:35).

72. Barrett notes that it would be possible to interpret "promises made to David" as "promises spoken by David" now reproduced in his dealing with the people of David's messianic descendant. See Barrett, *Acts*, 648. For a discussion on whether "David" is a subjective or objective genitive, see Lohfink, *Das Jüdische am Christentum*, 251n82.

73. Gentry writes, "The new covenant will accomplish what was promised in God's covenant with David." Gentry and Wellum, *Kingdom through Covenant*, 445.

74. Gentry and Wellum, *Kingdom through Covenant*, 421, 644.

75. Gentry and Wellum, *Kingdom through Covenant* (2nd ed.), 475. Gentry does not affirm the view of Eichrodt and Sommer, who argue for the democratization of the Davidic covenant to a "new Israel," based on an objective genitive reading of "my steadfast, sure love for David." For an explanation of the traditional supersessionist view of Isa 55:3, see Mackay, *Isaiah*, 392. Gentry interprets the phrase "my steadfast, sure love for David" as a subjective genitive, thereby resulting in the new David, who as an obedient son of God, succeeds in bringing Yahweh's torah to all humans, and shares his victory with the many, who are identified as "servants."

to the nations is through his death (Isa 53:5) and resurrection, which inaugurates the new covenant.

Gentry references Acts 13:34 as support for his interpretation that Isa 55:3 points to the future Davidic king who will administer new covenant blessings to Jewish and Gentile individuals in the NT church. Gentry notes that both Jews and Gentiles form the audience for Paul's sermon. In his summary of Israel's history, Paul cites three prophetic texts that prophesy Jesus' resurrection: Ps 2:7, Isa 55:3, and Ps 16:10. Gentry argues that a subjective genitive reading of Isa 55:3 ("sure mercies performed *by* David") fits with Paul's argument that the historical David serves as a "rubric" for the resurrected Messiah.[76] Paul's use of Isa 55:3 and Ps 16:10 indicate that Isaiah was not talking about the Davidic covenant blessings given to the historical David, in 2 Sam 7. Instead, Isaiah points to the new covenant blessings the new Davidic king (Jesus) will administer to the Gentiles because of his death and his resurrection, according to Gentry.[77]

Although Gentry appropriately illustrates how the Servant of the Lord refers to Jesus as the promised Davidic king, he connects Ps 2:7, Isa 55:3, and Ps 16:10 in a way that leads to a questionable interpretation of Isa 55:3. Paul quoted these OT texts (Ps 2:7; Isa 55:3; Ps 16:10) in order to establish that Jesus's resurrection confirms his identity as the Davidic king who fulfills the promises given to national Israel, the "children" of this promise (Acts 13:32–33).[78] Paul's first quotation, Ps 2:7, is linked with 2 Sam 7:14 with the expression "my son." Psalm 2 describes the opposition of the nations and their rulers against the Anointed of the Lord and Ps 2:7 refers to the legitimacy of Israel's king as a "son" of God.[79] By quoting Ps 2:7, Paul indicates that Jesus' sonship was made evident by his resurrection and that he is the "Anointed" of the Lord who will rule Israel and exercise dominion over the nations (Ps 2:2).[80]

---

76. Gentry and Wellum, *Kingdom through Covenant* (2nd ed.), 475.

77. Gentry writes, "The explanation that David served his *own* generation is a clear statement that the historical David is not in view in Acts 13:34. Instead, Isaiah refers to the Messiah. Since the pious deeds of David in the context of Isa 55:3 are the sufferings and death of the servant in Isa 53, the reference to the resurrection becomes clear." Gentry and Wellum, *Kingdom through Covenant* (2nd ed.), 478.

78. Keener, *Acts*, 2071.

79. Schnabel, *Acts*, 581.

80. Bock notes that Jesus did not become a "son" by adoption but that his sonship was confirmed with his resurrection. See. Bock, *Acts*, 456.

Paul's second OT quotation, Isa 55:3, also relates to 2 Sam 7:4–17. The "holy and sure blessings of David" refer to God's promise that he would establish in David's descendant an eternal kingdom for the benefit of Israel and the nations (cf. 2 Sam 7:13, 16).[81] God promises to renew these blessings at the time of restoration after exile by assuring Israel that he would yet give them the "sure love" for David (Isa 55:3).[82] Just as God made David a witness to the nations (Isa 55:4), so also will he establish Zion as a witness to the nations at her restoration (Isa 55:5, 12–13). Paul quotes Isa 55:3 to show that the permanent dominion of David's "throne" (2 Sam 7:16), as a witness among the nations, is possible only if the Davidic king lives forever and never sees "corruption" (Acts 13:35). This interpretation of Acts 13:34 is confirmed with Paul's quotation of Ps 16:10, in Acts 13:35.[83]

Paul connects Ps 16:10 with Isa 55:3 by means of the word "holy" which serves as a *gezerah Shewa,* one of the Hilell's rabbinic rules of interpretation where two passages are interpreted with a shared word.[84] Paul seems to imply that the "holy blessings" of David, from Isa 55:3, are connected with the "Holy One," from Ps 16:10. The connection becomes clear in Acts 13:36–37 when Paul states that Ps 16:10 could not have referred to the historical David since he died and saw "corruption." Psalm 16:10 reveals that the resurrection is the means by which God will establish the eternal kingdom of the offspring of David, who will rule from Zion and administer covenantal blessings to Israel and the nations, as Isa 55:3 promises.

Regarding the addition of Gentiles in the NT church, it is important to examine Paul's quotation of Isa 49:6 in Acts 13:47. Since Gentry interprets Isa 55:3 as a reference to the new covenant blessings Jesus administers to the NT church, he assumes that Isa 55:4–5 refer to individual Gentiles in the NT church. Isaiah 49:6 defines the servant's role with a twofold task: restore Israel and function as a "light to the nations." Paul quotes the second task, in Acts 13:47, to show that the Lord has commanded him, along with Barnabas, to undertake the role of bringing

---

81. Polhill, *Acts,* 304; Pillai, *Apostolic Interpretation of History,* 83–87; Schweizer, "'Son of God,'" 186–93.

82. Bruce, *Acts,* 260.

83. BDAG states that the quotation from Isa 55:3 is intended to show that the following quotation from Ps 16:10 could not refer to David himself, but must refer to his messianic descendant (Jesus). See Arndt et al., "ὅσιος," 728.

84. Bock, *Acts,* 458.

salvific light to the nations.[85] Luke has already identified Jesus as the Servant (Luke 2:20–32), which indicates that Paul views his own specific commission as an extension of Jesus' mission to the Gentiles.[86] By quoting the second half of Isa 49:6, Paul does not indicate that his mission replaces or redefines the Servant's task to restore national Israel. Instead, he highlights his participation in the Servant's mission to Gentile nations.[87] Furthermore, new covenant blessings for Gentile individuals in the NT church does not require a redefinition of national Israel as recipients of the first task of the Servant, as prophesied in Isa 49:6.

Gentry acknowledges that his subjective genitive reading of "David," in Isa 55:3, goes against the consensus view, which is an objective genitive interpretation of "David."[88] So, one may question the validity of interpreting Isa 55:3 as pointing to an "antitype of David" who applies new covenant blessings to Gentiles based on a subjective genitive interpretation. When the context of 2 Sam 7, Isa 55:3, and Acts 13 are examined together, it seems that Isa 55:1–5 state that just as God made the historical David a "witness to the peoples" (Isa 55:4), so now Zion will also become a witness to other nations (Isa 55:5) when the resurrected

---

85. See Köstenberger and O'Brien, *Salvation*, 148–49; Bird, "Light to the Nations," 127; Moore, "Lucan Great Commission," 57–58; Pao, *Acts*, 96–101; Ryan, "Church," 110–15; Thompson, *Acts*, 118–20; Beeblrs, *Followers of Jesus*, 156–57; Beale, *New Testament Biblical Theology*, 683–84.

86. This recalls Jesus' instruction to his disciples to go "to the ends of the earth" (Matt 28:19), which suggests that Jesus commissioned his followers to continue his function as a "light to the nations" by spreading the gospel light in his name.

87. James Meek concludes, based on his definition of typology, that "the prophecy of the servant finds fulfilment first of all in Jesus, but also through him in his church." See Meek, *Gentile Mission*, 53. Thomas Moore also suggests that the church is identified as the Isaianic Servant since Jesus fulfilled the individual aspects of the Servant, while the church fulfills the collective aspects of the Servant. See Moore, "Lucan Great Commission," 60. J. Ross Wagner argues that Paul's appropriation of themes from Isa 51–55 in the book of Romans, indicates that the larger story of Isa 51–55 was understood by Paul to prefigure his role as an apostle and missionary in heralding the gospel to Israel and to the Gentiles. See Wagner, "Heralds of Isaiah," 193–222. Frederick Bruce notes, however, that Paul's quotation of Isa 49:6 does not indicate that Paul's mission replaces the Servant's mission to restore Israel. See Bruce, *Acts*, 267.

88. Gentry writes, "We will argue, contrary to the consensus of scholarship, that the 'sure mercies' are *by David* rather than *for David.*" Gentry and Wellum, *Kingdom through Covenant*, 407. Joseph Blenkinsopp is an example of the consensus view. He writes, "The reference is therefore not to deeds performed by David himself on behalf of his people but to God's gratuitous acts of favor toward David." See Blenkinsopp, *Isaiah 40–55*, 370.

Davidic king will restore it and bring light to Israel and the nations from it (Isa 60:1–3).[89]

Isaiah 56

In Isa 56, God pronounces a blessing on anyone who keeps the Sabbath (v. 2), including foreigners and eunuchs (v. 6).[90] Gentry believes that the term "servants" in Isa 56:6 recalls the "servants" in Isa 54:17. Since the "servants" in Isa 54:17 are supposedly identified with the suffering Servant, from Isa 53, then the "foreigners" in Isa 56:6 reveal that the "servants" include Gentiles.[91] For Gentry, this inclusion of Gentiles in Isa 56:6 reveals the new "one people" concept where God unites Israelites and Gentiles to form a new corporate entity. Motyer highlights the progression of Gentile inclusion in Isa 56, which suggests to him, that God will form a new multiethnic community.[92] Motyer writes, "Note the progression in verse 7: they

89. The Davidic king, historically, was to testify to the nations of God's greatness according to Ps 18:50 and 22:28. See Eaton, *Kingship in the Psalms*, 182–84.

90. Gentry notes that Isa 56:6 presents foreigners in stark contrast with Israel. He writes, "At the beginning of the book of Isaiah, Israel, those who were born into the covenant community, the nation, physical Israel, were not Sabbath keepers. They were Sabbath-breakers. And now, it is the foreigners who are Sabbath keepers." Gentry also highlights that these foreigners are described as "ministers," which most commonly referred to Levites and priests in the OT. See Gentry and Wellum, *Kingdom through Covenant*, 448.

91. Gentry and Wellum, *Kingdom through Covenant*, 448. Gentry writes, "We were shocked to discover in 54:17 that those who are included in the new covenant community are called the servants of the Lord. The sins of the many have been borne by the servant, and the victory of the one servant is shared by the many so that in the end they become servants too." See Gentry and Wellum, *Kingdom through Covenant* (2nd ed.), 503.

92. Gentry remarks, "God will bring them to his holy mountain; he will give them joy in his house of prayer, and they will offer acceptable burnt offerings and sacrifices. There is a progression in these statements of belonging and being included . . . nothing could be clearer on just how far in the in-group are these foreigners!" Gentry and Wellum, *Kingdom through Covenant*, 448–49. Edward Young also notes that the "foreigners" will serve the Lord to the same capacity as Israelites priests and Levites, indicating the full inclusion of Gentile individuals into the Israelite priesthood. He adds that Isa 56:8 points to the NT church where Christ said, in John 10:16, that he came for "other" sheep to bring them into the "one flock." Thus, Young believes that Isa 56 refers to the NT church. See Young, *Book of Isaiah*, 390–94. Gentry, Motyer, and Young assume that the presence of Gentile "servants" implies that a new entity is portrayed in Isa 56:6. However, their interpretation does not account for Israel's historical precedence of not only welcoming Gentile individuals into their community as proselytes but also

are welcome to the place where the Lord is to be found (*my holy mountain*), into his presence and family (*my house of prayer*), and to those ordinances which effect and guarantee acceptance and fellowship (*my altar*) (cf. Ps 43:3–4)."[93] Gentry references the book of Acts as evidence that Isa 56 looks forward to the "new people of God," or the NT church, where foreigners are brought into the new covenant community.[94]

Clearly, in Deut 23, foreigners and eunuchs were excluded from Israel, as Gentry notes. However, it is not clear that their inclusion in Isa 56:3 points to a new type of "Israel." Several scholars see the "foreigners and eunuchs," from Isa 56:3, as Jewish proselytes.[95] Historically, Israel welcomed individual Gentiles to proselytize and join their community, while holding to a dominant Israelite ethnic core. As Joseph Blenkinsopp notes, "The example of the proselyte Ruth from Moab and the conversion to the Jewish faith of Achior from Ammon will suffice to remind us that laws do not always find universal acceptance or meet with universal compliance."[96] Gentry, however, believes that the presence of Gentile temple servants reveals a new type of "Israel."

---

allowing them to serve as temple servants.

93. Motyer states that Isa 56:1–8 portrays the gathering people in which "all are one, all are equal, all are welcome in the house of prayer." See Motyer, *Prophecy of Isaiah*, 463–67.

94. Gentry and Wellum, *Kingdom through Covenant* (2nd ed.), 504.

95. Brevard Childs writes, "Foreigners had always been seen as ethnically different from Israel, but at times were allowed to attach themselves to Israel (Isa 14:1; Zech 2:11). In 56:3 the foreigner at issue is specifically described as belonging to this class of proselytes." See Childs, *Isaiah*, 457. Westermann comments, "The term 'foreigner' reappears with the same meaning in Isa 60:10, 61:5, 62:8. This is obviously a designation for a proselyte current at the time." See Westermann, *Isaiah 40–66*, 312. Watts writes, "'The foreigner . . . who has joined himself to YHWH' came to be known in Judaism as a proselyte, a member of the synagogue who was not a Jew by birth. The position of the proselytes was a controversial one in Judaism. Not all Jews were prepared to grant them full covenant rights. Such openness to receiving Gentiles who would commit themselves to YHWH was actively resisted by some . . . in this passage YHWH assures those who voluntarily seek to join themselves to YHWH, i.e., to the covenant community of worship, of full acceptance." See Watts, *Isaiah 34–66*, 820. Blenkinsopp argues, "The term [foreigner] will eventually acquire a predominantly religious connotation, in the sense of a proselyte's adherence to the worship of the God of Israel." See Blenkinsopp, *Isaiah 56–66*, 136–37. Goldingay states, "The presence of individual foreigners in Israel in OT narrative seems to be quite uncontroversial. Regulations in the Torah presuppose that [they] may indeed become a member of the worshiping community." See Goldingay, *Isaiah 56–66*, 72.

96. Blenkinsopp, *Isaiah 56–66*, 138.

While it is true that Deut 23:1–8 prohibited Gentiles (i.e., eunuchs, Ammonites, Moabites, Edomites, and Egyptians) from entering the assembly of the Lord, Neh 7 lists several nationalities (Arab, Babylonian, Egyptian, and Edomite) among the temple servants of Israel.[97] John McKenzie notes that "the slaves of the preexilic temple were foreigners," which would suggest that Gentile ministers was not a completely foreign concept at the time of Isaiah.[98] Since some Gentile individuals did serve in the temple, historically, despite the restrictions listed in Deut 23, it is difficult to see how Gentry can claim that Isa 56 depicts a new "Israel" simply by virtue of the presence of Gentile ministers.[99] Isaiah 56:7 ("these I will bring to my holy mountain and make them joyful in my house of prayer") appears to be consistent with Solomon's petition in 1 Kgs 8:41–43, that God hears the prayer of foreigners at the temple, along with previous depictions of the nations' response to Yahweh in Isaiah (i.e., Isa 2).[100] The function of the temple as a house of prayer for all peoples does not entail the abolition of Israel's ethnic and national distinctiveness.[101]

Psalm 87

While examining Isaiah, Gentry chooses to cite Ps 87 as evidence for his interpretation of Isa 56.[102] He believes that Ps 87 supports his argument

97. Joseph Blenkinsopp writes, "The census of Ezra 2 (= Neh 7) lists several nationalities among the temple servants—Arab, Babylonian, Egyptian, Edomite, and possibly others (Ezra 2:43–54)—but the prohibition of foreigners in Ezek. 44:4–9, if it was then in force, may not have applied to such low-status individuals as the temple servants listed in Ezra and Nehemiah." See Blenkinsopp, *Isaiah 56–66*, 138.

98. McKenzie, *Second Isaiah*, 151.

99. Previously in Isa 44:5, individuals who see Israel's prosperity will eagerly seek to become members of God's people. Although this is not specifically stated, these individuals are most likely foreigners, or as Norman Whybray notes, "proselytes." See Whybray, *Isaiah 40–66*, 95.

100. Previously, the nations are depicted as confessing that there is "no other" God besides Yahweh (Isa 45:14) and turning from idols to worship the living God ("every tongue shall swear allegiance"; Isa 45:23). Yahweh himself invites all nations to "turn" to him to be "saved" (Isa 45:22). The nations' salvation consists not only of their worship of Yahweh but also of their living in a world in which Yahweh's justice is manifest (Isa 51:5). Far from dreading the establishment of Yahweh's kingdom, the nations wait with hope for this very thing (Isa 51:5; 42:4). See Van Winkle, "Isaiah 40–55," 457.

101. Goldingay, *Isaiah 56–66*, 84.

102. For an examination of the connection between Isaiah and the Psalms, see Lohfink and Zenger, *Israel and the Nations*. Andrew Abernethy notes that the motif of

that Gentiles will integrate with Israel to form a new one people. He argues that Ps 87 presents a "coherent and unified picture of Zion" situated on a "holy mount" (v. 1) and from where "springs" of life gush forth (v. 7). Gentry asserts that the term "springs" recounts the Gihon river, located outside of Eden (Gen 2:13) and the city walls of Jerusalem, thus indicating that the future Zion will possess the same source of water depicted in Eden signifying that the new Zion functions as an antitype to Eden.[103] Gentry adds that the "gates of Zion" (Ps 87:2) may refer to the gates of the temple, which would depict Zion as the "source of universal social justice and righteousness for the nations," which echoes Isaiah's eschatological vision of Zion from Isa 2.[104]

Within this picture of Zion, Gentry notes that the nations who are counted as citizens of Zion, according to Ps 87:4, correspond to the four compass points of the world: West (Egypt), East (Babylon), North (Philistia), and South (Cush).[105] He believes that the nations describe Gentiles

---

God bringing justice as a universal king to the nations in Isaiah connects with multiple passages from Psalms (72:1–7; 96:10–13; 97:2; 98:6–9; 99:4). See Abernethy, *Isaiah and God's Kingdom*, 26.

103. Gentry and Wellum, *Kingdom through Covenant* (2nd ed.), 506. The words of Ps 87:7 are addressed to Zion. "Springs" are often taken here as a symbol of divine blessing and life, but this reading does not relate to the preceding line. Instead, it seems better to translate כָּל־מַעְיָנַי as כֻּלָּם עָנוּ with the form עָנוּ being derived from עָנָה, "sing." This would mean that the "singers and dancers" all "sing" within Zion. Goldingay translates "springs are in you" as "the abode is in you," reading a form of משכנו in place of מַעְיָן. See Goldingay, *Psalms 42–89*, 632n6. Goldingay adds that "springs" may refer to the conception of children, which correlates with the idea that these Gentiles were fathered in Zion and are the words the singers and dancers speak in celebration for their citizenship in Zion. See Goldingay, *Psalms 42–89*, 639. Tate translates v. 7 as: "And they sing while dancing: 'All my springs are in you.'" See Tate, *Psalms 51–100*, 387. Kraus notes that "all my springs are in you" is a problematic reading of v. 7. It may be read as "they all, whose dwelling in you" or "all live in you," but Kraus prefers the following reading: "they all sing to you," based on a verb from the root "dwell" rather than "spring." See Kraus, *Psalms 60–150*, 185. Clearly, the meaning of "springs" is disputed, which questions Gentry's assertion that it refers to the Gihon River and alludes to the garden of Eden.

104. Gentry and Wellum, *Kingdom through Covenant* (2nd ed.), 506. For a discussion on how the "gates of Zion" can function as a metonymy for the Temple. See Steingrimsson, *Tor der Gerechtigkeit*, 134–39.

105. Gentry and Wellum, *Kingdom through Covenant* (2nd ed.), 506. Goldingay comments, contrary to Gentry, that the list of nations is not "actually a coherent collection of traditional enemies, nor do they represent the points of the compass, nor do they especially point to one historical period . . . the five peoples are just other peoples (cf. Isa 19:18–25). But all feature in the prophecies about foreign nations in

rather than Diasporic Jews. He writes, "[Psalm] 87 clearly teaches that the Lord will take the foreign nations, the enemies of Israel, and make them citizens of Zion."[106] He arrives at this conclusion because of the editorial arrangement of the Psalms and sees a connection between Pss 87 and 83 based on the theme of God's relationship with the nations.[107] By connecting Ps 87 with Ps 83, Gentry argues that Ps 86:8–10 prepares the reader for the vision in Ps 87, where David's appeal that the nations would recognize Yahweh's authority is fulfilled.[108] Gentry concludes his discussion on Ps 87 by referencing Isa 19:24–25 as further evidence that God will create a new entity that will include Israel's enemies as part of his people.[109]

---

the Prophets, which characteristically speak of calamity to come on them, though they also usually include some elements of hope of these peoples." See Goldingay, *Psalm 42–89*, 636.

106. Gentry and Wellum, *Kingdom through Covenant*, 454. Geoffrey Grogan affirms Gentry's interpretation of the nations listed in Ps 87:4. He writes, "The alternative view that the psalmist is writing instead about Jews born elsewhere who will be reckoned citizens of Zion, rather like 'Roman' citizens born in various parts of the Roman Empire, hardly fits a straightforward reading of the text." See Grogan, *Psalms*, 153. Tate writes that Ps 87 functions as an "amplification" of Ps 86:9. See Tate, *Psalm 51–100*, 389. Kraus, however, argues that the presupposition of v. 4 is that Israel is scattered throughout Egypt and Babel. He writes, "If we follow the trend of Yahweh's words that culminate in v. 5a, our interpretation should lean toward the view that Israelites are primarily thought of. Among the members of Israel—so Yahweh notes in the record—one is born here, another there. The people of God live in the Diaspora. Yahweh enumerates the nations among which Israel is dispersed." See Kraus, *Psalms 60–150*, 187–88. As Erich Zenger correctly notes, "Whether the psalm imputes a 'theological' citizenship on Zion to the diaspora Jews, individual proselytes, or the nations remains to this day open and contested." See Zenger, "Zion," 127. Depending on whether one interprets Ps 87 as an eschatological picture or a historical reference will affect one's conclusion on whether Ps 87:3 refers to scattered Israelites, proselytes, or Gentile nations.

107. Gentry comments that Ps 87 is connected to Ps 83 in the following ways: (1) the geographical designations "Philistia and Tyre" occur in Pss 83:7 and 87:4; (2) Ps 83 culminates with a statement that Yahweh will show that he alone is the "Most High" (83:18). Psalm 87:5 describes Yahweh as the "Most High" when he equips Zion as the center and the source of life for the nations; and (3) Yahweh intervenes against the assault of the nations against Israel, and according to Ps 83:18, the nations will acknowledge Yahweh, which Ps 87:4 also states. See Gentry and Wellum, *Kingdom through Covenant* (2nd ed.), 507–8.

108. Gentry and Wellum, *Kingdom through Covenant* (2nd ed.), 508–9. Grogan asserts that Ps 87 may be an exposition of Ps 86:9. See Grogan, *Psalms*, 153.

109. Gentry writes, "Yahweh has accorded a connection to Zion to the two great traditional enemy powers, Egypt (Rahab) and Babylon, as well as to the lands of Philistia, Phoenicia, and Cush in a legally binding way (with rights and obligations)." Gentry

He writes that "Isaiah predicts that the renewed and restored Zion will involve taking the worst enemies of Israel and incorporating them into the *one people of God*."[110]

Identifying how Ps 87 fits within the editorial arrangement of book 3 and its connection to book 4 is important in interpreting this psalm.[111] Psalm 87 fits within the end of book 3 (Pss 87–89), which depicts the collapse of the Davidic monarchy in history, followed by God's promise to reaffirm the Davidic covenant for Israel by recalling the Abrahamic covenant and attributing Davidic titles to Abraham and his descendants, in book 4.[112] As Bernard Gosse notes, the postexilic community would have

---

and Wellum, *Kingdom through Covenant* (2nd ed.), 506. Charles Feinberg notes that the chief offenders of Israel (during Isaiah's time) was Assyria and Egypt. God used them as instruments to judge Israel so that Israel would eventually bless them in return. Feinberg writes, "God in His plan and purpose has governed that after the time of the chastisement of Israel, He will bless the nations through her." See Feinberg, "Israel," 453.

110. Gentry and Wellum, *Kingdom through Covenant*, 454 (emphasis mine).

111. Examples of studies that address the editing and narrative function of nations within books 3 and 4 include, Wilson, *Editing of the Psalter*, and Wallace, *Book IV*.

112. Looking at Pss 2, 41, 72, and 89 (psalms which mark the beginning of book 1 and the ends of book 1, 2, and 3), one finds a progression in thought regarding the Davidic covenant. Psalm 2 introduces the idea of the Davidic covenant by alluding to language from 2 Sam 7:14. In Ps 41, David echoes the language of the rebellious kings of the earth from Ps 2. David speaks of Yahweh's protection over him in the face of enemies (Ps 41:1–2). The proclamation of Yahweh's covenant with his king, in Ps 2, is matched by David's assurance of protection in Ps 41. In Ps 72, petitions regarding justice, dominion over enemies, and a blessed life are given on behalf of the king's "son." So, the covenant Yahweh made with David, in Ps 2, which rests secure with David, in Ps 41, is passed to his "son" in a series of petitions, in Ps 72. Finally, Ps 89 makes explicit references to the Davidic covenant but is concerned with the extension of the covenant to the descendants of David. At the conclusion of Ps 89, the impression is that the Davidic covenant has not come to fruition and the cry of the Davidic descendants for hope is explicit in Ps 89:49. See Wilson, *Editing of the Psalter*, 209–13. In response to Wilson's interpretation of the end of book 3, Tremper Longman argues that since Ps 89 is attributed to Ethan the Ezrahite, it would not make sense for the psalm to be about the supposed "failure of the covenant" since Ethan lived during the time of Solomon. See Longman, "Messiah," 21–22. If Ps 2, along with Ps 1, forms the introduction to the Psalter as a whole and has been placed in this position at a date after the monarchy was no longer a political reality, then Wilson's interpretation of the ending message of book 3 seems preferable to Longman's. The intention of the editors who drew the Psalter together was to signal a future messianic hope, particularly because of the use of מָשִׁיחַ, in Pss 89:39 and 132:10. These two passages appear to offer hope of a future role for a Davidic king in an eschatological setting, particularly in Zion. Zenger notes that Ps 87 functions as a "messianic psalter" where it contrasts with David's historic monarchy to the trajectory of the monarchy of the "Messiah," from Ps 2. Psalm 89 enlarges the messianic perspective to include Israel as a people such that the covenant promises given

been struck by an enlarged application of Davidic titles to Abraham and his descendants in book 4, which is a response to the cry which concludes book 3 in Ps 89:49: "Lord, where is your steadfast love of old, which by your faithfulness you swore to David?"[113]

Despite the wavering stability of the Davidic monarchy in Israel's history, the future restoration of Zion, in book 3, prepares the readers for one of the themes of book 4: God's promise to reestablish his presence in Zion. Yahweh communicates his special love for Zion such that it surpasses any other location within Israel ("Mount Zion which he loves," Ps 78:68; "the Lord loves the gates of Zion more than all the dwelling places of Jacob," Ps 87:2). God's concern for Zion is closely connected with his love for his "son," who will reign from this city (cf. Ps 2:7). As Gerald Wilson points out, Ps 2 may serve as a key to the interpretation of the royal psalms within the entire Psalter.[114] God repeatedly depicts a future restored Zion (Pss 76:3; 78:68; 84:8), in book 3, following a description of the disaster that came upon it in Ps 74, since a restored Zion is the necessary setting for the Davidic king ("I have set my King on Zion, my holy hill"; Ps 2:6).[115] Psalm 87 fulfills the promise of Pss 2:8 and 86:9 where eventual multinational worship of Yahweh will take place in a restored eschatological Zion.[116] Included in this eschatological worship, according to Ps 87:4, are former national enemies of Israel. Interestingly, the description given to the incorporation of these foreign individuals into

---

to David are now applied to a "messianic" Israel. Since Ps 89:49 cites Isa 55:3, Zenger concludes that the Davidic promises are "democratized" to a future Israel, who are designated as "servants," in Isa 65–66. See Zenger, "Zion," 159–60, 160n68. Zenger's conclusion that the Davidic promises are "democratized" to a messianic Israel reflects similar argumentation to Gentry's and opens up the possibility that the future "Israel" refers to the NT church, although Zenger does not arrive at that conclusion. Instead of seeing the Davidic promises "democratized" to Israel, it seems preferable to interpret that the covenant promises are applied to a future Davidic king, who will then bless all nations from Zion, including Israel. In fact, Zenger arrives at a similar conclusion when he writes, "The 'world revolution' pictured in Ps 2 is transformed in Ps 87 into a 'world family,' when Zion as the mother of messianic Israel (Ps 2) and as the mother of all humanity (Ps 87) becomes the 'capitol' of the king of the world, Yahweh himself." See Zenger, "Zion," 160.

113. See Gosse, "Psaumes 90–106," 246.

114. Wilson, *Psalms*, 107–8.

115. Cole, *Message of Book III*, 160–61.

116. In Ps 86:9, the promise of an eventual universal worship of Yahweh was given. In Ps 87:4, some of those nations are named specifically. Just as Ps 83:18 desired that these nations "know" Yahweh, so Ps 87:4 listed among those who "know" him.

Zion (Ps 87:4–6) is similar to that used to describe the establishment of the king in Ps 2:7.[117] This may indicate a connection between God's concern for his "son," the Davidic king, who will reign from Zion, and the citizens of Zion, which will include Israel and Gentile nations.

Gentry's interpretation of Ps 87:4 assumes that when individuals from Gentile nations become citizens of Zion, their previous national identity disappears. However, as John Goldingay aptly notes, Ps 87:6 does not indicate that these individuals give up their former identity as citizens of Egypt (Rahab), Babylon, Philistia, Tyre, and Sudan (Cush), but become "peoples of dual citizenship."[118] Psalm 87:4 specifies that these individuals are still seen as people "born there" (Ps 87:4). When God "registers" these individuals, in Ps 87:5, he does not state that they are no longer citizens of their respective nations or that the territories of their respective nations become a part of Zion. Instead, these Gentiles become citizens of Zion when God records it in his "registry" (Ps 87:6). Daniel Smith posits that the "register," from v. 6, may correspond to the Assyrian practice of recording the "movement of peoples" involved in empire building.[119] If this is so, then the process in Ps 87:5–6 seems analogous to that of an Assyrian conquering king who declares foreign peoples as citizens of his kingdom without erasing their national and territorial affiliation.

Both the pictures of Ps 2:8, where a king inherits the nations while ruling in Zion, and Ps 87:6 depicts Zion as an international city with individuals from different nations.[120] There are both ethnic and territorial distinctions between the Israelite and Gentile citizens of Zion since the surrounding territories continue to remain even after these Gentile individuals become citizens of Zion. Although Gentry astutely observes that the citizens of Zion, in Ps 87:4, include individuals from Gentile nations, his conclusion of a one new people concept does not correlate with the language of territorial movement and national distinctions within this psalm. Individuals from these Gentile nations, located outside of Zion, must travel through the "gates" of Zion, indicating that the surrounding

---

117. Both king and foreigner are established in their present position by using the language of birth (Ps 2:7, יְלִדְתִּיךָ; Ps 87:4, 5, 6; יֻלַּד). The king's coronation in Ps 2 is accomplished by decree (אֲסַפְּרָה) and in like manner the declaration of citizenship is decreed (יִסְפֹּר). See Cole, *Message of Book III*, 166.

118. Goldingay, *Psalm 42–89*, 639.

119. Smith, *Religion of the Landless*, 29.

120. Allen writes that Ps 87 depicts a "multinational congregation in the Jerusalem temple." See Allen, "Psalm 87," 138.

territories remain distinct from Zion ("gates of Zion"; Ps 87:2).[121] The Gentile individuals are identified by the territories they were "born" in (Ps 87:4) and these territories continue to exist outside of Zion.[122] Gentry also mentions Isa 19:24–25 as further evidence that God will create a new entity that will include Israel's enemies as part of his people. Although Gentry appropriately observes the eschatological setting of Isa 19:24–25 and the participation of national entities outside of Israel, his conception of a "one new people" void of national distinctions fails to explain the language of territorial and national distinctions that are presented in Isa 19.[123]

Isaiah 61–62

Gentry claims that Israel lost its status as a priesthood because of their unfaithfulness to the Israelite/Mosaic covenant. As a result, a new covenant will create a new type of "Israel" that will include Gentiles.[124] Since

121. Ancient oriental iconography shows that cities, in the ANE, were distinguished from villages by their gates. If the "gates of Zion" connote a similar idea, then Zion is depicted as a distinct city compared to surrounding villages by its gates, thus implying territorial distinctions in the vision of Ps 87. See Uehlinger, "'Zeichne eine Stadt,'" 153–72.

122. Dwight Van Winkle argues that Isaiah consistently features nations, as national entities, participating in the eschatological kingdom. Isaiah 51:4–6 illustrates the salvation of the nations, Isa 49:22–23 expects their submission to Israel, and Isa 42:5–9 commissions Israel to become an agent of salvation for the nations. Van Winkle attempts to resolve the tension between universalism and nationalism by recognizing that the salvation of the nations does not preclude their submission to Israel. He writes, "The prophet does not envisage the co-equality of Jews and gentiles. He expects that Israel will be exalted and that she will become Yahweh's agent who will rule the nations in such a way that justice is established, and mercy is shown. This rule is both that for which the nations wait expectantly and that to which they must submit." See Van Winkle, "Relationship of the Nations," 457.

123. Isaiah 11:16; 35:8; and 49:11 describe territorial distinctions between Israel and Gentile nations by mentioning "highways" as the means by which God's people in Gentile territories travel to Zion. Anne Kaminsky and Joel Stewart observe that the inclusion of foreigners in no way erases the "privileged position" of Israel as a nation per se. They write, "First, while Isaiah contains many passages that speak of YHWH in cosmic and universalistic terms, it has little concern for the nations themselves aside from their role in asserting His sovereignty. Second, later passages in Isaiah show a growing interest in the fate of nations." See Kaminsky and Stewart, "God of All the World," 140–41.

124. Gentry writes, "Israel's role as a royal priesthood, lost through violation of the Israelite covenant, is restored by the new covenant." See Gentry and Wellum, *Kingdom through Covenant*, 456.

the label, "ministers," included foreigners in Isa 56:6 ("and the foreigners who join themselves to the Lord, to minister to him") and is then applied to "Israel" in Isa 61:6 ("but you shall be called the priests of the Lord; they shall speak of you as the ministers of our God"), Gentry infers that Gentiles gain the status that Israel lost through violating the Israelite/Mosaic covenant.[125] Gentry explains his argument accordingly: "In [Isa 61:6], which specifies the restored status as priests, [Israel] are called 'ministers of God,' exactly the same term applied to foreigners in 56:6. The double portion was the inheritance of the firstborn son—another connection to the role given to Israel in Exodus (4:22)."[126] According to his reading of Isa 61:6, Gentry believes that the role given to Israel in Exod 19:6, has now been given to a multiethnic community inclusive of foreigners in Isa 56:6, resulting in the recomposition of "Israel."

Gentry's interpretation, however, fails to recognize a shift that occurs from Isa 61:5 to 61:6, as demonstrated by the phrase "but you": "Strangers shall stand and tend your flocks; foreigners shall be your plowmen and vine dressers; *but you* shall be called the priests of the Lord, they shall speak of you as ministers of our God; you shall eat the wealth of the nations and in their glory you shall boast." The people addressed as "priests" and "ministers," in Isa 61:6, does not refer to the same group of people who will work as "plowmen and vine dressers," in 61:5.[127] Instead, v. 6 specifies that the Israelites in Zion will fulfill their role as priests (cf. Exod 19:6) because of the foreigners mentioned in v. 5.[128] Goldingay rightly concludes that vv. 5–6 echoes the historical model of the Levites in relation to the other tribes of Israel. The other clans, especially those in the Judean countryside, would take responsibility for farming the land thereby freeing the Levites to serve in the temple.[129] Isaiah 61:5–6 does not reveal the inclusion of Gentiles as priests, but that the support of Israelite priests in Zion will extend beyond the Judean countryside and include Gentile territories. Many recognize a motif here that is continued

125. Gentry and Wellum, *Kingdom through Covenant*, 456.

126. Gentry and Wellum, *Kingdom through Covenant*, 456.

127. Blenkinsopp, *Isaiah 56–66*, 226.

128. John Mackay writes, "In the changed conditions brought about by the Messiah, Israel will be able to fulfill the role for which they had originally been designated 'a kingdom of priests' (Exod. 19:6). So, they are presented not as a nation of conquerors, but as 'priests of Yahweh,' who have the privilege of mediating between Yahweh and the nations." See Mackay, *Isaiah*, 522–23.

129. Goldingay, *Isaiah 56–66*, 309.

from previous prophecies concerning the transfer of the "wealth of nations" to Zion.[130] The closest reference is found in Isa 60:5–16, where
Gentile nations bring their material resources in order to restore Zion
as a sign of their submission to the Davidic king, who reigns in Zion
(Isa 60:5). Accordingly, Isa 61:5–6 does not state that the foreigners, who
work as "plowmen and vinedressers," have become a part of Israel, thus
gaining the status and role of "priests and ministers," in v. 6. Instead, it
depicts foreigners bringing their "wealth" to Zion in order to restore it so
that the Israelites living in Zion can fulfill their roles as priests.

According to Gentry, Isa 62:12 ("And they shall be called The Holy
People, The Redeemed of the Lord; and you shall be called Sought Out,
A City Not Forsaken") confirms his interpretation of Isa 61:6 that the
renewed people of God are given in the new covenant what Israel lost in
violating the Israelite covenant. Gentry adds that the language utilized in
Isa 62:12 indicates that the new covenant community gained the status
of a "holy nation and royal priesthood."[131] However, when examining the
context of Isa 62, the focus is on the eschatological reversal of Zion and
not on the redefinition of national Israel with the inclusion of Gentiles.
Gentry seems to project his conception of the "one people of God" from
his interpretation of Isa 61:6 into his reading of Isa 62:12.

The language in Isa 62:5 continues the marriage imagery of Isa 61:10
("as a bridegroom decks himself like a priest with a beautiful headdress,
and as a bride adorns herself with her jewels") and communicates that
even though Zion feels "forsaken" by Yahweh (cf. Isa 49:14), God will
reverse that label ("you shall be no more be termed Forsaken"), by restoring
the conditions of its land ("your land shall be no more be termed Desolate"), in Isa 62:4.[132] God declares that the proof of his love for Zion will
be seen in the rebuilding of its walls, which is "continually" on his agenda
(Isa 49:16), and the abundance of her "children," though she considered
herself "barren" (Isa 49:20–21; 54:1–3). Claus Westermann observes that
the labels given to Zion, in Isa 62, reverses the earlier negative portrayals
of Zion in Isaiah:

---

130. Jones, "Wealth of Nations," 621; Blenkinsopp, *Isaiah 56–66*, 226. Charles
Cruise states that the "wealth of nations" concept is also manifested in Isa 18:7 and
45:14, where Gentiles bring their material resources to Jerusalem as a sign of their
submission to Yahweh. See Cruise, "Wealth of the Nations," 296.

131. Gentry and Wellum, *Kingdom through Covenant*, 456.

132. Oswalt, *Isaiah*, 581.

Until now it might have been said of Zion that she had been forsaken by her God and that in consequence her land had been laid waste and made desolate . . . now, however, Zion is called "my delight" or, to be more precise, "my delight is in her" . . . in verse 12 Isaiah leaves off quoting and goes back to the change in the name of verse 4, and so to the central statement made in [Isa] 62—God has now taken his chosen people back.[133]

When the textual details of Isa 60–62 are considered regarding Zion, it leads to a multinational paradigm of the kingdom rather than one where Israelites and Gentiles form a new "one people" concept. First, there are textual details that distinguish Zion from Gentile territories. In Isa 60, Jerusalem functions as a light that attracts the nations in a world of darkness.[134] Gentile nations (and kings) will come into the light in Jerusalem and the brightness of the presence of God will be seen in the Davidic king who reigns from Zion (Isa 42:4; 49:6; 51:4), indicating territorial movement. Isaiah 61:11 concludes with a description that the Lord will cause "righteousness and praise" to sprout up before the nations, which may allude to Isa 4:2 when the "branch of the Lord," referring to Davidic king, will bring forth "fruit" that will be the pride and honor of Israel ("in that day the branch of the Lord shall be beautiful and glorious, and the fruit of the land shall be the pride and honor of the survivors of Israel"). This detail suggests that the "fruit" comes from a particular location, Zion, to the nations, implying distinct territories outside of Zion.

Second, details within Isa 60–62 portray national distinctions between Israelites and Gentiles in Zion. When the Gentiles come to Jerusalem, they will bring their "wealth," which will be used to rebuild Zion (Isa 60:4–5). Kings from Gentile nations will "minister" in Zion (Isa

133. Westermann, *Isaiah 40–66*, 377–79.

134. McKenzie, *Second Isaiah*, 177. Goldingay notes the theme of light in Isa 60. He writes, "Themes include: image of light dawning on the dark city; power of light to attract makes possible a transition to talk of the nations' coming to this light; gathering of the city's scattered sons and daughters whom the nations and kings bring with them; nations and kings also bringing their resources to build up the city and its sanctuary." See Goldingay, *Isaiah 56–66*, 248. Oswalt notes that the light of Zion will be instrumental in Isa 60–62. He states that God will give light to his people and draw the nations through what they see of God in Israel. The nations will restore Zion's children and bring their "wealth" to Israel's God because of the light that comes from Zion. See Oswalt, *Book of Isaiah: 40–66*, 535. Blenkinsopp adds that Jerusalem is at the center of a dark world as a light. He observes that light is often associated with the glory of God and in this respect Isa 60:1–3 is the fulfillment of the promise made in Isa 40:5 and echoes Isa 24:23. See Blenkinsopp, *Isaiah 56–66*, 56–66; 210–11.

60:10) and Zion will "suck" the milk of nations and "nurse" at the breast of kings, reversing the historical reality of Zion's desolation at the hands of Gentile nations.[135] Nations will no longer oppress Zion but will serve as "shepherds, plowmen, and vinedressers" in order to support the Israelite priests in Zion (Isa 60:5–7).[136] A distinction in roles between Gentiles and Israelites will exist that is reminiscent of the Levites' distinct role from the other tribes of Israel.[137]

Third, descriptions of the Davidic king's role in Zion points to a multinational kingdom. Yahweh's faithfulness to Zion is expressed with a deliverance characterized by a "burning torch" signifying a light that will be visible to the nations and their kings (Isa 60:3, 11, 16). This "torch" may refer to the Servant of the Lord who will function as a "light to the nations" (Isa 49:6), which connects with the light imagery, from Isa 60, when the nations are drawn to Zion. God confirms his future restoration of Zion by addressing Zion's complaint, from Isa 49:14, and applying a marriage metaphor, from Isa 61:10, in Isa 62:4: "You shall no more be termed Forsaken, and your land shall no more be termed Desolate, but you shall be called My Delight Is in Her, and your land Married; for the Lord delights in you, and your land shall be married." Part of Zion's restoration includes Gentile nations submitting to Zion and their king, evidenced by Isa 62:8 when God swears by his "right hand" to no longer allow Gentile nations to exercise political control over Israel. Isaiah 62:12 concludes with a label for both Israel and Zion. God labels Israel, "a Holy People," which fulfills Exod 19:6 when God intended for Israel to become a "kingdom of priests" (Isa 61:6) and a "holy nation." Zion is labeled "a city not forsaken," addressing its self-proclaimed description (Isa 49:14) and reversing its character and condition. As John Oswalt notes, with the reversal of Zion's desolate condition, Isa 62 indicates the "condition and character" of God's salvation and restoration for national Israel and the Davidic king's impact on the nations.[138]

---

135. The nations and kings are depicted as a mother nursing her children. Restored Zion will be nourished by them as she receives their wealth as tribute. See Oswalt, *Book of Isaiah: 40–66*, 266; Jones, "Wealth of Nations," 621; Blenkinsopp, *Isaiah 56–66*, 226.

136. Oswalt, *Book of Isaiah: 40–66*, 571.

137. Israel's exalted position, as priests, fulfills what God promised in Exod 19:6 and Deut 33:10, which was to be a mediator between God and humans and assisting them to worship God (Isa 61:6).

138. Oswalt, *Isaiah*, 579.

Isaiah 66

According to Gentry, Isa 66:18–24 reiterates the theme of nations gathering to worship the Lord at Zion, as previously depicted in Isa 2:2–4 and 11:10, and later echoed in Zech 2:14.[139] Gentry argues that Isa 66:19 reveals how God will gather nations, namely through a "sign." Referencing Motyer's commentary, Gentry assumes that Isa 66 depicts the NT church, thus he argues that the "sign" most likely refers to the cross of Christ.[140] The "brothers" who come from these nations may refer to Israelites among the nations or Gentile converts (v. 20). Gentry opts for seeing them as Gentiles.[141] Based on his interpretation of "brothers," Gentry argues that Isa 66:18–25 describes a new covenant community that reconceptualizes national Israel because of the joining of "Jews and non-Jews into one family."[142]

---

139. Gentry writes, "This passage reminds us of [Isa] 2:2–4, where the nations are streaming to Mount Zion to receive Instruction or Torah from the Lord for daily living. It also reminds us of 11:10, where the Root of Jesse will stand as a banner for the peoples, who will then rally to him. A parallel passage is [Zech] 2:14, which speaks of many nations being joined to the Lord in the future day." See Gentry and Wellum, *Kingdom through Covenant*, 458.

140. Gentry and Wellum, *Kingdom through Covenant*, 458. Motyer writes, "Isaiah does not say what the *sign* is, but since in its biblical context this passage lies in the interim between the two comings of Jesus, the *sign* can only be the cross." See Motyer, *Isaiah*, 458.

141. Regarding Isa 66:18–24, Gentry writes, "Several considerations support the interpretation of 'brothers' as referring to Gentiles. Every word in the text of Isaiah is carefully chosen and motivated. Note, for example, [Isa] 58:7, where true fasting is defined. . . . Here Isaiah employs the term בָּשָׂר ('flesh') to show that the 'poor' are *family*. They are not other people; they are our own, and we must feed them with the same responsibility with which we would feed our own family. Likewise, in Isaiah 56:6 the text speaks of the foreigners as 'ministers' and 'servants' to show that they have the same status as priests. The same technique is employed in [Isa] 66:20, where אָח (brother) is used to show that those drawn from the nations are *family* as well." See Gentry and Wellum, *Kingdom through Covenant*, 459. Contrary to Gentry's view, McKenzie argues the "brothers" as a reference to Israelites. See McKenzie, *Second Isaiah*, 209. Goldingay agrees that the nations will bring the "Judahites" as an offering to Yahweh. See Goldingay, *Isaiah 56–66*, 517. John Watts notes that "survivors" can refer to those who survive among the nations or to survivors who are among the group in Jerusalem. He opts to see them as survivors among Jerusalem. See Watts, *Isaiah 34–66*, 940. John Oswalt argues that the "survivors" refers to those within Israel (Isa 4:2) who will go to the nations to gather the remnants of the Israelites ("brothers). See Oswalt, *Isaiah*, 697.

142. Gentry and Wellum, *Kingdom through Covenant*, 461.

One wonders whether Isa 66:18–25 describes a redefined, multi-ethnic "Israel," since Gentry's interpretation is based on several disputed points in Isa 66:18–25. First, the "survivors," in Isa 66:19, who are sent to the nations may refer either to Gentiles or Israelites ("and I will set a sign among them. And from them I will send *survivors* to the nations").[143] Within the context, it seems more likely that the "survivors" refers to the "remnant" within Israel who survive the Lord's judgment, detailed in Isa 66:15–16: "For behold, the Lord will come in fire, and his chariots like the whirlwind, to render his anger in fury, and his rebuke with flames of fire. For by fire will the Lord enter into judgment, and by his sword, with all flesh; and those slain by the Lord shall be many."

One theme reiterated in Isaiah is that of a surviving "remnant" within Israel following God's judgment. Isaiah 1:9 describes "survivors" God left in Judah following his judgment ("If the Lord of hosts had not left us a few survivors, we should have been like Sodom, and become like Gomorrah"). Isaiah 10:20–34 describe a "remnant of Israel" and the "survivors of the house of Jacob" who will return to the Lord after judgment ("for though your people Israel be as the sand of the sea, only a remnant of them will return"; v. 22). Finally, Isa 37:31–32 describes a similar scene to Isa 66:19 where a surviving remnant from Judah will go out from Jerusalem: "And the surviving remnant of the house of Judah shall again take root downwards and bear fruit upwards. For out of Jerusalem shall go a remnant, and out of Mount Zion a band of survivors." These texts seem to denote that Isa 66:19 recalls previous depictions of a surviving remnant within Israel who will go out to the nations following God's judgment.

Second, the "brothers" whom the "survivors" will gather, in v. 20, can refer to either Gentiles or Israelites, as Gentry observes. It seems better to view them as Israelites, instead of Gentiles, since this reading is consistent with the theme in Isaiah of God "signaling" the nations in order to gather Israelites back to Zion:

> He will raise a signal for the nations and will assemble the ban-
> ished of Israel, and gather the dispersed of Judah from the four
> corners of the eart.h (Isa 11:12)

---

143. Goldingay believes it refers to Gentiles since the word "survivors" connects with Isa 45:20, where they are explicitly survivors of the nations. See Goldingay, *Isaiah 56–66*, 514. However, the word "survivors" also appears in Isa 4:2 commenting on those who "survived" God's judgment in Jerusalem. Edward Young argues that the context "demands" that the survivors refer to the Jews described in vv. 16–17. See Young, *Book of Isaiah* 532.

Thus says the Lord God: "Behold, I will lift up my hand to the nations, and raise my signal to the peoples; and they shall bring your sons in their arms, and your daughters shall be carried on their shoulders." (Isa 49:22)

And nations shall come to your light, and kings to the brightness of your rising. Lift up your eyes all around, and see; they all gather together, they come to you; your sons shall come from afar, and your daughters shall be carried on the hip. (Isa 60:3–4)

Third, the phrase "some of them," in v. 21, could mean that some of the Israelite "brothers" included priests and Levites or that some Israelites from other tribes will serve as priests and Levites ("and some of them also I will take for priests and for Levites, says the Lord").[144] Even if "some of them" referred to Gentiles, this does not imply that the national distinctions between Israel and Gentiles have been abolished.[145] The inclusion of certain Gentile individuals as priests hardly demands a disappearance of the existing body of priests and Levites, who would presumably be Israelites.[146]

Gentry's interpretation of Isa 66:18–24 depends on a certain reading of "survivors," "brothers," and the phrase "some of them," which are disputed. Even if one assumes the presence of Gentile priests, the inclusion of these Gentiles does not indicate that the national entities these individuals traveled from disappear, as evidenced with the description of specific territories and languages affiliated with these individuals in Isa 66:18–19 ("nations and tongues"; "to Tarshish, Pul, and Lud, who draw the bow, to Tubal and Javan, to the coastlands far away").

144. Croatto, "Exegesis de Isaiahs 56," 91–110. See Klostermann, *Deuterojesaja*, 114. August Dillman argues that "some" may refer to take some Israelites as assistants ("Levites") for the priests. See Dillmann, *Der Prophet Jesaia*, 542. Blenkinsopp adds that one's interpretation of "some of them" in v. 21 is dependent on one's view of "them" in v. 19. See Blenkinsopp, *Isaiah 56–66*, 315.

145. As Goldingay observes, Gentile nations streaming to Zion does not imply that "Israel ceases to exist as a result of being assimilated to the nations." See Goldingay, *Isaiah 56–66*, 521. Although Goldingay agrees with Gentry's interpretation of the new Jerusalem, he recognizes the national distinction between Israelites and Gentiles in Isa 66. See Goldingay, *Isaiah 56–66*, 469.

146. Gentry may be overemphasizing the meaning of the terms "priests" and "Levites" in v. 21. "Levites," refers to a certain function within Zion, which has already been identified as a "house of prayer for all peoples" (56:7). See Watts, *Isaiah 34–66*, 940. As Westermann comments, "priests and Levites" denotes servants and may imply that the Gentiles will participate in ministerial activities alongside Jews. See Westermann, *Isaiah 40–66*, 426.

Isaiah 65

Gentry concludes his observations about Isaiah's eschatological kingdom with Isa 65. This chapter plays a significant role in Gentry's understanding of both the land and people who will inhabit the eschatological kingdom. According to Gentry, just as Isa 56:6 makes "plain" that individuals from nations are included as the servants of the Lord, Isa 65:15–16 shows that the promises to Abraham are fulfilled in the new covenant community.[147] Gentry states:

> First, note that it was in the covenant with Abraham in [Gen] 17 that Abram was given a new name, i.e., Abraham (Gen 17:5). Second, note that the covenant promised blessings for those who blessed Abram and his family. Third, note that there is a curse for the one—and it is specified in the singular—who rejects Abram's family. The blessing and cursing in [Isa] 65:15–16 clearly recall the promises of [Gen] 12:2–3, but they redefine them according to the new covenant community and its "God of Amen."[148]

Gentry believes that Isa 65:15–16 shows that the promises to Abraham find its fulfillment in the new covenant community, who are referred to as "servants of the Lord."[149] He argues that since individuals from Gentile nations are labeled as "servants of the Lord," in Isa 56:6, and the remnant of Israel, in Isa 65:8–10, is also labeled as the Lord's "servants," then the Abrahamic promises for national Israel are now given to the new covenant community comprised of both Jews and Gentiles.[150] In other words, Isa 65:15–16 functions as a conclusion to Isaiah's overall portrayal of God calling a "nation that was not called" (Isa 65:1) into a new "Israel." Gentry's conclusion of Isa 65:15–16, however, depends on a certain interpretation of Isa 65:1.

There is debate whether God is speaking to Israel or Gentiles in Isa 65:1 ("I was ready to be sought by those who did not ask for me; I was ready to be found by those who did not seek me. I said, 'Here I am, here I am,' to a nation that was not called by my name").[151] If one were to

---

147. Gentry and Wellum, *Kingdom through Covenant*, 465.

148. Gentry and Wellum, *Kingdom through Covenant*, 465–66.

149. Gentry and Wellum, *Kingdom through Covenant*, 465.

150. Gentry and Wellum, *Kingdom through Covenant*, 465.

151. Norman Whybray remarks that although Paul applies Isa 65:1–2 to Gentiles in Rom 10:20–21, Isa 65:1 was addressed to apostate Israel to acknowledge Yahweh.

see Gentiles as the intended audience, then this reading will affect how one interprets "servants" in Isa 65:8–10. Gentry interprets Gentiles as the intended audience of Isa 65:1, which explains his conclusion that Isa 65:8–10 refer to the new covenant community rather than national Israel. However, the context of Isa 65 suggests that national Israel is the intended audience in Isa 65:1. The repeated emphasis on God's calling and answering his people in Isa 65:1, 12, 24 demonstrates that there is a direct relationship between the earlier complaints, in Isa 63:7—64:12, with God's response in Isa 65:1–2. Previously, some within Israel lamented that they had not seen God's zeal in Isa 63:15 ("Look down from heaven and see, from your holy and beautiful habitation. Where are your zeal and your might? The stirring of your inner parts and your compassion are held back from me"). They also accused God of "hiding his face" from them in Isa 64:7 ("There is no one who calls upon your name, who rouses himself to take hold of you; for you have hidden your face from us and have made us melt in the hand of our iniquities"). Finally, they accused God of being "silent" to their outcry in Isa 64:12 ("Will you restrain yourself at these things, O Lord? Will you keep silent and afflict us so terribly?"). If the first two verbs, in Isa 65:1, can be understood as tolerative niphal verbs ("to be sought"; "to be found"), then God is defending himself against these false accusations from Israel by indicating that he has allowed himself to be "sought" after or "found" by Israel.[152]

See Whybray, *Isaiah 40–66*, 268. Goldingay notes that v. 1 relates back to the beginning of the prayer and Yahweh's relationship with Israel. See Goldingay, *Isaiah 56–66*, 443. Oswalt concurs with Goldingay and notes that Isa 65: 1–16 serves as an answer to the questions raised in the previous section (Isa 63:7—64:11) regarding Israel's judgment. God promises salvation for his "servants" within the context of an announcement of judgment on those who are physically connected to Israel but continue to rebel in idolatry. Oswalt sees that Gentiles can be included as God's servants, as Isa 56:6 states, however, the primary audience of Isa 65:1 remains national Israel. See Oswalt, *Isaiah*, 634–36. Blenkinsopp, however, argues that the Gentiles are the intended audience in v. 1. He writes, "Those who, without seeking, have found God and to whom, without asking, God has become manifest are the Gentiles, and their attitude is in contrast to the disobedient and contrary Jewish people to whom in vain God holds out his hands." See Blenkinsopp, *Isaiah 56–66*, 270. Like Blenkinsopp, Motyer notes that even though most commentators understand Isa 65:1 as referring to apostate Israelites, he concludes that Isaiah is referring to Gentile nations who have called to Yahweh and successfully found him. See Motyer, *Isaiah*, 523. Mackay also interprets the phrase "a nation that was not called by my name" as referring to non-Israelites. See Mackay, *Isaiah*, 585.

152. Smith, *Isaiah 40–66*, 700. If the verbs "to be sought" and "to be found" are read as tolerative niphals, then they express the idea that "the subject allows to happen to

One reason why some interpret the intended audience in Isa 65:1 as Gentiles is because Paul applies this verse, in Rom 10:20, to Gentiles during his day. So, it is important to examine the context of Rom 10:18–21 and how Paul utilizes OT quotations to see if he reinterprets Isa 65:1 as pertaining to Gentiles.[153] Beginning in Rom 10:18–21, Paul argues that Israel has known God's message, and yet, paradoxically, that they have stubbornly refused to know. The problem is that "not all have obeyed the gospel" and "believed" the gospel (Rom 10:16). Rather, by seeking "their own righteousness" (Rom 10:3), through the law, Israel has "not submitted to God's righteousness" (Rom 10:3).[154] Paul repeats the phrase "but I ask" in Rom 10:18–20, in order to connect his quotations of Ps 19:4, Deut 32:21, and Isa 65:1 and explain how Israel has certainly heard the gospel and cannot accuse God of not providing ample opportunity for them to respond ("have they not heard? Indeed they have"; Rom 10:18).[155] Paul has already quoted Hos 2:23 (a verse originally addressing national Israel), in Rom 9:25–26, as proof that since God is saving Gentiles ("those who were not my people"; Rom 9:25), a people who did not know God, then Israel has less of an excuse for they were given the "oracles of God"

---

himself or to have an effect on himself." This implies that God intends for those who seek and find him to successfully do so. See Waltke and O'Connor *Biblical Hebrew Syntax*, §23.4f–g.

153. A number of recent studies suggest that Paul's appropriation of Isaiah in Romans speak both to his own mission to the Gentiles and of Israel's present and future relationship with their God. See Wright, *People of God*; Swartley, *Israel's Scripture*; Watts, *Isaiah's New Exodus*; Marcus, *Way of the Lord*; Marcus, "Mark and Isaiah," 449–66; Allison, *New Moses*; Moessner, *Jesus and the Heritage*; Pao, *Acts*. Many scholars continue to believe that the use of Israel's scriptures by Paul and the other NT authors depends to a great extent on rather narrow connections between texts, often amounting to little more than shared terminology. This requires careful analysis of each of Paul's citations and allusions to derive Paul's intent and connection between the OT text and Paul's use of it.

154. Wagner, *Heralds of the Good News*, 188.

155. Wagner notes that the verbal resemblance between Rom 10:18–19 and Isa 40:21, 28 suggests that Paul deliberately framed his questions ("Have they not heard?"; "Did Israel not understand?") to recall Isaiah's challenge to unbelieving Israel in Isa 40:28 ("Have you not known? Have you not heard?"). Paul's allusion to Isa 40:21, 28 adds another Isaianic strand to his tightly-woven critique of Israel's unbelief, which repeats the theme in Paul's appeals to Isaiah in Rom 9–10. See Wagner, *Heralds of the Good News*, 182–84. Cranfield observes that Paul's question and positive answer, in Rom 10:18, must be understood in relation to what was said in Rom 10:2–3. The truth is that in one sense Israel knows and in another sense they do not know. See Cranfield, *Romans*, 538.

(Rom 3:2).[156] As he did with Hos 1:10 and 2:23 in Rom 9:25–26, Paul takes OT texts that speak of national Israel and applies them to the Gentiles, during his day, as a principle of analogy, in Rom 10:18–20.[157]

Paul introduces his quotation of Deut 32:21, in Rom 10:19, "first" in order to explain his quotation of Isa 65:1, in Rom 10:20.[158] As Frédéric Godet notes, Paul uses the word "first" not for the priority of Moses in time to Isaiah, but to explain Israel's rejection in light of Gentile salvation.[159] Paul cites Deut 32:21, from the Song of Moses, in order to portray God as provoked by jealousy because of Israel's idolatry. In response to Israel's idolatry, God will "provoke" them to jealousy by means of a people who are "not a nation," namely Gentiles.[160] The implication of Deut 32:21 is that Israel's lack of faith, during Paul's time, is equivalent to Israel's lack of faith during the time of Moses. Also, by referencing Deut 32:21, Paul reveals that the Gentiles' salvation, during his time, will be the means whereby Israel will be brought back to their God, just as God stated in the Song of Moses.[161] As Beale and Gladd state, "Paul identifies present Israel's judgment of hardening and the Gentiles' salvation followed by Israel's redemption with the same prophesied storyline in Deuteronomy."[162]

Paul then quotes Isa 65:1, in Rom 10:20, and builds upon the same theme from Deut 32:21. By explaining how God always intended to utilize Gentile nations in order to "provoke" Israel to salvation, Paul adds that Isaiah similarly stated the same principle in Isa 65:1–2. Paul divides

156. Schreiner, *Romans*, 572.

157. Moo, *Romans*, 668.

158. Dunn, *Romans 9–16*, 625.

159. Godet, *Romans*, 388.

160. Bruce, *Romans*, 197–98.

161. The theme of provoking Israel to salvation foreshadows Rom 11:11. God's purpose to call Gentile nations (Rom 9:25) will serve as the solution to Israel's rejection of the gospel. See Dunn, *Romans 9–16*, 625. Schreiner adds that Israel should have known from the OT that the Gentiles would be included within the circle of God's saving purposes and that Israel would resist his saving work. Thus, the Jews can level no objection against Paul's gospel because it is more successful among Gentiles than Jews. By quoting Deut 32:21, Paul insists that the state of affairs was predicted in the OT and was known to the Jews. See Schreiner, *Romans*, 573. Wagner notes that the Song of Moses is a witness to not only Israel's unfaithfulness, but even more importantly, to the faithfulness of the Lord, who refuses to abandon his people. By citing the Song of Moses, Paul connects a well-known poetic depiction of Israel's election, unfaithfulness, and redemption with his own account in Romans of Israel's stumbling and ultimate salvation. See Wagner, *Heralds of the Good News*, 194.

162. Beale and Gladd, *Hidden but Now Revealed*, 90–91.

Isa 65:1–2 in such a way where v. 1 comments on Gentiles' salvation (Rom 10:20), whereas v. 2 comments on Israel's rejection of the gospel (Rom 10:21). However, as many commentators observe, the original context of Isa 65:1–2 pertains to national Israel.[163] By bisecting Isa 65:1–2, Paul transforms Isa 65:1 from a declaration of condemnation for Israel into a proclamation of salvation for Gentiles, while continuing to read Isa 65:2 as a commentary on Israel's continual rebellion.[164] Interestingly, Paul omits the second sentence of Isa 65:1 ("I said, 'Here I am, here I am,' to a nation that was not called by my name") when he cites this verse in Rom 10:20. This omission may elucidate how Paul is applying Isa 65:1 to Gentiles during his day.

163. Bruce writes, "In their original context these words from Isa 65:1 seem to refer to rebellious Israel; but, as in his application of the Hosea prophecy, Paul recognizes here a principle which in the situation of his day is applicable to Gentiles." See Bruce, *Romans*, 198. Cranfield, Schreiner, and Moo concur that Isa 65:1–2 refer to Israel in its original context. See Cranfield, *Romans*, 539; Schreiner, *Romans*, 574; and Moo, *Romans*, 669. Moo argues that Isa 65:1 refers to national Israel based on a reading of the verbs in the MT as "tolerative niphals." This would translate the verbs as "I allowed myself to be sought," "I was ready to be found," and that the last phrase in the verse should be translated "a nation that did not call on my name." See Moo, *Romans*, 669n49. Others, who translate the last phrase as "a nation not called by my name" apply Isa 65:1 to Gentiles. See Alexander, *Isaiah*, 2:437–38; MacRae, "Isaiah 65:1," 369–76. Despite the context of Isa 65:1–2, several argue that Paul reinterprets or clarifies that the recipients are meant to be Gentiles. Godet does not agree that unbelieving Israel, in Isa 65:1, serves as a type of the Gentiles. Instead, he argues that the "simple and unbiased study" of the passage from Isaiah leads to the conclusion that the prophet really meant to speak of Gentiles in Isa 65:1. See Godet, *Romans* Godet 389. Dunn writes that although the original prophecy had Israel in mind, the language lends itself to being interpreted of non-Israelites. He argues that Isa 65:1 corresponds with the eschatological incoming of the Gentiles and Paul's success of his own mission to the Gentiles. See Dunn, *Romans 9–16*, 626. Gentry seems to argue along the same lines with Dunn's and Godet's reading of Isa 65:1 by viewing it as a prophecy of the addition of Gentiles into the new covenant community.

164. See Wagner, *Heralds of the Good News*, 211. Wagner comments that Paul's reinterpretation of Isa 65:1 involves two distinct moves: first, finding the Gentiles in a text originally dealing with disobedient Israel; second, turning an ironic lament over Israel's obduracy into a positive celebration of Gentile inclusion in the people of God. Wagner argues that Paul's hermeneutical lens allows him to find Gentiles in the midst of divine oracles about Israel because of his conviction that God is calling Gentiles as well as Jews to be his redeemed people in Christ. Thus, according to Wagner, Paul's most common interpretive strategy is to find negative descriptions of Israelites, who are estranged from God, and locate Gentiles in those passages. See Wagner, *Heralds of the Good News*, 211–13.

Within Paul's account of Israel in Rom 9–11, Paul comments on a believing "remnant" within national Israel ("only a remnant of them will be saved"; Rom 9:27). Paul develops the concept of a remnant within Israel by citing Isa 10:22 and 28:16 in Rom 9:27 and 9:33 to highlight a division between those who "believe" and those who will "put to shame." Romans 9:27–29 seems to support the interpretation that the "remnant," in Isa 65:8–10, refers to the believing core of national Israel since Paul alludes to Isaiah to argue that God preserved a believing remnant within national Israel.[165] Paul highlights the "remnant" within Israel's history as a guarantee or confirmation that he will eventually save the nation as a whole.[166] This reading of the "remnant," as the believing core of national Israel, fits conceptually with the "firstfruits" and olive tree illustration in Rom 11:13–24.

In Rom 11:16, Paul mentions that the remnant of Israel functions as a "firstfruits" of what God will do for the "whole batch," that is, the nation. The "remnant" is not an end in itself but guarantees and anticipates the salvation of the nation as a whole.[167] Paul parallels the "firstfruits" of a dough with the "root" of an olive tree.[168] In Paul's olive tree illustration, the "natural branches" refers to Israel, while the "wild" branches refer to Gentiles (Rom 10:21). Paul states that if God has the power to "graft"

165. "And Isaiah cries out concerning Israel: 'Though the number of the sons of Israel be as the sand of the sea, only a remnant of them will be saved, for the Lord will carry out his sentence upon the earth fully and without delay.' And as Isaiah predicted, 'If the Lord of hosts had not left us offspring, we would have been like Sodom and become like Gomorrah'" (Rom 9:27–29). The Apostle Paul is showing from the OT that prophecy itself has spoken of the remnant and of the seed as those to whom salvation belonged and apart from whom the nation would have suffered the destruction of Sodom.

166. Rydelnik, "Jewish People," 264.

167. The concept of "firstfruits" within a lump of dough is found in Num 15:17–21. There is debate over whether the "firstfruits" refer to the remnant or patriarchs. It seems more likely that "firstfruits" refers to the remnant since the focus of Rom 11:1–6 is on a believing remnant within national Israel ("so too at the present time there is a remnant, chosen by grace"; Rom 11:5).

168. Some interpret the concept of "root" referring to Abraham and the patriarchs since this allusion was well-established in Jewish literature. Others see Paul making use of a long-standing metaphor of the olive tree as a symbol for Israel. See Mauer, "ῥίζα," 6:987–89. Anthony Hanson cites rabbinic use of the figure of the olive tree and goes so far as to argue that Rom 11:17–24 is a midrash on Jer 11:16–19. See Hanson, *Paul's Technique and Theology*, 121–24. The olive tree, however, must be broader than Israel since it includes both Israel and Gentiles. Israel, in Paul's analogy, corresponds to the natural branches, not the tree itself.

in wild branches to the olive tree, then he also has the power to graft in the "natural" branches again if they do not continue in unbelief (Rom 10:23). Paul affirms that God has the ability and willingness to save Israel if they are willing to repent and that the "remnant" functions as a preview of what God will do for the nation as a whole ("if the dough offered as firstfruits is holy, so is the whole lump"; Rom 11:16).[169]

When Paul appeals to the "provoking" motif from the Song of Moses and Isa 65:1–2, in Rom 10:19–20, he is not stating that Gentiles were the original recipients of Isa 65:1 or that Gentiles will unite with Jews to create a new multiethnic "Israel" in the eschatological kingdom. Instead, Paul argues, by way of analogy, that the God who can be found by Gentiles during Paul's day is both willing and able to reverse the unbelief of national Israel

169. In Rom 9:33 and 11:26, Paul refers to a "deliverer" coming "from Zion" and alludes to Isa 28:16 and 59:20. Paul changes "for Zion" to "from Zion," perhaps influenced by Pss 14:7; 53:6; and 110:2, pointing to Christ's second coming. Particularly in Rom 11:26, Paul references Isa 59:20, where Jesus will come to Zion and to those "in Jacob" who turn from their sin, indicating a distinction between Israel and Gentiles because of how Paul utilizes this verse in his argument for a future salvation of Israel in Rom 11:26. For a thorough analysis on the phrase "in this way all Israel will be saved," from Rom 11:26, see Vlach, *Has the Church Replaced Israel?* Non-supersessionists believe that Rom 11:26 affirms their view that national Israel will be saved. See Burns, "Future of Ethnic Israel," 190; Hoehner, "Romans 9–11," 153–58; Kaiser, "Assessment of 'Replacement Theology,'" 16; Blaising, "Future of Israel," 437–38; and Fruchtenbaum, *Israelology*, 552. Supersessionists argue that Rom 11:25–26 does not refer to national Israel. Their interpretation is based on a certain reading of οὕτως. They interpret οὕτως as comparative and referring to the manner in which God is saving "Israel." There are two possible options about the preceding point of reference: (1) the remnant of Jewish believers being saved in this age; or (2) entrance of the Gentiles into the community of the saved. Through the salvation of individual Jews and Gentiles, "Israel" is redeemed. See Robertson, *Israel of God*, 181. Dumbrell views οὕτως referring to the manner in which the remnant will be saved. He synthesizes Rom 11:25–26 with Eph 2:12–20, suggesting Christians now enjoy the privileges that was exclusive to Israel. See Dumbrell, *End of the Beginning*, 158. The second interpretation is that οὕτως is temporal and refers to the order of salvation. This interpretation sees Israel's salvation as following the Gentiles'. This translates to a sequential understanding of Israel's salvation as outlined in Rom 11:11–24. The preferred interpretation of οὕτως is viewing it as correlative with καθὼς, connecting Rom 11:26 with Isa 59:20. Darrell Bock explains, "In [Rom] 11:26, the term οὕτως is best interpreted with a view to 'just as' indicating that the salvation of 'all Israel' (most definitely a national reference in light of the contextual use of the term Israel) will take place as predicted by the prophets." See Blaising and Bock, *Progressive Dispensationalism*, 318. Romans 15:8–9 seem to strengthen this view of οὕτως and "Israel" as a reference to national Israel: "For I tell you that Christ became a servant to the circumcised to show God's truthfulness, in order to confirm the promises given the patriarchs, and in order that the Gentiles might glorify God for his mercy."

in the future. In fact, God will use the Gentiles as way to "provoke" Israel to repent and be restored as a nation. When Paul quotes Isa 65:2 in Rom 10:21, he remarks that God continues to "stretch" his hands out, waiting for Israel's salvation.[170] In Rom 11:1, Paul explicitly states that God has not rejected Israel ("I ask, then, has God rejected his people? By no means! For I myself am an Israelite"), thus confirming the understanding that his use of Isa 65:1 does not negate God's desire and willingness to restore national Israel in the future. It seems that Paul does not reinterpret Isa 65:1 as applying to Gentiles at the expense of national Israel. Instead, he cites Isa 65:1 in order to show that since God has the willingness to save Gentiles during Paul's day, he also has the same willingness to save national Israel in the future, which has been guaranteed with the preservation of a believing "remnant" within Israel during the time of Paul.[171]

Paul's concept of the "remnant," within Rom 9–11, corresponds with Isaiah's depiction of a remnant. When commenting on the remnant motif, Isaiah typically employs specific language indicating the national entity

170. Paul reverses the order of the two clauses from Isa 65:1 and substitutes the verb "seek" with "ask for."

171. For analysis on the different views of the relationship between Israel and the church, in Rom 9–11, see *Three Views on Israel and the Church*. Michael Vlach provides a "non-typological future-mass-conversion view," Fred G. Zaspel and James M. Hamilton Jr. provide a "typological future-mass-conversion view," while Benjamin Merkle provides a "typological non-future-mass-conversion view." Regarding Paul's use of Isa 65:1, Vlach writes that since "Isaiah often refers to Gentile salvation (19:24–25) and the situation in 65:1 contrast with that of unbelieving Israel in 65:2," then Gentiles could be in view. See Vlach, "Non-Typological," 37. Fred Zaspel and James Hamilton write that Isaiah "echoes" Moses in announcing that God would "show his favor to the Gentile nations who were not even seeking him while Israel stubbornly refused his kind offer. Paul takes up this 'jealousy' theme again in chapter 11, but here he highlights it to demonstrate once more that God's word has not failed but is being fulfilled." See Zaspel and Hamilton, "Typological Future," 107. Benjamin Merkle writes that Paul quotes Isa 65:1 in reference to Gentiles in order to "demonstrate that it was God's desire all along to include the Gentiles into his plan of redemption." See Merkle, "Typological Non-Future," 166. Merkle adds that he does not believe that the "privileged status of Israel is now transferred to the church," but that the promises to Israel are fulfilled in Christ, the "blameless Israelite," who transfers these blessings to whoever is "grafted" into the olive tree by faith in Christ. See Merkle, "Typological Non-Future," 167. Gentry's view seems to correspond with Merkle's since he also affirms that Christ is the "first and foremost" fulfillment of Israel and the church becomes the "Israel of God" because of their union with Christ. See Gentry and Wellum, *Kingdom through Covenant*, 106. The writer opts to affirm Bruce and Moo's view that Paul uses Isa 65:1, as a "principle of analogy," to reveal that just as God is willing to save Gentiles, he is also willing to save national Israel in the future and he confirms this promise with a preservation of a "remnant." See Bruce, *Romans*, 198; Moo, *Romans*, 619.

he has in mind.[172] When Isaiah utilizes the remnant motif in connection with Gentile nations, he explicitly labels the remnant with a particular nation. He mentions a "remnant of Syria" (Isa 17:3); a "remnant from Philistia" (Isa 14:28–32); and a "remnant" from Moab (Isa 15:9; "those who remain," Isa 16:13–14).[173] This indicates that when the "remnant" motif is applied to Gentiles, it is explicit. Gentry's interpretation of Isa 65:8–10 as depicting a "remnant" that consists of both Jews and Gentiles (new covenant community) is foreign to the remnant motif presented within Isaiah. Instead, it seems to be more consistent to read Isa 65:8–10 as describing the remnant as the believing core of national Israel.

Isaiah 65:8–10 also provides textual details that imply that the "servants" envisioned in that passage refers to the believing core of Israel. Isaiah 65:9 states that "Jacob" will have "descendants," and "Judah" will possess the "land" of promise. Leaving aside Gentry's interpretation of "servants" for the moment, nowhere in Isa 65:9–10 is there evidence that the blessings of the Abrahamic covenant are given to a "new" community that replaces national Israel. Instead, it would seem to be more consistent to understand Isaiah as predicting that the eschatological remnant of national Israel will possess the Abrahamic promises, according to Isa 65:8–10.[174]

Gentry interprets Isa 65:13–16 as describing the differences between national Israel and his envisioned new covenant community. However, Isa 65:13–16 can also be read as describing the differences between those who reject God versus those who seek after God within national Israel. Oswalt describes this distinction accordingly:

> Thus, 65:13–16 details the differences between "you" (i.e., those who have been trying to manipulate God for blessings) and "my servants" (i.e., those who seek God for himself with changed lives). In fact, the very blessings that the manipulators sought

---

172. For a survey of the remnant motif in ANE literature and its parallels found in the Hebrew Bible, see Hasel, "Remnant." Hasel notes that Isaiah utilizes the remnant motif in both a "non-eschatological and eschatological" sense depending on the context. For example, in Isa 10:20–23, the "remnant" of Israel refers to those left after the eschatological judgment will have fallen upon Israel, while Isa 28:5 refers to the "remnant" of Israel during the time of Hezekiah's plan to join an alliance with Egypt. Hasel, "Remnant," 400. Whether referring to the eschatological or historical remnant of Israel, both instances refer to national Israel.

173. Hasel, "Remnant," 401.

174. Westermann, *Isaiah 40–66*, 405.

and were denied will fall on the servants who seek God first and his blessings only secondarily'[175]

Regarding the New Jerusalem, introduced in Isa 65:18, Gentry proposes that the land originally promised in Gen 12:7 has here been expanded to include the entire earth in order to accommodate Gentiles in the kingdom.[176] According to Gentry's interpretation of Isa 65, the new heavens and a new earth is synonymous with the new Jerusalem.[177] Gentry writes:

> A great nation cannot exist apart from a place to call home. This is actually made explicit in [Gen 12:7], where God promises to Abram the land of Canaan. Nonetheless, as the history of the divine dealings with Abram show, God's priority is to create a covenant people first rather than settle the issue of the land where they will dwell. . . . Isaiah announces that the people of

175. Oswalt, *Isaiah*, 682.

176. Colin Chapman concurs with Gentry's reading of the land promise from the Abrahamic covenant to be typologically fulfilled in Christ and the church. Colin Chapman writes, "[The promised land] was intended to be the scene of God's gradual revelation of himself, which would lead eventually to the coming of Jesus, and to blessing for all peoples of the world. Since the New Testament speaks of all followers of Jesus as Abraham's seed and heirs according to the promise' (Gal 3:29), it must mean that all four aspects of the covenant—the land, the nation, the covenant relationship between God and his people, and the blessing for all peoples of the world—find their fulfillment in Jesus and in those who put their faith in him." See Chapman, *Whose Promised Land?*, 226.

177. Gentry and Wellum, *Kingdom through Covenant*, 468. Motyer affirms Gentry's interpretation that the new Jerusalem is synonymous with the new creation. Motyer writes, "The new creation (v. 17) is now *Jerusalem*, the new city. The City (Gen 11–19) was humankind's earliest effort to organize the world for its own security and stability. With Isaiah we watched the same human urge move from the imperialist Babylon that he knew (13–14), to the Babylon principle at work in ongoing history (21:1–10) and, at its end, to the fall of the world city where meaning had ceased to exist (24:1–10). By contrast, he showed us another city—of joy and provision (25:6–9), strength and salvation (26:1–3). It is in this way that the new creation becomes the new Jerusalem: the Lord's perfect organization of his new creation as a perfect setting for his new people. *Its people* are *my people*." Motyer argues that the new Jerusalem symbolizes God's new kingdom, which stands in contrast with Babel and other earthly kingdoms. He states that the description of infants no longer dying prematurely is a "metaphor" for how death will have less power in the new creation. See Motyer, *Isaiah*, 450–51. Alexander also supports this interpretation of the new Jerusalem. He writes, "Significantly, in verses 17–18 the creation of the 'new heavens and a new earth' parallels the creation of Jerusalem (cf. Isa. 24:23). The repeated use of the Hebrew verb בָּרָא, 'to create,' suggests that Jerusalem is deliberately equated here with the new heavens and the new earth. They are one and the same." See Alexander, *From Eden*, 53–54.

the new Zion will be far more numerous than those of the old (barren woman, Isa 54:1–3) because the nations will be drawn in to the new Zion. Implicit in this is the fact that more land will be required than just the real estate entailed in historical Israel. How can the new Zion find enough space in the new Jerusalem/ Israel? [Isa] 65 solves the puzzle: new Jerusalem and the new creation will be coextensive.[178]

Gentry interprets Zion, Israel, and the new creation as synonymous because of his assumption that the new Jerusalem functions as an antitype to Eden and Sinai. When analyzing Isa 2, Gentry states that since the torah will come from Zion, it functions as an antitype to Sinai, where God formalized his relationship with Israel through the giving of the Israelite/Mosaic covenant.[179] Thus, the future Zion has "assumed roles earlier played by Eden and Sinai," and functions as the new dwelling place of God (temple) where his people will gather to worship through a new covenant.[180] When commenting on Isa 11, Gentry points to the depiction of peace that will exist in Zion as an allusion to the garden of Eden. Gentry references Ezek 28:13–14, where Eden is described as a mountain, as proof that the new Zion, in Isa 11, will function as an antitype of Eden.[181] Gentry imposes the images of Eden and Sinai into his reading of Zion within Isaiah (Isa 2:1–4; 4:2–6; 11:1–10; 25:6–12) and concludes that the new Jerusalem functions as an antitype of Eden and Sinai.[182] In so doing,

178. Gentry and Wellum, *Kingdom through Covenant*, 468.

179. Gentry and Wellum, *Kingdom through Covenant*, 469.

180. Gentry and Wellum, *Kingdom through Covenant*, 470.

181. Gentry and Wellum, *Kingdom through Covenant*, 469. All of the occurrences of "Eden" either signify the actual garden of Eden or serve as a metaphorical descriptive term. None of them provide the textual foundation for understanding the land promised in the Abrahamic covenant as a typological reference to Eden. "Eden" occurs fourteen times in the OT and six times in Gen 1–4 (2:8, 10, 15; 3:23, 24; 4:16). "Eden" occurs as part of God's metaphorical description of the king of Tyre (Ezek 28:13) and is part of the description of Assyria in Ezek 31:9 ("and all the trees of Eden envied it, that were in the garden of God"). As part of his pronouncement of judgment on Assyria, Ezekiel refers to the trees of Eden in the underworld/Sheol, chopped down by some previous arrogant rulers (Ezek 31:16, 18 [2x]). The prophet, Joel, compares the coming Day of the Lord to a vast consuming fire. Before the raging fire hits, the land is compared to the Garden of Eden and behind the fire the land is a desert wilderness (Joel 2:3). Two passages describe God changing the land of Israel from a desert wilderness to a beautiful garden, like the garden of Eden (Isa 51:3; Ezek 36:35). In Ezek 36, the prophet uses this term, "garden of Eden," to describe his restoration of Israel to the actual land of promise (from which he had evicted them through covenant curse).

182. Gentry argues, "The first (2:1–4) pictures the Temple Mountain higher than

Gentry blends the concept of a city (Jerusalem), nation (Israel), and earth (new creation) into the new Jerusalem image because it supposedly functions as an antitype of Eden and Sinai and does not refer to the actual city of Jerusalem within the new creation.[183]

A consistent reading of Jerusalem in Isaiah, however, leads to a different interpretation. Instead of depicting the new Jerusalem as coextensive with the new creation, Isaiah seems to depict Jerusalem as a particular location blessed together with the new creation. Isaiah 2:1–3 states that Zion functions as a gathering place for Gentile nations so that they can be taught from the word of the Lord (2:3). Isaiah 11:16 describes a "highway" from Assyria, located outside of Zion, that the remnant, from the "four corners of the earth" (Isa 11:12), can travel on to reach Zion, which Isa 35:8–10 describes as the "Way of Holiness" (Isa 35:8). Isaiah 19:23 describes a highway between Assyria and Egypt, which is located outside of Zion, while Isa 27:12–13 reiterates that Israelites outside of Zion will travel in order to gather in Zion. Isaiah 60:11 mentions that the gates to Zion will remain open so that nations and their kings can continually enter the city. Finally, Isa 66:18–19 describes God sending "survivors" to the nations, located in territories outside of Zion (Tarshish, Pul, Lud, Tubal, Javan). These textual details suggest that Zion is not synonymous with the new creation but as a specific location within the new creation.

Gentry provides exegetical support for his interpretation of the new Jerusalem by citing T. Desmond Alexander. He argues that Jerusalem, in Isa 65:18, is "deliberately equated" with the new heavens and the new earth, in v. 17, because both are preceded by the same verb, בָּרָא.[184] The

---

all others, with the nations streaming to it to receive instruction (Torah). The second (4:2–6) combines images of a fruitful land, a city devoted to the Lord, and a place of worship overshadowed by a canopy of glory as in the exodus. The third (11:1–10) portrays the future as an Edenic paradise (recall that Eden was on a mountain). The fourth (25:6–12) paints the scene of a mountain banquet with aged wine where death is swallowed up forever. The last (65:17–25) combines the new creation and the new Jerusalem together in one tableau." Gentry and Wellum, *Kingdom through Covenant*, 468–69.

183. Gentry and Wellum, *Kingdom through Covenant*, 470.

184. Gentry and Wellum, *Kingdom through Covenant*, 467. Regarding the seeming inconsistency between Isaiah's announcement that God will create a new heavens and a new earth while focusing on the new Jerusalem, Westermann comments that either v. 17 is the "language of exaggeration" and the speaker was not conscious of the inconsistency or vv. 17 and 25 has been made into a description that is apocalyptic. Westermann concludes that 65:17 is an exaggeration of what is actually described in 65:18. See Westermann, *Isaiah 40–66*, 408. Jon Levenson views these verses as synonymous

repetition of בָּרָא, for Gentry, provides the basis to equate the new Jerusalem as synonymous with the new creation. However, the repeated use of בָּרָא does not mean that the objects of this verb are synonymous. The word בָּרָא is utilized in Isa 40–48 when describing God's creation of darkness and light (Isa 45:7), the heavenly bodies (Isa 40:26), the earth and its inhabitants (Isa 40:28; 42:5; 45:12, 18), and Israel (Isa 43:1, 7, 15).[185] Clearly, the repetition of בָּרָא does not indicate that darkness, light, heavenly bodies, and Israel are synonymous with the new creation. Also, Gentry's interpretation seems to be based on a certain construal of Hebrew poetic parallelism.

Hebrew poetic parallelism can be categorized semantically, linguistically, and/or syntactically.[186] It functions as a linguistical tool that

---

statements and questions the recreation in 65:17 as universal. See Levenson, *Creation*, 89–90. Gary Smith, rightly notes, that although the temple in Jerusalem was the center of God's presence which impacted the world, the temple and the world are not synonymous locations. See Smith, *Isaiah 40–66*, 719. Andrew Abernethy provides a convincing explanation on why the new Jerusalem and new creation should not be viewed as synonymous. He notes that the use of *bara* in vv. 17–18 creates "a parallel between God's creation of the universe and God's creation of a particular place, Jerusalem." According to Abernethy, by focusing on Jerusalem, a particular location within the new creation, God is providing a "sample of what he will do throughout the entire heaven and the earth." See Abernethy, *Isaiah and God's Kingdom*, 175–76.

185. Blenkinsopp writes, "The threefold use in vv. 17–18 of the verb *bara*, a technical term for divine creative activity, indicates dependence on Isa 40–48, which speak of the creation of darkness and light (45:7), the heavenly bodies (40:26), the earth and its inhabitants (40:28; 42:5; 45:12, 18), and Israel (43:1, 7, 15)." See Blenkinsopp, *Isaiah 56–66*, 286. Whybray notes that the verb *bara* in v. 17, appears to build upon the use of the verb in Isa 41:20; 42:5–9; 43:7–15; and 45:8. He adds that the use of *bara*, in v. 18, may be compared with Isa 62:7 in order to imply that the city will be more than simply a restoration of the old or a "reestablished" city but one that will share in the same "new" characteristics as the heavens and the earth described in v. 17. See Whybray, *Isaiah 40–66*, 276.

186. Robert Lowth laid down the foundations of a systematic inquiry into parallelism and categorized according to three semantic categories: synonymous, antithetic, and synthetic. See Lowth, *poesi hebraeorum*; Lowth, *Isaiah*. Adele Berlin notes that most contemporary scholars have abandoned the models of Lowth and are seeking new models for a reassessment of biblical poetry. Almost all of them, according to Berlin, have looked to linguistics for a model. See Berlin, *Dynamics of Biblical Parallelism*, 18. She notes that there are (1) morphological parallelism (pairings from different word classes, and pairings form the same word class with different morphologic elements) and (2) syntactic parallelism (syntax of the lines is equivalent and where pairing of lines in which a transformation has occurred). See Berlin, *Dynamics of Biblical Parallelism*, 31–63. James Kugel destroys the notion of a distinct number of semantic categories and replaces it with a general overarching semantic concept which

helps structure the text. As Jonathan Culler comments, "Linguistics is not hermeneutics," so one should not assume a certain interpretation based on parallelism alone.[187] Instead, parallelism is a linguistical device that expresses "one thought" in multiple expressions.[188] Through repetition (word, phrase, syntactical markers, etc.), an idea is expressed. However, what the repetition communicates concerning the overall thought is debated.[189] As Robert Alter writes, "Repetition is not simply a restatement

---

may be realized in so many different ways that they defy most superficial description. See Kugel, *Biblical Poetry*, 51–54. David Tsumura categorizes Hebrew poetic parallelism into the following categories: (1) Superimposition, (2) Chiastic Word Order; and (3) Ellipsis. By superimposition, Tsumura means that two lines often constitute a compound sentence, with the syntactical images of two lines being perfectly superimposed. In this synonymous parallelistic structure, two colons of the same syntactical image are superimposed on each other and express the meaning. In contrast, antithetic parallelism, in which two contrastive elements are dealt with is an example of superimposition of the opposite sides of the same coin, not of two contradictory thoughts. Regarding chiastic word order, Tsumura states that each colon has the same syntactical image but with a chiastic word order, that is interrogative pronoun + verb + prepositional phrase // conjunction, interrogative pronoun + prepositional phrase + verb. The object of the participle of a transitive verb in the first line corresponds to the subject of the intransitive verb in the second line. The synonymous parallelistic structure also achieves "a result reminiscent of binocular vision." Finally, ellipsis is where the "superimposition" of the syntactical image of two lines can be realized even if there is a gapping of element in one of the parallel lines. In sum, Tsumura argues that parallelism is the device of expressing one thought through two lines as well as the linguistic unit that constitutes one sentence through two lines. See Tsumura, "Verbal Grammar of Parallelism," 170–71.

187. Culler, *Structuralist Poetics*, 31. As Culler states, "The fact that parallelism exists tells us nothing about the meaning of the verse."

188. David Toshio Tsumura writes, "I define parallelism, semantically, in the simplest way, as a device expressing 'one thought through two lines.'" He adds that grammatically, however, the parallelism may be defined as a linguistic unit that constitutes "one sentence through two lines." See Tsumura, "Verbal Grammar of Parallelism," 167–71. Based on his analysis of Proverbs, Alviero Niccacci came to the following definition of parallelism: "Lines consist of parallel grammatical units, that normally constitute a complete sentence." See Niccaci, "Analyzing Biblical Hebrew Poetry," 89. Luis Alsonso Schökel writes, "Parallelism is, above all, a formal resource for the articulation of discourse, and in its most basic form it is dyadic, through three- and four-part divisions are not uncommon. Beyond four begins a series." See Schökel, "Isaiah," 168. Adele Berlin adds, "Parallelism may involve semantics, grammar, and/or other linguistic features, and it may occur on the level of the word, line, couplet, or over a greater textual span." See Berlin, *Dynamics of Biblical Parallelism*, 25–26.

189. Regarding word repetition, Adele Berlin notes that a word may elicit a number of different associations. For example, the repetition of "Zion" and "cities of Judah" in Lam 5:11 reveal a subordinate relationship where Zion refers to one city among the

of the same idea, but a new statement that may intensify, specify, comple-
ment, qualify, contrast, or expand the initial verse in its repetition."[190]
When Gentry argues that the repetition of בָּרָא indicates that the new
Jerusalem is synonymous with the new creation, he seems to assume that
repetition consistently communicates synonymous concepts. It is possible that the repetition of בָּרָא signifies that the new Jerusalem functions
in a subordinate relationship to the new creation and specifies how the
conditions of the new creation will look based on the conditions described in the city.[191] Also, several linguists do not cite Isa 65:17–18 as an
example of Hebrew parallelism, which brings into question the validity of
Gentry's argument that the repetition of בָּרָא communicates that the new
Jerusalem is coextensive with the new creation.[192]

---

cities of Judah. The effect of the second word pair is to expand the meaning in this case.
See Berlin, *Dynamics of Biblical Parallelism*, 71, 80–81. Luis Alsonso Schökel argues
that by means of repetition, the poet is able to analyze one situation in two ways.
He can dwell upon and show first one side and then the reverse of the same reality.
In the corresponding half he may introduce an alternate rhythm. He adds that since
parallelism is found so frequently in all genres of Hebrew poetry, it is best to focus on
those examples composed with a particular end in mind. See Schökel, "Isaiah," 168.
DeClaissé-Walford, Nancy J., Rolf A. Jacobson, and Beth LaNeel Tanner note that parallelism can repeat and pair many things together: synonyms or antonyms; questions
and responses; a singular noun and a plural noun; a masculine noun and a feminine
noun; a statement with a supporting reason; an abstract concept with a concrete reality. As they note, the variations are "practically inexhaustible." See DeClaissé-Walford
et al., *Psalm*, 40–41. Elcanon Isaac argues that after each thought there is a reaction in
which the idea is embodied in a less intense form, so that the minor parts of the verses
form a background on which the major parts stand out. He proposes three degrees of
parallelism: (1) where the intensity is great in the major member, in which case there is
a tendency for the minor member to repeat the idea in substantially the same metrical
form and verbal arrangement; (2) where the intensity is not so great, but where in addition there is a lyrical quality; and (3) where the intensity is not great and the contrast
less, but where the thought is meditative. See Isaacs, "Nature of Parallelism," 116–19.

190. Alter, *Art of Biblical Narrative*, 122.

191. Gentry writes, "Jerusalem is not only at the centre of the new world, but in
fact is coextensive with it. The new creation is the new Jerusalem and vice versa. This
conclusion is clear from Isaiah 65:25, where the new creation is described as God's
holy mountain—Mount Zion has become the new Eden!" See Gentry and Wellum,
Kingdom through Covenant, 467. However, as Watts observes, one can interpret Jerusalem as the "focal point" of the new creation rather than as synonymous with it. See
Watts, *Isaiah 34–66*, 925.

192. Berlin cites Isa 1:3, 4, 9–10, 19–20; 2:4; 3:1, 8; 4:5; 5:1; 6:11; 9:19; 10:3; 14:25;
15:19; 16:5, 7; 24:10, 12, 17–18; 28:10, 13, 21; 29:5, 17; 30:13; 31:8–9; 33:1; 34:6, 9–11;
35:5–6; 38:18; 40:3–4, 9, 12, 18; 41:8–9, 26; 42:1, 13, 16; 43:10, 18; 44:1, 2, 8, 26; 45:1,
12; 48:13; 51:6; 52:2–3, 15; 54:2, 4, 7–8; 57:20; 58:8; 60:16; 61:5; 65:9, 15, 21; 66:8,

Although Gentry acknowledges that there are other ways to interpret Isa 65:18, he points to Rev 21 as support for his interpretation that the new Jerusalem will be coextensive with the new creation. When one examines Rev 21, however, the textual details support a multinational paradigm where the new Jerusalem is distinct from surrounding Gentile nations. The new Jerusalem comes down out of heaven, not as the new earth, but will be located on the new earth, clearly indicating a distinction between Jerusalem and the new earth (Rev 21:1–2). Revelation 21:25 mentions that the gates will never be shut, which implies a territorial limit to the new Jerusalem and a distinction between it and surrounding territories. Finally, Rev 21:24 portrays nations and kings traveling into Jerusalem in order to bring their "glory and honor," again indicating that the new Jerusalem is a distinct location from the surrounding Gentile territories.

There are several intertextual details between Rev 21 and Isa 60 which indicate that both passages describe the same city. Revelation 21:23 and Isa 60:19 both mention that the city will have no need for the sun or moon since the Lord will be an "everlasting light" (Isa 60:19) by illuminating the city with the "Lamb" (Rev 21:23). Revelation 21:24 mentions and kings bringing their "glory" into the new Jerusalem, while Isa 60:11 describes nations and kings bringing their "wealth" to rebuild the city. Finally, Rev 21:25 state that the gates of the new Jerusalem will "never be shut," while Isa 60:11 states that Zion's gate will remain open "day and night." The textual parallels between Rev 21 and Isa 60 seem to reveal that Isa 60 describes the new Jerusalem portrayed in Rev 21. If so, then the textual of details provide insight on the nature of the new Jerusalem.

According to Isa 60:4, when the nations travel to Jerusalem, they will bring Zion's "sons" and "daughters," which is a theme repeated throughout Isaiah (Isa 11:12; 14:1–2; 45:13–14; 49:22–23; 66:20), along with their "wealth" (Isa 60:4–5), which will be used to rebuild Zion (60:10).[193] The "sons" and "daughters" refers to Israelites who will become "planted" back in their land, which will happen through the Davidic king ("the shoot of Jesse"; Isa 11:1) who will "raise up the tribes of Jacob" (Isa 49:6). Isaiah 60:21–22 transitions form a description of the city to the condition of its citizens: "Your people shall all be righteous; they shall possess the land

13, 23 as examples of Hebrew parallelism. Yet, she does not cite Isa 65:17–18 as an example. See Berlin, *Dynamics of Biblical Parallelism*, 171–72. Schökel cites Isa 1:4–7; 16–17; 2:12–19; 5:11, 22; and 29:1 but omits Isa 65:17–18 as examples of Hebrew parallelism in Isaiah. See Schökel, "Isaiah," 168–74.

193. Jones, "Wealth of Nations," 621.

forever, the branch of my planting, the work of my hands, that I might be glorified. The least one shall become a clan, and the smallest one a mighty nation; I am the Lord; in its time I will hasten it." Israel is assured of their permanent possession of their land (Isa 60:21), which connects with Isa 61:3, when God will plant them as "oaks of righteousness," when they were previously described as an oak whose "leaf withers" (Isa 1:30). Isaiah 60:22 alludes to the Abrahamic promise that all nations will be blessed through Abraham's offspring (cf. Gen 18:18).[194] The textual details from Rev 21 and Isa 60 both portray a new Jerusalem as a specific city within the new creation and Israelites and Gentiles with national distinctions.

Clearly, Gentry interprets Isaiah's vision as displaying a single worldwide city rather than a multinational kingdom. Gentry assumes that the new covenant transforms the nature and identity of Israel because of the presence of Gentiles and that the new Jerusalem becomes coextensive with the new creation. It seems that Gentry does not provide a plausible reading of Isaiah built up from the details of the text but imposes certain hermeneutical presuppositions into his reading of Isaiah to arrive at his conclusion.

Hermeneutical Assumptions of Gentry's Interpretation of Isaiah's Kingdom

Gentry consistently interprets passages in which Gentiles are included in the people of God and participate with Israel in worshipping Yahweh as evidence that the concept of Israel has been transformed with Gentiles integrated into a new multiethnic "Israel." Key to his interpretation is a certain conception of typology that leads him to this conclusion. His co-author, Wellum, states this explicitly:

> In order to discern properly how Old Testament types/patterns are brought to fulfillment in God's plan, we must first observe not only how those types are *intertextually* developed *within* the Old Testament but also how they are applied and developed under the new covenant. In other words, Jesus and the new

---

194. Like Gentry, Edward Young interprets Isa 60 as a vision regarding the increase of the NT church rather than a reference to a multinational kingdom. He believes that the "smallest one," in v. 22, refers to individuals from Israel who will now host a multitude of individual Gentiles in Zion. According to Young, the growth of Zion recalls Isa 54 and points to Gentile inclusion in the NT church. See Young, *Isaiah*, 457.

covenant becomes the hermeneutical lens by which we interpret the fulfillment of the types/patterns of the Old Testament.[195]

There are two approaches to typology. The first approach centers on the idea of "prefiguration," where a type prefigures a truth connected in Christianity. The second centers on the idea of "correspondence," where a type demonstrates the correspondence between various stages in the fulfillment of God's purpose.[196] In his definition of typology, Wellum includes aspects of both "prefiguration" and "correspondence," as well as adding an element of "intensification." He defines typology as "the study of Old Testament salvation historical realities or 'types' (persons, events, institutions) which God has specifically designed to *correspond* to, and predictively *prefigure*, their *intensified* antitypical fulfillment aspects (inaugurated and consummated) in New Testament salvation history."[197] Based on his

195. Gentry and Wellum, *Kingdom through Covenant*, 606.

196. Regarding the first approach, see Fritsch, "Biblical Typology," 214. Regarding the second approach, see Lampe, "Typological Exegesis," 202. Benjamin J. Ribbens describes these two approaches as "*prefiguration* typology" and "*correspondence* typology." See Ribbens, "Typology of Types," 84–85. There is a non-evangelical approach to typology, which Davidson labels the "post-critical neo-typology" view, which argues that typology is basically the result of drawing analogies or correspondences within the uniform pattern of God's activity and possesses no prospective aspect. Advocates of a "post-critical neo-typology" view formed "to bring together elements of the traditional typology with the findings of modern critical scholarship." See Hoskins, *Jesus as Fulfillment*, 27; Ninow, *Indicators of Typology*, 43–44; and Hugenberger, "Notes on Typology," 331–41. Critical scholars who affirm the "post-critical neo-typology" view include Gerhard von Rad, Hans Walter Wolff, and M. D. Goulder. See Rod, "Typological Interpretation," 174–92; Wolff, "Hermeneutics of the Old Testament," 160–99; and Goulder, *Type and History*, 1–13. Evangelicals who affirm a "correspondence" approach, without affirming the critical view of the historicity of the type and antitype, include France, *Jesus and the Old Testament*, 39–42. The "correspondence" approach can include a "prospective" or "prophetic" quality or can be identified retrospectively. Brent Parker notes that a traditional conception of biblical typology affirms that the original prototypes and types in Scripture possess a prospective quality leading to the antitype. On the other hand, post-critical neo-typology advocates do not find types to be predictive or prophetic in any way. Instead, the biblical writers apprehended the typological relationship retrospectively since a type has no predictive element. See Parker, "Israel-Christ-Church," 60–61.

197. Gentry and Wellum, *Kingdom through Covenant*, 103 (emphasis mine). Gentry and Wellum adopt their definition of typology from Davidson, *Typology in Scripture*, 397–408. Greg Beale writes that typology is "the study of analogical correspondences among revealed truths about persons, events, institutions, and other things within the historical framework of God's special revelation, which, from a retrospective view, are of a prophetic nature and are escalated in their meaning." See Beale, *Handbook on the New Testament*, 14. Based on this definition, Beale lists five essential characteristics

definition of typology, Wellum claims that typology exhibits a twofold character. First, typology involves a "repetition of the 'promise-fulfillment' pattern of redemptive history in which all types find their fulfillment in Christ."[198] Second, typology exhibits an *a fortiori* quality, which is to say that there is an escalation as the type is fulfilled in the antitype.[199]

---

of a type: (1) analogical correspondence, (2) historicity, (3) a pointing-forwardness, (4) escalation, and (5) retrospection. John Currid lists four characteristics found in typology: (1) it must be grounded in history; both type and antitype must be actual historical events, persons, or institutions; (2) there must be a historical and theological correspondence between type and antitype; (3) there must be an intensification of the antitype from the type; and (4) some evidence that the type is ordained by God to foreshadow the antitype must be present. See Currid, "Use of Typology," 121. Brent Parker argues that most evangelicals agree that typology (1) involves the study of real and organic historical and theological correspondences of types—identifiable as OT persons, events, or institutions; (2) possesses a divinely intended quality with prophetic or prospective import (OT types and typological patterns point forward to later persons and events) that are progressively unpacked across successive epochs of biblical revelation culminating in NT counterparts (generally denoted as *antitypes* and routinely identified with Jesus Christ or the salvation or new covenant realities he secures); and (3) exhibits a significant resemblance, as well as an escalation (an *a fortiori* quality) or qualitative progression, that is detected between the type and antitype. See Parker, "Israel-Christ-Church," 5–7. Baker notes that any approach to typology should include two principles: history and correspondence between the type and antitype. Based on these two principles, Baker provides the following definition for typology: "A type is a biblical event, person or institution which serves as an example or pattern for other events, persons or institutions; typology is the study of types and the historical and theological correspondences between them; the basis of typology is God's consistent activity in the history of his chosen people." Baker, *Two Testaments, One Bible*, 171. Interestingly, Baker does not include escalation or an intensification of a type as a necessary element in his definition of typology.

198. Gentry and Wellum, *Kingdom through Covenant*, 105. Others who also argue that a type always refer to Christ and his redemptive activity include Goppelt, *Typos*, 17–18; Hugenberger, "Notes on Typology," 337; Carson, "Mystery and Fulfillment," 404–7; Marshall, "Assessment of Recent Developments," 15–17; Bruce, "Typology," 1214–15; and Amsler, "Typologie de l'Ancien Testament?," 75–81.

199. Stephen Wellum writes, "It is important to note that escalation across time does not occur incrementally from the original type to each 'little' installment and then to Christ, as if there were a straight line to increase. Rather escalation occurs fully only with the coming of Christ. The previous typological patterns point forward to the greater one to come (Rom. 5:14), but the greater aspect is realized only in Christ." See Gentry and Wellum, *Kingdom through Covenant*, 106. "Escalation" means that the OT type and NT antitype are not on the same plane as there is an element of intensification or qualitative progression. For a discussion of the escalation of typological patterns, see Goppelt, *Typos*, 18, 177, 199–202, 220; Davidson, "Eschatological Hermeneutic," 36–44. Others, such as David Baker, question whether a type must always include the two aforementioned qualities. Baker notes that "progression" or "heightening" from

Certainly, there are cases where an escalation of a type results in the antitype rendering it obsolete (i.e., animal sacrifices). However, it is possible for a type to escalate such that the antitype does not transform or replace the type.[200] As Feinberg notes, "Even if Israel is an OT type, it does not follow that its role as a national and ethnic entity is eclipsed by the church in the new covenant era. Israel typology could be understood in a manner such that certain OT promises to Israel still remain as the

---

the type to its antitype is an aspect of the progression from OT to NT and not a necessary characteristic of a type. A type, at its essence, is exemplary and it is possible for one thing to be a type of its opposite or for something more advanced to be typical of something less advanced. See Baker, *Two Testaments, One Bible*, 183. He adds that types can include other themes besides Christ redemptive activity. Brent Parker notes that not all typological patterns are directly Christocentric (i.e., flood typology of 1 Peter 3:18–22), but instead are "Christotelic." By "Christotelic," Parker utilizes Peter Enns's definition without adopting Enns's view of Scripture. See Parker, "Israel-Christ-Church," 72n117. Enns defines "Christotelic" as reading the Old Testament "already knowing" that Christ is "somehow the end." See Enns, *Inspiration and Incarnation*, 154; Enns, "Fuller Meaning," 213–15. William Lane notes that types do not always include an *a fortiori* quality, but can function as examples, patterns, or illustrations. Hebrews 8:5 seems to reverse the order so that Moses patterns the earthly things (i.e., tabernacle), which are merely a "copy and shadow of the heavenly things," after the heavenly things. In other words, the heavenly things serve as a type of the earthly things, the antitype. Lane comments, "The fact that it was only a copy of the heavenly reality consigns the earthly sanctuary to the realm of the changing and transitory, which has only limited validity because it must ultimately pass away." See Lane, *Hebrews 1–8*, 206.

200. Brent Parker notes that the typological temple pattern is appropriated to the church but takes further shape and additional realization in the new heavens and new earth with God's presence fully realized as Jesus, the perfect temple, who dwells with his people for eternity (Rev 21:22). Parker concludes that typological patterns are always "either completely fulfilled" with the coming of the Christ or they are initially inaugurated by Christ with "further fulfillment" through the church. See Parker, "Israel-Christ-Church," 76–77. Parker seems to undermine his earlier argument when he states that since Israel functions as an OT type of Christ, then Christ's arrival in the NT consists of the completion and fulfillment of the type, Israel, such that the unconditional promises for them have been fulfilled in Christ. See Parker, "Israel-Christ-Church," 4. If the typological pattern for the temple can include a both/ and fulfillment in the church and Christ, then why does Parker assume that a similar typological pattern cannot exist for national Israel? Although Parker acknowledges that not all antitypes require the complete fulfillment of a type, thus allowing a future fulfillment to continue, he does argue that there is always a "transformation" of the type with its fulfillment because of his understanding that typology must include a characteristic of "escalation." Thus, his conception of Israel escalates in its composition with the introduction of Gentiles because he assumes that typology always includes an element of escalation from type to antitype.

pattern of realization even if it functions as an OT type."[201] To assume that an escalation of a type requires its replacement or transformation by an antitype, without clear textual markers, will lead to unwarranted exegetical conclusions.[202]

Wellum explains how Israel functions as a typological pattern of which Christ is the "first and foremost" fulfillment and the church becomes the "Israel of God" because of their union with Christ.[203] As a result, the covenant promises given to Israel are applied to the church since Christ takes on the role of Israel and the new covenant community unites with him. Gentry and Wellum's hermeneutical argument is evident when Wellum explains how the land promises for Israel will be fulfilled. He writes:

> There are exegetical grounds both in the immediate context and across the entire Canon to argue that the "land" was never intended by the biblical authors to be understood *merely* within the limited confines of specific geographical boundaries. In other words, "land," when placed within the biblical covenants and viewed diachronically, was intended by God to function as a "type" or "pattern" of something greater, i.e., creation, which is precisely how it is understood in light of the coming of Christ and the inauguration of the new covenant.[204]

---

201. See Feinberg, "Systems of Discontinuity," 72. For how Jesus can be thought of as the antitype of Israel but in a way that secures national Israel's future restoration, see Vlach, "What Does Christ," 43–54.

202. Baker, *Two Testaments, One Bible*, 175–78.

203. Gentry and Wellum, *Kingdom through Covenant*, 106. Brent Parker argues that since Israel is a type of Christ and derivatively of the church, the escalation and heightening characteristics intrinsic to typological patterns means that instead of interpreting the church-Israel relationship in strict continuity, the church has a qualitative difference in possessing better spiritual realities as a regenerate community than historical Israel. He adds that the characteristics of the Israel-Christ typology reveal that the mediatorial and national role of OT Israel has reached its terminus and fulfillment in Jesus Christ, and derivatively to the church as the "renewed/new Israel." See Parker, "Israel-Christ-Church," 9–10. Both Wellum and Parker assume that a certain type of escalation is intrinsic with every type and applies this form of typology to Israel.

204. Gentry and Wellum, *Kingdom through Covenant*, 706. Seth Erlandsson also proposes a reading of Israel's land as a type. He writes, "To rightly understand the true meaning of these prophecies, it is important to pay attention to the following: the difference between God's Israel during the time of the old covenant and the true Israel, the difference between the old and new covenants, and the difference between a theocratic nation in a specific geographical land and God's true Israel which cannot be seen with physical eyes (Luke 17:20)." See Erlandsson, "Isaiah 2:1–4," 268.

Wellum argues that the promised land is fulfilled in the new creation through the redemptive work of Jesus instead of referring to a specific territory for national Israel. He adds:

> In the New Testament, it is our contention that the land promise does not find its fulfillment in the future in terms of a specific piece of real estate given to the ethnic nation of Israel; rather it is fulfilled in Jesus, who is the true Israel and the last Adam, who by his triumphant work wins for us the new creation. That new creation has "already" arrived in the dawning of the New Covenant in individual Christians (2 Cor. 5:17; Eph. 2:8–10) and the church (Eph. 2:11–21) and it will be consummated when Christ returns and ushers in the new creation in its fullness (Rev. 21–22).[205]

Gentry posits that the NT supports his reading of Israel, in Isaiah, as a type of the eschatological kingdom. However, the textual details in Isaiah seem to portray Israel as a nation within a multinational kingdom. Even if the NT allegedly supports Gentry's interpretation of Israel as an OT type, he does not demonstrate how the details from Isaiah supports his interpretation. Instead, Gentry and Wellum presuppose a certain metanarrative, which influences their exegesis. They write:

> The metanarrative we bring to these texts determines our exegetical outcomes . . . furthermore, we argue that already in the OT, especially in the prophets, the land is viewed as a type that looks back to Eden and forward to the new creation. The people of Israel, as God's chosen people, serve as the privileged means by which God brings about his redemptive purposes to the nations. Even now, God is not finished with them, as Romans 9–11 makes plain. At the same time, the meaning of Israel and Jerusalem is being transformed to speak of the people of God, which will include both ethnic Jews and Gentiles.[206]

---

205. Gentry and Wellum, *Kingdom through Covenant*, 607. It has been noted by several that, while the book is presented as a whole-Bible theology, there is a noticeable lack of extended interaction with and discussion of NT passages, especially that which demand an explanation in light of the authors proposed metanarrative. See Bock, "Kingdom through Covenant"; Moo, "Kingdom through Covenant"; and Vlach, "Have They Found a Better Way?," 10–12. The issue was also addressed at the Dispensational Study Group meeting at the Evangelical Theological Society in San Diego, 2014: Blaising et al., review of *Kingdom through Covenant*, November 2014.

206. See Gentry and Wellum, "'Kingdom through Covenant' Authors Respond."

For Gentry and Wellum, typology and a certain canonical metanarrative appears to function as a lens filtering out national and territorial
distinctions in Isaiah's eschatological kingdom.[207] If it is true that Gentry
and Wellum build their argument regarding Israel as an OT type from
their exegetical observations, then one questions how they reconcile the
textual details from Isaiah with their understanding of the metanarrative
of Scripture.[208] It may be the case that Gentry and Wellum, along with
other theologians (i.e., Herman Ridderbos), argue that the territorial and
national details presented in certain prophecies function as idiomatic expressions.[209] If this is so, one wonders how those who affirm "prophetic

207. Brent Parker explicitly states that a multinational eschatological kingdom
does not affirm a "one people of God" concept, which is why he rejects such a notion.
He states that the church is a "singular entity" comprised of people from every nation
and is one congregation, one new humanity in Christ. Yet, a multinational kingdom
has many peoples of God who keep their national status. He views the incorporation
of Gentiles into the church as depicting an expansion of the people of God from what
was an ethnic, political nation (Israel) to an international, transnational community
that is one body. See Parker, "Israel-Christ-Church," 186n145. Parker does not explain
how a multinational paradigm of the kingdom, as opposed to a multiethnic one, undermines the "one people of God" concept. If the kingdom is depicted as an international community, as Parker states, then why would national distinctions need to be
dismissed in order to uphold a unified people of God concept? If the kingdom people
could be unified, despite their ethnic differences, it is not much of a leap to conclude
that the people can also be unified, despite their national distinctions, especially since
territorial distinctions exists in the kingdom.

208. Blaising offered a review of *Kingdom through Covenant* and noted how Gentry and Wellum utilize a certain form of typology as a way of establishing the divine
plan in Scripture. See Blaising, "Critique," 120–24. In response to Blaising's critique,
Brent Parker notes that Gentry and Wellum do not assert typology as the means of
establishing the divine plan. Instead, they are tracing the storyline of Scripture, as it
is progressively unfolded, and observing the escalated realities that come with what
Christ has accomplished by inaugurating the kingdom and bringing forth the dawning
of the new creation era. Parker adds that a type is "exegetically" discovered either in
the immediate context or through intertextual development in the canon of Scripture
and seems to imply that Gentry and Wellum are basing their conclusions about typology based on their exegetical observations and not from their assumption of a certain
form of typology. See Parker, "Israel-Christ-Church," 63, 185n44.

209. Ridderbos explains this concept as "prophetic idiom." Ridderbos writes,
"The function of prophecy is consequently not that of a detailed projection of
the future but is the urgent insistence on the certainty of the things to come. . . .
This limitation of the perspective . . . is connected with the fact that the prophet
paints the future in the colors and with the lines that he borrows from the world
known to him, i.e., from his own environment. It is also true that the nations, the
inhabited world, etc., occur in the eschatological picture. But this does not imply
that the prophet has been equipped with geographical omniscience, that his view

idiom" can determine what details of a prophecy will be fulfilled the way it is portrayed and which ones function as idioms. Gentry and Wellum insist that their conclusion regarding Israel as an OT type are based on exegetical observations. Yet, in my estimation, they do not explain how the national and territorial details, presented in Isaiah, leads to their conclusion that the NT church redefines national Israel in the eschatological kingdom.

Conclusion

The purpose of this chapter was to examine Gentry's view of Isaiah's eschatological kingdom from *Kingdom through Covenant* (1st and 2nd editions), as a case study, since his arguments are indicative of how other scholars support their conception of a mono-national, multi-ethnic kingdom.[210] Several issues with Gentry's interpretation were

---

comprises continents in their qualities and differentiation, and that he is now able to give a universal geographical picture of the world. Just as the time of the future is ultimately contracted to one point, so the world-space is to him a totality and not an accurately differentiated magnitude. We see the prophets paint the future with the palette of their own experience and project the picture within their own geographical horizon." See Ridderbos, *Coming of the Kingdom*, 524–25. Charles Lee Irons argues that Zech 14 is an example of a prophetic idiom. The depiction of the eternal state (both in blessedness for the elect and in judgment for the reprobate) by means of the language originally employed by Moses on the earthly, typological level. He writes, "Thus, the wicked are described as having no rain (Zech 14:17–18; cf. Deut 11:17; 1 Kings 8:35). Likewise, the spotless purity of the redeemed citizenry of heaven is presented in typological language borrowed from the Mosaic covenant . . . those elements found in the last portion of Zechariah 14 which to the premillennialist or postmillennialist appear as limitations and qualifications incompatible with the perfection and sinlessness of the eternal state turn out instead to be easily explainable as instances of prophetic idiom." See Irons, "Prophetic Idiom," 3.

210. See Muilenburg, "Book of Isaiah," 5:504; Dumbrell, *End of the Beginning*, 119–20; Hays, *From Every People*, 106; Moo, "Creation and New Creation," 45; Young, *Isaiah*, 275; and Goldsworthy, *According to Plan*; Dempster, *Dominion and Dynasty*, 233–34. Dempster adds that a promised Davidic king will mediate blessings to this future kingdom. He connects the Abrahamic covenant with the new Adamic/Davidic king. The Davidic king will restore a new world order, which will end the cosmic battle between the seed of the woman and the serpent. In other words, the new David will lead the people into a new kingdom. It must be noted that Dempster draws upon Ps 2 to show how the new Davidic king will rule over the nations thereby fulfilling the Abrahamic covenant. Dempster, *Dominion and Dynasty*, 176. Similar to Dempster, Desmond Alexander affirms a multiethnic people in the new creation because of his understanding of the Abrahamic covenant. Alexander writes, "Citizens of the new earth will be drawn from all ethnic groups of this earth." See Alexander, *From Eden to Jerusalem*, 165.

highlighted in this chapter. First, Gentry's assumption that Israel functions as an OT type of the church underlines his interpretation of the Abrahamic covenant. Gentry argues that the use of גּוֹי, as opposed to עַם, in Gen 12:2, signifies that God will create a future kingdom or a "great nation," through Abraham, out of the chaos of Babel. Based on his view of typology, this "nation" will function as a type of Jesus and the NT church. Genesis 17, according to Gentry, predicts that Israel will expand to include individuals from many nations with its land expanding to encompass the entire world.

Second, in his analysis of Isaiah's eschatological visions, Gentry assumes that the presence of Gentiles in the kingdom indicates that Jews and Gentiles unite to form a new "one people" concept. Gentry connects the phrase "servants of the Lord" from Isa 54:17 with the suffering Servant from Isa 53. He claims that a "one in many" paradigm exists such that the blessings ascribed to the Servant apply to the many who identify with him, including Gentiles. The Abrahamic and Davidic blessings previously promised to national Israel are redefined by a future Davidic king who will bless the new covenant community known as the "servants of the Lord." However, several textual details within Isaiah consistently portray national distinctions between Israel and Gentiles in the eschatological kingdom, which undermines Gentry's new "one people" concept. Gentry also contends that Isa 65 depicts the new Jerusalem as coextensive with the new creation. Yet, a closer look at the details of Rev 21 and Isa 60, as well as the texts leading up to Isa 65, reveals that Isaiah consistently presents Zion as a distinct city within the new creation.

Third, Gentry presupposes a certain form of typology, where an escalation of a type becomes replaced by its antitype. Then he applies this concept to Israel and concludes that Israel "escalates" to become a new covenant community, comprising of Israelites and Gentiles individuals. By applying a certain form of typology to Israel, it seems that Gentry imposes his assumption of the metanarrative of Scripture into his reading of Isaiah. The issue with Gentry's (along with other theologians') interpretation of Isaiah is not his affirmation of typology but his insistence that Isaiah portrays Israel as an OT type of a particular conception of an eschatological kingdom, even though the textual details do not seem to support his interpretation. Instead, in the following chapter, I will show how Isaiah envisions Israel as a particular nation within a multinational paradigm.

6

Isaiah's Multinational
Eschatological Kingdom

I WILL PRESENT A reading of Isaiah's eschatological kingdom that interprets the kingdom consummation as a multinational reality, composed
not just of individuals, but of individuals with distinct ethnic and territorial affiliations. Although I cannot provide a comprehensive treatment
of Isaiah, I will offer an interpretation of several passages Gentry utilizes
that has better explanatory power in dealing with the details of Isaiah.
I will describe three themes within Isaiah's eschatological visions that
contribute to a multinational picture of the eschatological kingdom: (1)
Zion, (2) Israel and Gentile nations, and (3) messianic king. Then, informed by these three themes, I will analyze several passages that affirm a
multinational portrayal of Isaiah's eschatological kingdom.

Zion

The concept of an empire, during Isaiah's time, informs his vision of a
multinational kingdom. As Ben Ollenburger describes, Isaiah's prophetic
visions "relate to the particular history of Israel" and its relations to other
nations.[1] In the ANE, rulership was associated with deity so that the defeat of a nation was viewed as the defeat of their ruling deity. For example,
when Judah was defeated by the Babylonians, it appeared that Marduk was
victorious over Yahweh. Isaiah, however, boldly continues to proclaim that

---

1. Ollenburger, *Zion*, 157.

Yahweh's sovereignty extends beyond to the nations and their gods.[2] Isaiah envisions a kingdom that will not only include Israel but also all the nations of the earth. God's kingdom will include nations such as Philistia (Isa 14:28–32), Moab (Isa 15:1—16:14), Damascus (Isa 17:1–14), Ethiopia (Isa 18:1–7), Egypt (Isa 19:1–17), Tyre (Isa 23:1–18), Edom (Isa 34:5–17; 63:1–6), Babylon (Isa 13; 14:3–22; 47:1–15), and Assyria (Isa 14:24–27).[3] As Joy Hooker argues, the historical context of Isaiah falls under the "shadow of the Assyrian, Babylonian, and Persian empires."[4] Thus, Isaiah's prophecies of a multinational kingdom communicates to the empires of his world that God will establish a new kingdom or empire, from Zion, where all nations will submit to him. (Isa 10:12).

An empire, in the ANE, primarily ruled through domination. As Gerald Janzen remarks, "Imperial society was a reflection of this creative process involving conflict, whereby justice was generally enforced by military might and domination."[5] This is why the king of Assyria would act as the principal land owner and determine who would receive land.[6] However, Isaiah presents Zion as a concept of God's kingdom that challenges the ANE concept of an empire ruled by domination.[7] Instead of forced submission, nations will desire to obey their king because of their ethical righteousness. Nations will travel to Zion as an act of obedience, which displays a "new reality."[8] Thus, God's eschatological kingdom does not imitate the ruthless domination seen in ANE empires. Instead, his kingdom envision a new world order where a multitude of nations will choose to submit to their new king who reigns from Zion.

When examining depictions of Zion within Isaiah's eschatological visions, several observations can be made. First, God promises to reverse Zion's present desolate condition in the future.[9] Although Zion complains that it feels "forsaken" and "forgotten" (Isa 49:14), God comforts Zion (Isa 40:1–11) and promises to use Cyrus to rebuild Jerusalem (Isa 44:28;

---

2. Hooker, "Zion as Theological Symbol," 118.

3. Hooker, "Zion as Theological Symbol," 110.

4. Hooker, "Zion as Theological Symbol," 119.

5. Janzen, "Nature of God's Power," 461.

6. Smelik, "Distortion of Old Testament Prophecy," 80.

7. Hooker, "Zion as Theological Symbol," 119.

8. Hooker, "Zion as Theological Symbol," 120.

9. The Lord comforts Zion, in Isa 51:2–3, by pointing to the promise he gave to multiply Abraham's offspring (Isa 51:2) as proof that his promises to restore Zion will certainly occur.

45:13). God adds that it is impossible for him to abandon Zion just as a nursing mother would not forget about her child (Isa 49:15) and a person could not forget about a cut on his hand (Isa 49:16). God declares that the proof of his love for Zion will be seen in the rebuilding of its walls, which is "continually" on his agenda (Isa 49:16), and the abundance of her "children," though she considered herself "barren" (Isa 49:20–21). The promise of Isa 49:19 is reaffirmed in Isa 54:1–3, where Zion, who was once considered "barren," will have more children than a "married woman," which will require her to "enlarge" her tent (Isa 54:2).

Second, Zion is described as a distinct location in the new creation. Isaiah 2:1–3 states that in the new creation, Zion, is to be elevated above all other mountains of the world in order to symbolize the importance given to Jerusalem.[10] Zion plays a central role in the kingdom as a gathering place for Gentile nations so that they can be taught from the word of the Lord (Isa 2:3). Just like God provided a "highway" for Israel when they left Egypt, during the exodus, Isa 11:16 describes a "highway" from Assyria on which the remnant can travel on from the "four corners of the earth" to Zion (Isa 11:12). Isaiah 35:8–10 describes a highway called "Way of Holiness" that connects the "redeemed" and "ransomed" of the Lord to Zion. When people travel on this highway and arrive at Zion, they will obtain "gladness" and "joy" and their "sorrow and sighing" will disappear (Isa 35:10; 51:11). Isaiah 66:18–19 describes God sending "survivors" to the nations, located in territories outside of Zion ("Tarshish, Pul, Lud, Tubal, Javan"). When God introduces the "new heavens and the new earth," in Isa 65:17, he focuses on Jerusalem in order to depict the conditions for the new creation as a whole. As Andrew Abernethy aptly writes, "In Isaiah the realm of God's kingdom is universal, but the universal, cosmic scope of God's kingdom has a centre point in Zion. Zion, then, is not just an illustration of God's plan for the rest of the world, but it is also a hub around which the rest of God's kingdom finds its orbit."[11] These texts suggest that Zion is not synonymous with the new creation but envisages Zion as the capital city of God's multinational kingdom.

Third, not only is Zion depicted as a central location within the kingdom, but also as a place where both Israelites and Gentiles experience blessings. Isaiah 25:6–12 depicts an eschatological feast in which God's people respond to the victory he will win over his enemies and for

---

10. Oswalt, *Book of Isaiah: 1–39*, 118.

11. Abernethy, *Isaiah and God's Kingdom*, 176–77.

the establishment of his reign as king over the world. In addition to the blessings of food for all peoples in the kingdom, God will do three additional things: (1) swallow up and destroy death (v. 7); (2) wipe away all tears (v. 8); and (3) remove the reproach of his people (v. 8).[12] The setting of this eschatological scene occurs on "this mountain" (v. 6), which suggests that this scene is closely connected to the events in Isa 24:23, when God reigns as king from Mount Zion. Isaiah declares that God is exalted in Zion and fills the city with justice, security, salvation, and wisdom (Isa 33:5–6). The people of Zion will behold their king[13] and his city as one of joyous festivals, peace, and security (Isa 33:17, 20, 22).[14] In Isa 35, the glory of the Lord is revealed from Zion, which is a common motif in Isaiah (Isa 4:5; 11:10; 40:5; 60:1; and 66:18). Pilgrims on their way to Zion had to pass through territories typically controlled by Gentile nations. However, in this eschatological scene, people with all types of physical ailments (i.e., "weak hand," "feeble knees," "anxious hearts," "blind," "deaf," and "lame") will travel on a highway to Zion and be healed of their infirmities because of the waters that come from Zion (Isa 35:5–10).[15]

When these textual details from Isaiah are surveyed, it is clear that Zion has a central role in God's kingdom. God promises to reverse Zion's condition and establish it as his dwelling place. Zion is not portrayed as

12. Smith, *Isaiah 1–39*, 433.

13. There is debate over the identity of this king. Brevard Childs and Edward Young believe the kings refers to the Messiah from Isa 32 based on the royal ideology of Pss 45 and 72. See Childs, *Isaiah*, 248; Young, *Isaiah*, 2:421. John Hayes and Stuart Irvine identify the king as Hezekiah. See Hayes and Irvine, *Isaiah*, 369. Hans Wildberger views the announcement of God as king in Isa 33:22 as a key to identifying the king in v. 17. See Wildberger, *Isaiah*, 2:300–301. John Oswalt believes that this king was fulfilled in "multiple ways." He writes, "First, it was fulfilled immediately when Hezekiah, was delivered by God. Second, it was fulfilled when God delivered his people from Babylonian captivity and restored them to their own land. Third, it was fulfilled in the more distant future when God revealed his Messiah in Jesus Christ. Finally, it will be fulfilled in the eschaton when the Messiah rules the earth by the rod of his mouth." See Oswalt, *Isaiah*, 379. Based on Isa 33:22 and the allusion to Isa 6, where Isaiah saw the Lord, as king, it seems that the king of Isa 33:17 refers to the messianic king, from Isa 11.

14. The depiction of Zion as an indestructible permanent tent (Isa 33:20) is consistent with its portrayals in Pss 48:1–14 and 132:13–18. See Smith, *Isaiah 1–39*, 562.

15. Isaiah 40:9 describes Zion as the messenger of good news to the surrounding cities that God will return to Jerusalem. Isaiah 35 reveals how God's presence in Zion will draw the "redeemed" and "ransomed" in order to receive healing to their physical ailments. This scene may correlate with Rev 22:1–2, which describes the river of the water of life flowing through Jerusalem which will give "healing" to the nations.

synonymous with the new creation, but as a specific city within the kingdom to which both Israelites and Gentiles travel in order to be blessed by God. The next theme will highlight the national distinctions that will continue to exist between Israelites and Gentiles in the eschatological kingdom.

Israel and Gentile Nations

When examining depictions of Israel and Gentile nations within Isaiah's eschatological visions, several observations can be made. First, God promises to gather and restore national Israel together with Zion. Isaiah 27:12–13 reiterates God's promise to gather Israelites from the four corners of the earth, such as the "Euphrates" in the north, the "Brook of Egypt" in the south, the land of Assyria, and those driven out of the land of Egypt to Zion. In Isa 30, God promises that he will establish his people in Zion (Isa 30:19), and despite their previous trials (Isa 30:20), he will give them spiritual blessings (Isa 30:19–22), physical blessings (Isa 30:23–26), and victory over their enemies ("nations"; Isa 30:27–33). In Isa 41:8, God identifies Israel as his "servant," "the offspring of Abraham," and as those he "has chosen." Though Israel experienced God's judgment through exile, he reassures them that he will continue to be with them: "Fear not, for I am with you; be not dismayed, for I am your God; I will strengthen you, I will help you, I will uphold you with my righteous right hand" (Isa 41:10). In Isa 43:5–7, the promise first made in Isa 11:11 is reiterated: God will recover Israelites from all the nations where they have been taken. God reiterates this with vivid imagery in Isa 46:3–4. Even though many within Israel have trusted in Babylonian idols and will be "carried" off into captivity (Isa 46:1–2), God reminds Israel ("house of Jacob"; Isa 46:3) that he has "carried" them since their conception and promises to continue to do so until their "old age" (Isa 46:3–4). Finally, God promises to "plant" Israel in their land as "oaks of righteousness" (Isa 61:3), when they were previously depicted as an "oak whose leaf withers" (Isa 1:30).

There seems to a close correlation between Zion's and Israel's future restoration. As Marvin Sweeny notes, "The book of Isaiah is fundamentally concerned with Zion or the city of Jerusalem, insofar as Jerusalem is the site of YHWH's holy Temple, which in turn symbolizes YHWH's role as the sovereign creator of the entire universe, including

Israel, Judah, and the nations at large."[16] In Isa 26, there is a reference
that in the day that Zion will be restored, a song will be sung in the
"land of Judah" (Isa 26:1). Though Zion feels abandoned (Isa 49:14),
God promises that her children will soon come home, even with kings
and queens serving as their "foster fathers" and "nursing mothers" (Isa
49:22–23). In Isa 49:14, Zion identifies itself as "forsaken" by God, yet
God promises, in Isa 49:17–21, to enlarge the city with an abundance
of "descendants" though she viewed herself "barren" (Isa 49:21). God
tells those within Israel, who "pursue righteousness" and "seek the
Lord" (Isa 51:1), to remember the Abrahamic covenant and creation
(Isa 51:2–3). Since God has the power to create Eden and Israel, then
he also has the power to restore Zion (Isa 51:3). Part of the promise to
restore Zion includes God's promise to restore his "nation." When God
restores his "nation" (Isa 51:4), his law will go forth (cf. Isa 2:3) and
his justice will become a light to the peoples (Isa 51:4; cf. 42:4). In Isa
44:21–22, God comforts Israel by stating that he will never forget them
and has "redeemed" them by blotting out their sins. This connects with
Isa 49:15–16, when God comforts Zion by saying that he will never
forget them just as a nursing mother would never forget her child. As
Zion experiences blessings that are analogous to King David's, nations
will come to Zion because of the beauty that God will display from this
city (Isa 55:5). These passages indicate that the restoration of Zion is
closely connected with the gathering and restoration of national Israel.[17]

Second, part of God's restoration of Israel includes the reversal of
their relationship with Gentile nations from political submission to mutual submission to a Davidic king in Zion. Isaiah 11:14 describes that
after God regathers Israel and unites them with Judah (Isa 11:11–13),
he will reestablish the kingdom with Gentile nations ("But they shall
swoop down on the shoulder of the Philistines in the west, and together
they shall plunder the people of the east"). The Davidic king will signal
Gentile nations to inquire of him (Isa 11:10) and scattered Israelites will
be gathered to Zion in order to worship him (Isa 11:12). Although Israel's enemies have made numerous attempts to enslave Israel, God has

16. Sweeney, "Book of Isaiah," 180.

17. The restoration of Zion also has an effect on nations in the eschatological kingdom. Pilgrims come to worship in Zion (Isa 60:6) and foreigners build up Zion's walls
(Isa 60:10). Upon witnessing God's kingship when he judges all evil and restores Zion
and Israel, nations will come to align themselves with the king in Zion (Isa 40:5; 52:10;
60:1; 66:18). See Abernethy, *Isaiah and God's Kingdom*, 196.

"increased" Israel and "enlarged" their land (Isa 26:13–15). God promises that the nations who fight against Jerusalem will become like "small
dust" and "passing chaff" (Isa 29:5). Isaiah 19:23–25 describes Egypt and
Assyria worshipping Yahweh, implying their submission to the Davidic
king. In Isa 62:8, God swears by "his right hand" to no longer allow Gentile nations to exercise political control over Israel. One of the curses for
Israel included their enemies consuming their harvest (Deut 28:30–33;
Lev 26:16). However, God promises, in Isa 62:8, that the time of curses
from the law has passed and Israel's enemies will no longer take their
grain or drink their wine ("The Lord has sworn by his right hand and
by his mighty arm, 'I will not again give your grain to be food for your
enemies, and foreigners shall not drink your wine for which you have labored'"). Isaiah 60:11 and 61:6 describes nations bringing their "wealth"
and "foreigners and kings" ministering in Zion as a sign of their submission to the Davidic king.

Isaiah 54:3 adds that Zion's offspring will "inherit the nations." The
phrase "inherit the nations" may be an allusion to Ps 2, where God promises that his king ("son"; Ps 2:7), who will reign from Zion, will inherit
the nations as his "heritage," implying their political submission (Ps 2:8).
The theme of the Davidic king within Isaiah will be addressed later in
this chapter, but it is sufficient to note that Gentile nations will submit to
Israel's king, who reigns from Zion. These details reveal that the Gentile
nations' worship of Yahweh and submission to the Davidic king are also
signs of their submission to Zion, for it is from Zion that Yahweh is revealed to the nations, and it is from Zion that he is worshipped.

Third, Israel and Gentile nations are unified by peace in a kingdom
that rules them all. One of the main themes reiterated throughout Isaiah
is the emphasis on God's plan to redeem the nations (Isa 11:12; 14:1–2;
19:20–25; and 66:18–21).[18] The beginning (Isa 2:2–4) and the end of
Isaiah (Isa 66:18–24) envision how the nations will be a part of God's
kingdom.[19] Isaiah 2 portrays nations as participants, and not simply as

18. Smith, *Isaiah 1–39*, 129. Davies notes that Isaiah is often entitled a "prophet to
the nations." See Davies, "Nations," 105.

19. Andrew Abernethy writes, "In both Isa 2:2–4 and 66:18–24 God's prominence
in Zion serves as a reference point for why the nations would come there. By closing
the book of Isaiah on this note it is unmistakable that a major feature of the book's
message is that God's kingdom community will consist of many nations, though these
passages aim to evoke jealousy and repentance within Israel simultaneously." See Abernethy, *Isaiah and God's Kingdom*, 194.

onlookers, in Israel's salvation who will enjoy its benefits (Isa 2:3).[20] In Zion, the Lord will bring peace between nations, as portrayed with the replacement of "swords" with "plowshares" (Isa 2:4). Isaiah calls Israel, during his time, to repent and imitate what the nations will do in the kingdom (Isa 2:5).[21] The vision of Isa 19:17–25, as first revealed in Isa 2, is that Zion will become a place of blessing for Israel and Gentile nations. Isaiah, more than any other prophet, outlined the judgment of God upon the Gentile nations who were oppressing Israel. The chief oppressors of Israel at that time were Assyria and Egypt.[22] However, Isa 19:19 describes an altar to the Lord in the land of Egypt and Isa 19:21 explicitly states that Egypt will know the Lord and Egypt and Assyria will travel back and forth to one another's countries in order to worship Yahweh. Between the two nations of Assyria and Egypt, Israel will fulfill God's promise to Abraham that his descendants will be a "blessing in the midst of the earth" (Gen 12:3; Isa 19:24).[23] This prophecy indicates,

20. Clements, "Light to the Nations," 69. Ramsdell also observes that Isaiah recognizes that the Gentile world is longing for the establishment of the reign of righteousness, as illustrated in Isa 2. See Ramsdell, "Missionary Future," 195.

21. In this picture, there is universal peace and homage to Israel. Jeremiah 3:17 also says that Gentile nations will call Jerusalem "the Throne of the Lord" and will gather in Jerusalem and call on the name of the Lord. See Vasholz, "Israel's Future," 47.

22. Ramsdell observes that Egypt and Assyria stood in Isaiah's mind as representatives of the Gentile world. He writes, "The truth, which he clothes in language peculiar to his day, is that the heathen shall eventually share the same salvation as Israel and shall be equally dear to the heart of God." See Ramsdell, "Missionary Future in Isaiah," 192. Shawn Aster outlines Assyria's negative portrayal within Isaiah: "In several places in Isaiah, Assyria is portrayed as an unwitting agent of YHWH. In Isa 6:13, YHWH takes credit for deportations, which are clearly accomplished in practice by Assyria. In Isa 7:17–19 and in Isa 8:7, YHWH takes a direct role in instigating an Assyrian invasion of Israel. And in the most famous expression of this theology, Assyria is called a 'rod of YHWH's wrath' in 10:6." See Aster, "Isaiah 19," 466.

23. Gordon Wenham notes that the unique construction ("be a blessing") from Gen 12:2 occurs in two other passages: Isa 19:24 and Zech 8:13. This would support the interpretation that Isa 19:24 fulfills the Abrahamic covenant by depicting Gentile nations as blessed by Israel. See Wenham, *Genesis 1–15*, 276. Beaulieu notes how this passage fulfills the intention of the Abrahamic covenant with the phrase "blessing in the midst of the earth" (Isa 19:24). He writes, "Isaiah can refer to both Egypt and Assyria as recipients of covenant blessing (Isa 19:25) because the elective covenant with Abraham and his descendants was to be a channel of blessing to all nations (Gen 12:3; 22:18). The Abrahamic covenant always had a universal purpose that was to be more fully actualized in the future. This points in the direction of a universalism that is more fully developed throughout the book of Isaiah (cf. Isa 2; 11; 25:5–9; 42:1–9; 44:1–5; 45:6, 14–17; 60:1–3)." See Beaulieu, "Egypt as God's People," 218.

in part, that these Gentile nations will be God's people along with Israel. This is evident where titles usually reserved for Israel ("my people"; "work of my hands"; and "my inheritance") are ascribed to Assyria and Egypt (Isa 19:25).[24]

Peter Gentry mentions Isa 19:24–25 in his exegesis of Ps 87. In Ps 87, Zion is described as the gathering place for people from Babylon, Philistia, Tyre, and Cush. Like Isa 19:24–25, Ps 87 foresees that Gentile nations not normally associated with Yahweh will be a part of his kingdom.[25] Psalm 87:4 specifies that these Gentiles individuals are still seen as people "born there" ("'This one was born there,' they say"; Ps 87:4), yet Ps 87:5–6 indicates that they become people of "dual citizenship" when God "registers" them as citizens of Zion ("And of Zion it shall be said, 'This one and that one were born in her'; for the Most High himself will establish her; Ps 87:5).[26] In Isa 5:6, God mentions that "briers and thorns" will grow in Israel's land when he punishes them, but then, in Isa 27:4–5, God says that the briers and thorns could "make peace" with him. God previously stated that he will remove his protective hedge around his "vineyard," which will result in its destruction (Isa 5:5), but in Isa

24. Gary Smith points out that this prophecy ascribes three titles, traditionally belonging to Israel, to Assyria and Egypt. See Smith, *Isaiah 1–39*, 363. Edward Young comments about the importance of the titles ascribed to Egypt and Assyria. He writes, "['My people'] is normally applied to Israel (cf. Exod 3:7, 10; 5:1; 7:4; Deut 7:6; 1 Pet 2:9). Isaiah 19:25 is the only verse where 'my people' refers to Egypt. Furthermore, two other nations are being blessed along with Egypt: Assyria and Israel; therefore, one can conclude that Egypt and Assyria can also be redeemed by God because he is their God. God blesses Egypt as a representative of the people of the world . . . , Isaiah expands on the promise of God to Abraham in Gen 12:1–3 that all the families of the earth shall be blessed through his descendants (cf. Gen 28:14). God sees Abraham's descendants as spreading throughout the world and taking the gospel to all people. Fulfillment of this promise takes place in the book of Exodus when God delivers the Israelites from slavery along with Egyptians who choose to join them (Exod 12:38)." See Young, *Isaiah*, 45.

25. Israel is depicted as a distinct nation among Gentiles nations rather than an entity that engulfs other nations to form a new entity. Andrew Abernethy also observes that Isa 19:24–25 and Isa 25:8 indicate that the inclusion of Gentile nations does not redefine national Israel. He writes, "While all peoples will come to the feast and benefit from the death of death, pointing to inclusivism, the promise to 'remove the reproach of his people' refers to Israel. While some Reformed readers may quickly set 'Israel' aside as a 'type of the church,' this passage reminds non-Jewish readers that amid the incorporation of Gentiles into the king's people, his commitment to remove the shame of Israel continues and will come about in due course." See Abernethy, *Isaiah and God's Kingdom*, 39.

26. Goldingay, *Psalm 42–89*, 639.

27:6, Jacob's "vineyard" will take "root" and "blossom" and "fill the whole world with fruit." In Isa 56:3, 6, Isaiah describes "foreigners" who have "joined themselves to the Lord." God pronounces a blessing on anyone who keeps the Sabbath (Isa 56:2), including foreigners and eunuchs (Isa 56:6). Foreigners have joined themselves with Israel, just like the proselyte Egyptians (Exod 12:38, 48–49); Rahab, the Canaanite (Josh 2:8–13); Ruth, the Moabite (Ruth 2:10); and Uriah, the Hittite (2 Sam 11:11).[27] The future blessings promised to the foreigners and eunuchs reiterates the theme of Gentiles gathering in Zion (Isa 2:2–3; 66:18–21).[28] In Isa 60:10, foreigners will build up the walls of Jerusalem, while others will serve as shepherds, plowmen, and vinedressers, in Isa 61:5. Isaiah 61:6 specifies that the Israelites in Zion will fulfill their role as priests (cf. Exod 19:6) because of the foreigners mentioned in v. 5.[29] Isaiah 61:5–6 echoes the model of the Levites in relation to the other tribes of Israel. The other clans, especially those in the Judean countryside, would take responsibility for farming the land thereby freeing the Levites to serve in the temple.[30] What is new, in Isa 61:5–6, is not Gentile inclusion as priests, but the support of Israelite priests in Zion extending beyond the Judean countryside to Gentile territories. This picture portrays a peaceful relationship between Israel and Gentile nations where Gentile nations will see Zion's righteousness and glory (Isa 62:2) for it will become a beautiful "crown" in God's "hand" (Isa 62:3).

When these eschatological visions of Isaiah are read together, it is clear that God promises to restore national Israel in his kingdom. Included in God's restoration of Israel is a return to their land, a reversal of the conditions of Zion, and a change in the relationship between Israel and Gentile nations from animosity to harmony. Instead of living as political

27. Although "foreigners and eunuchs" were prohibited from joining Israel, according to Deut 23, there were instances throughout Israel's history where Gentile individuals were allowed to serve in the temple (Neh 7). So, Isa 56 does not depict a future reality concerning a "new" Israel with the inclusion of Gentile ministers. Instead, Isa 56 portrays the new Zion as a "house of prayer for all peoples" (v. 7), which includes foreigners and eunuchs, who were typically marginalized in society.

28. Smith, *Isaiah 40–66*, 534–35.

29. John Mackay writes "In the changed conditions brought about by the Messiah, Israel will be able to fulfill the role for which they had originally been designated 'a kingdom of priests' (Exod. 19:6). So, they are presented not as a nation of conquerors, but as 'priests of Yahweh,' who have the privilege of mediating between Yahweh and the nations." See Mackay, *Isaiah*, 522–23.

30. Goldingay, *Isaiah 56–66*, 309.

slaves to other nations (i.e., Assyria), Israel will be restored under her own king in Zion, the same one to whom the Gentile nations will submit. Although both Israel and Gentile nations will gather in Zion to worship God, they are not depicted as a part of a new "one people" concept void of national distinctions. Instead national and territorial distinctions remain, which illustrates a similar multinational picture seen with other ANE empires during Isaiah's time.

Messianic King

A unifying theme in Isaiah is that of the messianic king who will rule, from Zion, over Israel and Gentile nations in the eschatological kingdom. The title "Messiah" comes from the verb משח and refers to a person who has been anointed by God for a specific purpose.[31] Mark Boda notes that a messianic figure, in the OT, may be defined according to a "particular sociological role" and "temporal reference."[32] It is the "temporal reference" of certain OT passages that make it difficult to identify clearly a messianic figure.[33] If one reads OT messianic prophecies as eschatological, then a messianic figure refers to an eschatological king who will play an authoritative role in the kingdom. However, if one reads OT messianic

31. The idea of a messiah may be associated with passages that do not use either מָשִׁיחַ or a form of the verb משח. Some scholars, such as van Groningen, adopt broad understanding of messianic expectation so that any anticipation of Jesus in the OT is labeled relevant. See van Groningen, *Messianic Revelation*. In the torah, the word מָשִׁיחַ is almost exclusively used of an anointed priest and in the Writings of an anointed king. Particularly in the psalms, the verb "anoint" (משח), has to do with a king (Pss 2:2; 18:50; 20:6; 28:8; 45:7; 84:9; 89:20, 38; 132:10, 17). Also, the "anointed priests" in the Pentateuch and "anointed king" in the Psalms usually refers to the contemporary human king. See Longman, "Messiah," 16–24. Nicholas Perrin argues that although the sage is never described as anointed with oil, wisdom is connected with an endowment of the Holy Spirit and in that sense may be described as anointed. See Perrin, "Messianism," 37–60.

32. Boda, "Figuring the Future," 37. Mark Boda observes that some passages, such as Pss 2; 89:39; and 132:10, may reveal that references to a "messianic" figure may have referred to "present" figures in their historical context, but have been taken up to encourage future hope in an eschatological figure. Boda, "Figuring the Future," 40.

33. Walther Eichrodt sees the eschatological at the heart of prophetic religion. See Eichrodt, *Theology of the Old Testament*, 1:385. Sigmund Mowinckel, however, limits the eschatological to texts that express a clear break between the historical and eschatological eras. He traces the development of prophetism from historically oriented prophecy of the preexilic period to the futurism of Deutero-Isaiah. See Mowinckel, *He That Cometh*, 125.

prophecies within their immediate historical context, then a messianic figure refers to a religious or political leader at that time.[34] This dynamic is evident within Isaiah where certain prophecies refer to Cyrus, a historical figure (Isa 45:1–3), while others refers to an eschatological figure (Isa 9:7; 11:4–5; 32:1–2).[35] For the purposes of this book, I will utilize the title "messianic king" as a reference to the eschatological king who will exhibit authority over Israel and Gentile nations.[36]

The messianic king is identified with different terms within Isaiah. Isaiah 4:2 introduces the "branch of the LORD," which has been used in several OT passage as a reference to the messianic king (cf. Jer 23:5; 33:15; Zech 3:8).[37] This imagery continues, in Isa 14:19, when God refers to the

34. John Collins defines "Messiah" as "a future figure who will play an authoritative role in the end time, usually the eschatological king." See Collins, *Scepter and the Star*, 11. James Charlesworth defines "messiah" as referring "to a present, political and religious leader who is appointed by God, applied predominantly to a king, but also to a priest and occasionally a prophet." See Charlesworth, *Messiah*, xv. Collins and Charlesworth provide definitions of a "Messiah" based on their understanding of the historical or eschatological nature of certain OT passages.

35. Gerhard von Rad argues that one should apply "a concept of time to the prophets' teaching of which they themselves are quite unaware." In so doing, von Rad states that an interpreter may incorrectly assume that certain OT passages were historical in reference when it can refer to both within history and foretelling a future event. See Rad, *Old Testament Theology*, 2:115.

36. John Collins notes that there are four kinds of messianic figures in the Dead Sea Scrolls: king, priest, prophet, and heavenly messiah. A messianic king referred to the expectation of an eschatological king of the Davidic line, which the commentary on Isaiah (*pesher*; 4Q285) references with the title "Branch of David" and "Prince of the Congregation," which allude to messianic prophecies in Isaiah and Ezekiel. See Collins, *The Scepter and the Star*, 57–58. Collin states that this concept of the Davidic messiah also includes elements of a "warrior king" who will destroy the enemies of Israel and institute an era of unending peace. See Collins, *The Scepter and the Star*, 68. Collins does remark, however, that these four messianic paradigms are not always distinct and can have overlap with one another. A messianic figure can be both priestly and prophetic and the heavenly messiah may also be a king. See Collins, *The Scepter and the Star*, 114–15, 164, 167, 173. Despite the fluidity of these four types of messianic figures in the Dead Sea scrolls, Al Wolters comments that what was "clear" for the Jewish community was an understanding of a "future royal messiah who would deliver Israel from its enemies." See Wolters, "Messiah," 80. It is according to this understanding of a messianic figure that I will comment on the prophecies in Isaiah.

37. John Watts argues that the "branch of the LORD" parallels "the fruit of the land," thus referring to the actual land. See Watts, *Isaiah 1–33*, 75. Samuel Amsler connects צמח to the vocabulary of plant life and translates the verb "to sprout, cause to grow, bloom" and the noun "sprout." He recognizes a specialized royal Davidic usage of the term to represent the expectations of a future king, though he does not classify

rejected Babylonian king as a "loathed branch," and Isa 11:1 describes the messianic king as a "shoot" from which its "branch" will bear fruit. In Isa 4:4, the "survivors of Israel" and those "left in Zion" will be made "holy" by the Lord when he "washes" the filth and "cleanse the bloodstains" from his people ("when the Lord shall have washed away the filth of the daughters of Zion and cleansed the bloodstains of Jerusalem from its midst by a spirit of judgment and by a spirit of burning"; Isa 4:4).[38] The Lord's presence will be evident in Zion, as depicted with a "cloud by day" and a "smoke" and "flaming fire by night" (Isa 4:5), recalling God's presence with Israel in the wilderness (cf. Exod 13:21–22; 14:19). This vision differs from Isa 2:1–5 in that it focuses on the purification of Israel in Jerusalem and not on the Gentile nations who will hear from God's law. If the "branch of the LORD," in Isa 4:2, refers to the messianic king, then he will be the agent the Lord uses to purify Israel and reveal his glory from Zion.

The messianic king, within Isaiah, is depicted as possessing both divine and human attributes. In Isa 6:1, the Lord is described as a king who sits upon his "throne" ("In the year that King Uzziah died I saw the Lord sitting upon a throne, high and lifted up; and the train of his robe filled the temple"). Later in Isa 7:14, God promises a "son" from a virgin as a sign that it was unnecessary for Judah to trust in Assyria for deliverance from Syria and Israel ("Therefore the Lord himself will give you a sign. Behold, the virgin shall conceive and bear a son, and shall call his name Immanuel"). In Isa 9:7, this birth carries the message forward with the revelation that this "son," known as a "Wonderful Counselor, Mighty God, Everlasting Father, and Prince of Peace," will rule the nations with justice from the throne of David ("of the increase of his government and of peace there will be no end, on the throne of David and over his kingdom, to establish it and to uphold it with justice and righteousness from this time and forevermore"). Isaiah 9:1–7 reveals that the future human

---

Isa 4:2 in this category. See Amsler, "צמח‎," 3:1086. However, Edward Young considered "fruit of the land" as an indication of the earthly origin of the Messiah, while "branch of the Lord" refers to his divine nature. See Young, *Isaiah*, 173–78. Gary Smith argues that the two clauses in Isa 4:2 refer to two parallel acts of God that will transform Zion. God will cause his messianic Branch to spring forth, and also bring fertility to the land. God will reverse the situation depicted in Isa 2:6—4:1 and replace the proud leaders of Israel with a "branch of the LORD" and replace the desolation of the land with great fertility. See Smith, *Isaiah 1–39*, 156.

38. The term "holy" can refer to God's original plan, in Exod 19:6, to establish Israel as his "treasured possession" and "holy nation."

king/son will rule as "mighty God" in an eternal kingdom. Psalm 2 and 2 Sam 7:14 has already prepared the reader for a human king who will be understood as God's "son." Isaiah 9 informs the reader that this same "son" possesses divine attributes.

Isaiah 11:1 describes a future Davidic ruler who is a "shoot from the stump of Jesse" and will spring forth after God will "cut down" the forest of Assyria (Isa 10:33–34). This new ruler from Jesse's line will bestow "the Spirit of knowledge and the fear the Lord" (Isa 11:2), judge righteously ("with righteousness he shall judge the poor"; Isa 11:4), signal the nations ("In that day the root of Jesse, who shall stand as a signal for the peoples"; "He will raise a signal for the nations"; Isa 11:10, 12), and restore Israel and Judah from the "four corners of the earth" ("and will assemble the banished of Israel, and gather the dispersed of Judah from the four corners of the earth"; Isa 11:12).

In Isa 32, a righteous king is introduced who will protect God's people (Isa 32:2) and will bring justice and peace for all (Isa 32:15–19).[39] The identity of this king has been debated, but it seems to point to a messianic figure because Isa 32 alludes to earlier messianic passages.[40] Gary Smith appropriately details the shared language between Isa 32 and previous messianic passages. He writes:

> Both the messianic figure and this king in 32:1–2 will rule in righteousness and justice (9:7; 11:4–5), while 1:26 mentions other officials who will function in the future restored Jerusalem. Also, the protective characteristics in 32:2 are parallel to images of protection that God will provide when he sets up his kingdom (4:6; 25:4). The time when God opens the eyes of the blind (32:3; 29:18; 35:5; 42:18), pours out his Spirit (11:1), transforms nature (30:23–26), and brings in a new age of security and peace (2:2–4; 9:6; 28:12) are all connected to a future era when God will change the world and the Messiah will reign in Zion.[41]

When these passages are read together, the messianic king is depicted as a future Davidic ruler who will be born as a man but possesses divine attributes. The identity of the messianic king is confirmed with

39. This future time is contrasted with the present period in Jerusalem that will lead to mourning, no fertility, and no peace (Isa 32:9–14).

40. Paul Wegner provides an extensive list of various proposals for interpreting the king in Isa 32 but concludes that this prophecy "was intentionally shaped to engender messianic ideas." See Wegner, *Kingship and Messianic Expectations*, 275–301.

41. Smith, *Isaiah 1–39*, 539.

the birth of Christ (Matt 1:23) when Matthew quotes Isa 7:14. Jesus, as the messianic king, will fulfill Isaiah's descriptions of divine and human kingship since he will rule from Zion as God incarnate.

After establishing the identity of the messianic king, there are several observations that can be made regarding his function in the kingdom. First, there seems to be a connection between the messianic king and the Lord's Spirit. The messianic king is called Wonderful Counselor, which comments on the miraculous works and wisdom that God will display through him (Isa 9:6). The Spirit will rest upon this king and give him wisdom, understanding, counsel, and might (Isa 11:1–2). God promises, in Isa 32:15, that his Spirit will reverse Israel's present condition, as detailed in Isa 32:9–14. One of the primary changes that the Spirit will introduce will be a period of righteousness and justice (Isa 32:16–17), which correlates with Isa 9:7 and 11:4.

Second, the messianic king will play a pivotal role in uniting both Israel and Gentile nations with peace. Isaiah 2:2–3 predicted a day when the nations will come to Jerusalem, though a Davidic king is not mentioned. Isaiah 11 provides information indicating that the "root of Jesse" (Isa 11:1) plays a central role in gathering the nations (Isa 11:10). This Davidic king will also gather Israelites, from all over the world, to Zion (Isa 11:11–12) and establish a type of peace that removes the original curse between man and creation, alluding to the conditions of Eden (Isa 11:6–9; cf. Gen 3:14–19). Within his kingdom, there will be peace among all nations (Isa 2:3–4; 19:24–25) and within creation itself (Isa 11:6–9). These depictions do not indicate that the nations will join Israel to become "one people" but that a reversal of present hostilities between the nations and Israel will occur because of this king.

Third, this messianic king seems to function as the Servant of the Lord. God promises to send Israel's savior "from the east" (Isa 41:2), which is later revealed as Cyrus the Persian king who will conquer Babylon and facilitate in the rebuilding of Jerusalem's temple (Isa 44:28). God's commission to his "anointed" one, Cyrus, includes political hegemony over other "nations" (Isa 45:1) so that Cyrus would know the Lord (Isa 45:3) and that his work would be for the benefit of God's servant, "Jacob" (Isa 45:4). Woven throughout these passages about Cyrus are descriptions of another servant who will fulfill Cyrus's mission to a greater degree. This servant will "raise up the tribes of Jacob" and be a "light to the nations" (Isa 49:6) and will open the eyes of the blind (Isa 42:7), which echoes Yahweh's divine work in the kingdom (Isa 29:18; 35:5).

The Servant will perform tasks that also identify him as the messianic king. By functioning as a "light to the nations" and a "covenant to the people" (Isa 49:6), he will restore national Israel ("tribes of Jacob") and provide worldwide blessings for the nations (Isa 49:6).[42] Isaiah 55:1–13 depicts the worldwide effects of the messianic king's work to bring "salvation to the ends of the earth" (Isa 49:6). The way he will bless the nations is seen in Isa 52:15 when he "sprinkles" them ("so shall he sprinkle many nations"), presumably with his blood, by being "pierced" for their transgressions: "But he was pierced for our transgressions; he was crushed for our iniquities; upon him was the chastisement that brought us peace, and with his wounds we are healed" (Isa 53:5). Luke 2:31–32 confirms that Jesus is the Servant who will function as a "light to the nations" because he is the promised Davidic king from 2 Sam 7 (cf. Luke 1:69). The reference to the root, in Isa 53:2 ("like a root out of dry ground"), is a clear

42. There are some who dispute this interpretation since Isa 49:3 mentions Israel as the servant. There are three different interpretations regarding Isa 49:3: (1) the passage is referring to the nation, (2) to the prophet, or (3) to some ideal Israel. Alec Motyer views "Israel" as a reference to the Messiah as a fulfillment of what national Israel was supposed to function. Since the term originally referred to an individual (Jacob), Isaiah presents another individual who will restore Israel after the exile. See Motyer, *Isaiah*, 386. John Oswalt also views "Israel" as a reference to the Messiah who will display the Lord's "splendor" (49:3), and in so doing, he will be the one "who restores the tribes of Jacob" to the Lord. See Oswalt, *Isaiah*, 547. John Goldingay and John Watts agree that the servant refers to national Israel who will draw Gentile nations to him. Goldingay writes, "Jacob-Israel will be restored and transformed. It will fulfill its vocation to be 'a covenant for the people' (Isa 49:8)—that is, the world's people (as in Isa 42:6) at vocation has not been taken away from it; God's involvement with the prophet-servant is only an interim arrangement. Precisely in restoring Jacob-Israel, Yahweh will shine a light on the nations. In a striking formulation, Yahweh finally speaks of the lot that will be enjoyed by his servants—plural (Isa 54:17)." See Goldingay, *Isaiah*, 73. Watts adds the following about Israel's role to the nations: "If there is a development it is perhaps that the scope of the vision is greater: what had transpired in a more local setting in the past would now take place on a grander and universal scale, though even Solomon's accounts have a universal tinge (1 Kgs 5:14). Nevertheless, the principle is still the same: salvation (i.e., fellowship with the creator and enjoyment of his justice, mercy, and wisdom) was to be found in Yahweh alone and thus mediated through submission to his chosen and now restored agent, Israel, as his people enjoy the blessings promised to David." See Watts, "Echoes from the Past," 506. Brevard Childs presents an argument for an "ideal Israel," but he avoids identifying this figure with a specific person. See Childs, *Isaiah*, 383–85. It seems preferable to interpret the servant, in Isa 49, as a reference to the messianic king, since the descriptions of this servant do not correlate with previous descriptions of Israel (Isa 41:18–20). Also, the servant, in Isa 52:15, will "sprinkle many nations" and "shut" the mouths of kings because he will be "pierced" for his people's transgressions, which is a clear reference to Christ.

reference to the Davidic king from Isa 11:1, 10. The Servant is described as one who has been anointed by the Spirit ("The Spirit of the Lord God is upon me, because the Lord has anointed me"; Isa 61:1), an allusion to the Davidic king in Isa 11:2 ("And the Spirit of the Lord shall rest upon him"), who will transform Israel to become "oaks of righteousness" (Isa 61:3), in contrast to when they were described as "oak whose leaf withers" (Isa 1:30).[43] As the Lord's "anointed" one, the messianic king will function as a mediator of the Lord's Spirit and covenant blessings to his people (Isa 42:6; 49:8; 59:21).

When these texts are read together, it is clear that the messianic king, who reigns from Zion, will serve as a mediator of blessings for both Israel and Gentile nations. In sum, the three aforementioned themes merge together and depict a picture of a multinational kingdom. Utilizing these three themes, I will show how several passages in Isaiah consistently portray a kingdom with national and territorial distinctions between Israelites and Gentiles.

Pictures of a Multinational Kingdom

Isaiah 11

This chapter returns to the theme of God's kingdom provisions and the messianic hope for the world, corresponding to Isa 9:1–7. Although Israel may presently suffer under Assyria's oppression, they are called to trust God because of what he will do in the future when he delivers them from Assyria ("And there will be a highway from Assyria for the remnant that remains of his people, as there was for Israel when they came up from the land of Egypt"; Isa 11:16). Isaiah 11 depicts a future kingdom and ruler set in contrast to the Assyrian kingdom and its ruler, depicted in Isa 10:5–14.[44] What is promised in Isa 2:2, the pilgrimage of the nations to Zion, has been focused specifically on the king in Isa 11.

Isaiah 11:1 identifies this king as the "shoot from the stump of Jesse." The term "shoot" is used in other OT prophecies as a reference to the

---

43. Kings, in Israel's history, included the anointing of the Spirit of Yahweh (1 Sam 10:6; 11:6; 16:13; 19:9; 20:23). The king is Yahweh's servant and an official representative authorized to carry out divine rule upon earth. This king will have Yahweh's Spirit "rest" upon him and is known as "Wonderful Counselor" (Isa 9:6), a reference to the miraculous work of the Spirit. See Wildberger, *Isaiah 1–12*, 471.

44. Smith, *Isaiah 1–39*, 267.

Messiah (cf. Jer 23:5; 33:15; Zech 3:8; 6:12). The fact that the stump of a tree is able to produce shoots testifies to Yahweh's divine action, which Isaiah terms "wonderful" (Isa 28:29; 29:14) and is a title given to the messianic king ("Wonderful Counselor"; Isa 9:6).[45] The Spirit of Yahweh gives the king the abilities (i.e., wisdom, might, and understanding) necessary to carry out the demands of his office (Isa 11:2). The reign of this king will be one of "justice" because he will condemn the wicked with his word (Isa 11:4) and will bind "righteousness" and "faithfulness" to himself like a man binds his belt and loincloth to his body (Isa 11:5). The theme of "righteousness" and "faithfulness" are connected within the enthronement songs, where Yahweh is celebrated as king. If the Messiah is described with similar terms, then Isaiah seems to apply divine attributes to this earthly king.[46]

The result of this king's reign will be a peace that unifies that which was formerly divided. Descriptions of a "young lion roaming with a calf," "the old lion eating straw like a cow," and a "small child leading wild animals" (Isa 11:6–9), portray a type of peace that coincides with the one described in the "new heavens and new earth," in Isa 65:17. Isaiah 11:9 confirms that this king will dwell on "this mountain," which is the same phrase in Isa 65:25, referring to animals living in eschatological peace in Zion ("'The wolf and the lamb shall graze together; the lion shall eat straw like the ox, and dust shall be the serpent's food. They shall not hurt or destroy in all my holy *mountain*,' says the Lord"; Isa 11:9). In this kingdom, the "knowledge of the Lord" will fill the earth and "cover" the waters, which alludes to Isa 2 where nations will stream to the "mountain" of the house of the Lord to be taught his word ("They shall not hurt or destroy in all my holy mountain; for the earth shall be full of the knowledge of the Lord as the waters cover the sea"; Isa 11:9).

Isaiah 11:10 transitions to what the messianic king will do for both Israel and Gentile nations: "In that day the root of Jesse, who shall stand as a signal for the peoples—of him shall the nations inquire, and his resting place shall be glorious." Worldwide recognition of this king would finally fulfill what had been promised to the kings in Jerusalem from Israel's history (cf. Pss 2:8; 18:41; 72:8). The glory promised in the new kingdom connects with the gifts which the nations and the kings are to bring to the king in Zion in Isa 60:9: "For the coastlands shall hope for

---

45. Wildberger, *Isaiah 1–12*, 472–74.
46. Wildberger, *Isaiah 1–12*, 478.

me, the ships of Tarshish first, to bring your children from afar, their silver and gold with them, for the name of the Lord your God, and for the Holy One of Israel, because he has made you beautiful."[47]

In Isa 11:11, the Lord will extend his hand, which connects with Isa 10:13 and 49:22, in order to "recover the remnant," from all over the known world at the time. These nations represent places from the south (Egypt and Cush), the north (Assyria and Hamath), the east (Elam and Babylon), and the west (coastlands of the sea).[48] Before Yahweh gave a "signal" to Israel's enemies to attack Jerusalem (Isa 5:26), but in the eschatological kingdom, he will give the nations the signal to bring his "sons" and "daughters" to Zion (cf. Isa 43:6; 49:22; 60:4).

The king will not only gather Israelites who have been scattered but also reconcile the two divided "brothers" (Isa 11:13; cf. 27:6). The result is the unification of the kingdom and the reestablishment of its sovereignty over its neighbors, fulfilling the conditions of the kingdom previously promised to David.[49] This vision concludes with God's direct intervention to remove the natural barriers for Israel to return to Zion. His power parallels the crossing of the Red Sea when Israel left Egypt under Moses and the result is a "highway" from Assyria through Egypt that crosses Canaan for the remnant's return (Isa 11:16).[50]

Isaiah 11 describes a future Davidic king who will reign from Zion and establish a peace that is reiterated in the "new heavens and new earth," in Isa 65, confirming that the messianic kingdom is in view. In this kingdom, there will be a peace that unifies the cosmos and all people (i.e., "wolf and lamb"; "Ephraim and Judah"). This eschatological vision affirms a multinational paradigm with territorial distinctions between Zion and surrounding Gentile areas and national distinctions between the "banished of Israel" and "dispersed of Judah" versus the "nations" who will bring them to Zion.

Isaiah 60

In Isa 60, Jerusalem functions as a light that attracts the nations in a world of darkness. Gentile nations (and kings) will come into the light in

---

47. Kaiser, *Isaiah 1–12*, 263.

48. Smith, *Isaiah 1–39*, 276.

49. Watts, *Isaiah 1–33*, 217.

50. Watts, *Isaiah 1–33*, 217–18.

Jerusalem and the brightness of the presence of God will be seen in the Davidic king who reigns from Zion ("light to the nations"; cf. Isa 42:4; 49:6; 51:4). When the nations come to Jerusalem, they will bring Zion's "sons" and "daughters," which is a theme repeated throughout Isaiah (Isa 11:12; 14:1–2; 45:13–14; 49:22–23; 66:20). Along with bringing Zion's children, the nations will bring their "wealth" (Isa 60:4–5), which will be used to rebuild Zion (Isa 60:10).[51] Previously, Zion accused Yahweh of abandoning it (Isa 49:14), which Yahweh acknowledges (Isa 54:6–7) while also promising to restore them (Isa 41:17; 42:16). Isaiah 60 reveals that God fulfills his promise to restore Zion by using Gentile nations and their wealth. In Isa 60:16, Zion will "suck" the milk of nations and "nurse" at the breast of kings, reversing the historical reality of the desolation of Jerusalem at the hands of Gentile nations. Also, the "gates of Zion" will remain open so that Gentile kings can freely enter with their wealth in order to restore Zion, which correlates with the description of the new Jerusalem in Rev 21:24 (Isa 60:11).[52]

Isaiah 60 reaches its climax, in vv 19–20, with references to the light of God, recalling vv 1–3. Isaiah 60:19 indicates that Zion will no longer need the sun or moon since the Lord will be an "everlasting light," which Rev 21:23 reiterates when describing the new Jerusalem. The final two verses, vv 21–22, transitions from a description of the city to the condition of its citizens. The "branch" planted by Yahweh is an ideal projection of the people of Israel as they were intended by God to be from the beginning ("the branch of my planting, the work of my hands, that I might be glorified"; Isa 60:21), which will happen via the messianic king ("the shoot of Jesse"; Isa 11:1) who will "raise up the tribes of Jacob" (Isa 49:6).

Isaiah 60:21 recalls the terms and conditions of the promised land for Israel from the Abrahamic covenant, while Isa 60:22 alludes to the Abrahamic promise that all nations will be blessed through Abraham's offspring (cf. Gen 12:3): "Your people shall all be righteous; they shall possess the land forever, the branch of my planting, the work of my hands, that I might be glorified. The least one shall become a clan, and the smallest one a mighty nation; I am the Lord; in its time I will hasten it" (Isa 60:21–22).[53] Within this chapter there are several descriptions of

51. Jones, "Wealth of Nations," 621.

52. On the use of Isa 60–62 in Revelation, see Fekkes, *Isaiah and the Prophetic Traditions*, 264–76.

53. Like Peter Gentry, Edward Young interprets Isa 60 as a vision regarding the increase of the NT church. He believes that the "smallest one," in v. 22, refers to

national and territorial distinctions between Israelites and Gentiles. Gentile nations (and kings) will come into the light in Jerusalem, signifying territorial movement. When Gentile nations come to Jerusalem, they will bring Zion's "sons" and "daughters," referring to Israelites, along with their "wealth" (Isa 60:45), displaying national distinctions between Israelites and Gentiles.

Isaiah 61

Isaiah 61–62 opens with the messianic king's announcement of his role and concludes with a call for his people to embrace their role as a "holy people" (Isa 62:10–12).[54] Earlier in Isa 11:1–9, the Spirit "rest" upon the shoot from the stump of Jesse, then in Isa 42:1–4, God places his Spirit upon his Servant who will bring forth "justice to the nations." Isaiah 61 brings these images together by portraying a messianic king, who will fulfill the role of the Servant, by bringing justice and righteousness on the earth through the power of the Spirit (Isa 61:1–7). This messianic king will mirror Yahweh's actions previously depicted in Isaiah. He will "bring good news" to the poor, which typically referred to the afflicted people God would comfort (Isa 41:17; 49:13; 51:21; 54:11). In Isa 30:26, Yahweh promised to "bind" up the people's brokenness and the Messiah promises to do the same in Isa 61:1. The Messiah will "open" the prison of those who are bound (Isa 61:1), recalling descriptions of Yahweh opening the eyes of the blind (Isa 42:7), which both relate to the idea of liberation.[55]

Isaiah 61:2 describes this liberation as "the year of the Lord's favor." This alludes to Isa 49:8–9, where Yahweh speaks of a time of favor, expressed in the freeing of prisoners and to the Servant's work. This image parallels the description of the Jubilee year (cf. Lev 25:8–17) when debts were canceled, and slaves were freed every fiftieth year.[56] The Messiah will also execute a "day of vengeance" (Isa 61:2), which also appears in Isa

---

individuals from Israel who will now host a multitude of Gentiles in Zion. The growth of Zion recalls Isa 54 and points to Gentile inclusion in the NT church. See Young, *Isaiah*, 457.

54. Oswalt, *Book of Isaiah: 40–66*, 562.

55. Goldingay, *Isaiah 56–66*, 301.

56. For discussion of the allusion to the year of Jubilee (Lev 25) in Isa 61:1–2, see Bruno, "Jesus Is Our Jubilee," 92–94. Bruno writes, "In Isa 61, the Jubilee is seen as a pointer to the eschatological restoration of Israel, when all of God's people will be permanently free from their captivity." See Bruno, "Jesus Is Our Jubilee," 94.

34:8 and 63:4 and closely resembles the "Day of the Lord" when Yahweh will exact justice on the enemies of his people.[57] Isaiah 61:3 expresses the means by which the promises from Isa 60:21 will be realized: "to grant to those who mourn in Zion—to give them a beautiful headdress instead of ashes, the oil of gladness instead of mourning, the garment of praise instead of a faint spirit; that they may be called *oaks of righteousness*, the planting of the Lord, that he may be glorified." The Messiah will plant Israel as "oaks of righteousness" and will comfort those who mourn, referring to the end of oppression (cf. Isa 25:8).[58] Isaiah 61:4 reiterates the promise that no matter how devasted the ruins, nor how desolate the land, God will rebuild Zion just as he promised in Isa 54:3 and 58:12 ("They shall build up the ancient ruins; they shall raise up the former devastations; they shall repair the ruined cities, the devastations of many generations"; Isa 61:4). Nations will no longer oppress Israel, according to vv 5–7, but instead, they will serve as "shepherds, plowmen, and vinedressers," indicating their submission to the Davidic king, in Zion, by participating in positions typically relegated to the Judean countryside.

Isaiah 61:8 mentions an "everlasting covenant," which is a particular result of the work of the messianic king (Isa 49:8; 54:10; 55:5) and alludes to the "covenant of peace" (Isa 54:10; 55:3). The result of this covenant includes a recognizable offspring from Israel who will be made known among the nations, which is a reference to the messianic king who will bring forth justice to the nations (cf. Isa 32:15–19). Isaiah seems to speak as Zion, in v. 10, voicing her praise for what God has done for her through this king: "I will greatly rejoice in the Lord; my soul shall exult in my God, for he has clothed me with the garments of salvation; he has

57. Jesus quoted Isa 61:1–2 and 58:6 in Luke 4:18–19 and identified himself as the servant king who fulfills the time declared in Isa 61. Jesus' presence will usher in a period of favor like the message of comfort that Isaiah brought to Israel (Isa 40). Interestingly, Jesus does not mention the "day of vengeance," in Luke 4:18–19, which suggest that he distinguishes the time between the "year of the Lord's favor" and the "day of vengeance." It seems that he views his first coming as correlating to the year of favor, where he brings freedom and deliverance while associating his second coming with the "day of vengeance," when he will return to exact justice (Rev 16:14). See Bock, *Luke 1:1—9:50*, 394.

58. Barry Webb comments that the phrase "oaks of righteousness" alludes to Isa 6:13, indicating that the remnant, the eschatological inhabitants of the new Zion, are the final outgrowth of the stump. See Webb, *Message of Isaiah*, 235. Beuken, however, states that the phrase connects with Isa 60:21, which seems to be a preferable interpretation because it is the closest reference to Isa 61:3. See Beuken, "Theme of Trito-Isaiah," 71–72.

covered me with the robe of righteousness, as a bridegroom decks himself like a priest with a beautiful headdress, and as a bride adorns herself with her jewels." The image of a bride is familiar as Jerusalem has already been portrayed as a bride in Isa 49:18. Isaiah's vision concludes with a description that the Lord will cause "righteousness and praise" to sprout up before the nations, which may allude to Isa 4:2 when the "branch of the Lord," referring to the Davidic king, will bring forth "fruit" that will be the pride and honor of Israel.

The details in Isa 61 envision a multinational paradigm of the kingdom. Gentiles will have different roles and functions from Israelites in Zion. There are territorial distinctions between Zion and its surrounding areas seen with foreigners traveling to Zion with the "wealth" they bring from their respective territories. Finally, a messianic king will reign from a specific location and bring forth "righteousness and praise" to the nations, implying that the particular location of Jerusalem is envisioned as a portion of the new creation. He will also "plant" Israel as "oaks of righteousness" in their land further indicating both national and territorial distinctions between Israelites and Gentiles.

Isaiah 62

God confirms his promise, from Isa 60:1–9, that the nations will see Zion's glory, which is manifested by the change of condition and character of the city, evidenced by a new name: "The nations shall see your righteousness, and all the kings your glory, and you shall be called by a new name that the mouth of the Lord will give" (Isa 62:2). Yahweh's faithfulness to Zion is expressed with a deliverance characterized by a "burning torch" ("her salvation as a burning torch"; Isa 62:1) signifying a light that will be visible to the nations and their kings (Isa 60:3, 11, 16). This "torch" may refer to the Servant of the Lord who will function as a "light to the nations" (Isa 49:6), which continues the light imagery, from Isa 60, when the nations are drawn to Zion. In Isa 62:3, God specifically calls Zion a "crown of beauty" and a "royal diadem," which alludes to Isa 28:1–5, where God states that he is Israel's "crown of glory" and "royal diadem." This reveals that Yahweh will become Israel's glory by "wearing" Zion as his crown and royal diadem resulting in his light shining to the nations. Part of Zion's restoration includes Gentile nations submitting to the king in Zion and thereby come into peace with Israel.

In Isa 62:10, God uses an image of a "highway" which has different connotations within Isaiah: "Go through, go through the gates; prepare the way for the people; build up, build up the highway; clear it of stones; lift up a signal over the peoples." A "highway" could have negative overtones, such as in Isa 7:3 and 36:2, when a highway was the place where Israel will face enemy occupation and destruction. A "highway" could also have positive overtones, such as in Isa 11:16; 35:8; and 49:11, when a "highway" refers to the means by which God's people return to Zion.[59] In Isa 62, Isaiah may be stating that the highway refers to God realizing his promises ("your salvation comes"; Isa 62:11); or to the redeemed walking into Jerusalem ("prepare the way of the people"; Isa 62:10); or to the nations flowing to Zion while bringing Zion's children with them ("signal over the peoples"; Isa 62:10). It seems that a "highway," in Isa 62:10, refers specifically to the nations traveling to Zion while bringing Zion's children (Israelites) with them with the use of the phrase "signal to the peoples." The previous time "signal" appeared was in Isa 11:10–12 and Isa 49:22. Both times they depicted the Davidic king signaling the nations to bring Israelites to Zion.

Isaiah 62:12 concludes with a label for both Israel and Zion: "And they shall be called The Holy People, The Redeemed of the Lord; and you shall be called Sought Out, A City Not Forsaken." God labels Israel, "a Holy People," which fulfills Exod 19:6 when God intended for Israel to become a "holy nation." Isaiah 4:3–4 explains how Israel becomes "holy" by revealing that the "branch of the Lord" will "wash" their filth, pointing to the suffering servant who will be "pierced" for his people's transgressions (Isa 53:5). Zion is labeled "a city not forsaken," addressing its self-proclaimed description (Isa 49:14). Within this eschatological vision, there are both territorial and national distinctions. Nations will witness Zion's glory, indicating that Zion is distinct from the territories of Gentile nations. God will reverse Israel's political condition, implying national distinctions between Israel and Gentiles. Finally, the messianic king will "signal" the nations to travel on a "highway" to Zion, indicating territorial borders within the kingdom.

---

59. Oswalt, *Book of Isaiah: 40–66*, 588.

Isaiah 65

Isaiah 65:1–2 opens with God's response to Israel, in Isa 65:1, 12, 24, to their earlier complaints, in Isa 63:7—64:12. Previously, some within Israel lamented that they had not seen God's zeal (Isa 63:15), accused God of "hiding his face" (Isa 64:7), and accused him of being "silent" to their outcry (Isa 64:12). God states, with two tolerative niphal verbs ("to be sought"; "to be found"; Isa 65:1), that he can be sought after and found in order to defend himself against the false accusations from Israel. After defending himself, God focuses on his "servants" within Israel who have responded to him, in Isa 65:8–10. Isaiah 65:9 mentions that God will fulfill his promises to Abraham since he will bring forth an "offspring" from Jacob in order to inhabit the promised land: "I will bring forth offspring from Jacob, and from Judah possessors of my mountains; my chosen shall possess it, and my servants shall dwell there." This does not mean that everyone who descended from Israel will share in this promise. The term "servants" designates, in Isa 65:8–16, to the believing core of Israel.[60] Thus, Isa 65:17–25 reveals that those within national Israel, whose character reflects Yahweh's standards, will receive the blessings from the Abrahamic covenant, particularly possession of the promised land.

The language of Isa 65:17–25 closely relate to the vision of the messianic kingdom from Isa 11, where the Davidic king will reign over the nations.[61] The focus of Isa 65:17–25 is upon Jerusalem and its people because it is the capital of the multinational kingdom. This does not mean, however, that the eschatological kingdom is only concerned about Zion but emphasizes the central role and importance of Zion for both Israel and the nations. Even if one assumes that the increase of Zion refers to the NT church, the new Jerusalem is depicted as the center of the new creation rather than coextensive with it.[62]

---

60. Blenkinsopp, *Isaiah 56–66*, 275.

61. Richard Schultz notes how Isa 11:6–9 serves as an intertext to Isa 65:17–24. He argues that each statement in Isa 11:6–9 is reflected in Isa 65:25, but each incompletely and each to a different degree. Isaiah 65:25 contains only the first and the fifth animal pair from Isa 11. The restored animal harmony is apparently an integral part of the new creation, the call/answer language in v. 24 perhaps replacing the reference in Isa 11:9 to the pervasive knowledge of God. See Schultz, "Intertextuality," 34.

62. Edward Young argues that the word בָּרָא implies something fundamentally new as a result of God's creative activity. He adds that Jerusalem functions as "the focal point" of the new creation and of the kingdom of God. See Young, *Isaiah*, 513–14.

In the new Jerusalem, there will be a reversal of the effects from the fall. There will be neither earthly sorrow nor untimely death such that a person who dies at a hundred years old would be considered "young" in this kingdom (Isa 65:20). Two of the conditions from the fall included painful childbirth and the futility of working on a cursed earth (cf. Gen 3:17), which are both reversed since people will no longer "labor in vain" or "bear children for calamity" in this vision (Isa 65:23). Isaiah 65:25 recalls the description of the eschatological kingdom in Isa 11:6–9. Although the messianic king is not given prominence in this passage, it is the same kingdom that is spoken of, and the blessings portrayed here are those that are made available because of the messianic king who reigns in Zion. The one element presented in Isa 65:17–25 that is not seen in Isa 11:6–9 is the phrase "and dust shall be the serpent's food" (Isa 65:25). This may be another allusion to Gen 3:15 and indicates that the peace pictured in the new Jerusalem is also true of the new creation as a whole.

The joy portrayed in the new Jerusalem (Isa 65:18) is indicative of the peace that will exist among the entire new creation and promised through the "covenant of peace" (cf. Isa 54:10). The "days of Noah," from Isa 54:9, functions as an allusion to the flood when God reversed the "chaos" of the flood and confirmed his peace on earth with an everlasting sign ("rainbow"). In the same way, the "covenant of peace" will serve as a confirmation that God will reverse the "chaos" from the exile and confirm his peace in the new creation with an everlasting sign, namely the covenant of peace. The peace accomplished by this "everlasting covenant" includes unifying what was formerly divided. The language of a "wolf" and "lamb" grazing together recalls the language of Isa 11:6–9, which also depicts the messianic kingdom. Isaiah 65 provides a preview of the type of peace that the Davidic king will provide for the entire new creation.

Some argue that Rev 21 reveals that the new Jerusalem, as described in Isa 65:17–24, is coextensive with the new creation.[63] However, the textual details of Rev 21:23–26 undermine this interpretation:

> And the city has no need of sun or moon to shine on it, for the glory of God gives it light, and its lamp is the Lamb. By its light will the nations walk, and the kings of the earth will bring their glory into it, and its gates will never be shut by day—and there will be no night there. They will bring into it the glory and the honor of the nations. (Rev 21:23–26)

---

63. Gentry and Wellum, *Kingdom through Covenant*, 467.

Nations and kings are mentioned as streaming to Jerusalem just as in Isa 60:3 and Isa 2:2–3. There is both territorial and national distinctions exhibited in Rev 21:24, where a plurality of kings and nations travel from their land to Jerusalem. There are "walls" surrounding the New Jerusalem (Isa 21:14), implying a limit to its territorial space. If Rev 21 should be read together with Isa 65, then territorial and national details presented in both Isa 65 and Rev 21 illustrate a multinational picture of the kingdom.[64]

Isaiah 66

Isaiah 66 provides a final picture of the eschatological kingdom. When God comes to earth in all his power and glory (Isa 66:15), he will first execute justice by destroying the wicked and they will live forever in a place of unending fire and undying worms (Isa 66:24). God announces to his people that those who tremble at his word will find great joy and comfort in it (Isa 66:2). God's word includes a message of hope for Zion, in vv 7–9. God presents a woman who gave birth so quickly that she bypassed labor pains (Isa 66:7), and he identifies this woman as Zion. Zion will "give birth" to her "children" even though she was believed to be barren (Isa 26:19; 37:3; 54:1). God has promised repeatedly that he has the power to reverse Zion's fortunes (Isa 40:8; 55:10–11) and bring her "children" home (Isa 11:12; 14:1–2; 49:22–23; 66:20).

Isaiah 66:12 introduces a "peace" that God promises to his people, which was made available to them through the messianic king's work: "For thus says the Lord: 'Behold, I will extend peace to her like a river, and the glory of the nations like an overflowing stream; and you shall nurse, you shall be carried upon her hip, and bounced upon her knees.'" God promises that when Zion recognizes her king, instead of the "river of Assyria" rising in all its glory against her (cf. Isa 8:7), a "river" of peace and "glory of the nations" will stream to her (cf. Isa 60:11; 61:6). Yahweh comforts his people like a mother comforts her child (Isa 66:13) by telling them that Jerusalem will be the location of his comfort (cf. Isa 40:1–2; 49:13–14; 51:3; 52:9). In sum, there will be joy in the new Jerusalem, where there will never be any need: "You shall see, and your heart shall rejoice; your bones shall flourish like the grass; and the hand of the Lord

64. Whether Isa 65 refers to the millennial kingdom or the eternal state is a topic beyond the scope of this book. For the purposes of this book, it is sufficient to conclude that the eschatological kingdom is a material kingdom. For a detail of the distinction between the millennial and eternal kingdom, see McDougall "Revelation 21:9 to 22:5."

shall be known to his servants, and he shall show his indignation against his enemies (Isa 66:14)."

Isaiah 66:18–24 reiterates the theme of Gentile nations gathering to worship the Lord at Zion, which fulfills the hope of postexilic Judaism.[65] There is debate over several issues in this section. First, the "survivors" who are sent to the nations can refer either to Gentiles or Jewish survivors (Isa 66:19).[66] Within the context, it seems more likely that the "survivors" refers to the "remnant" within Israel who survive God's judgment from Isa 66:15–16. One theme reiterated in Isaiah is that of a surviving "remnant" within Israel following God's judgment. Isaiah 1:9 describes "survivors" God left in Judah following his judgment ("If the Lord of hosts had not left us a few survivors, we should have been like Sodom, and become like Gomorrah"). Isaiah 10:22 describe a "remnant of Israel" and the "survivors of the house of Jacob" who will return to the Lord after judgment ("for though your people Israel be as the sand of the sea, only a remnant of them will return"). Finally, Isa 37:31–32 describes a similar scene to Isa 66:19 where a surviving remnant from Judah will go out from Jerusalem ("And the surviving remnant of the house of Judah shall again take root downwards and bear fruit upwards. For out of Jerusalem shall go a remnant, and out of Mount Zion a band of survivors").

Second, the "brothers" whom the "survivors" will gather, in Isa 66:20, can refer to either Gentiles or Jews. It seems better to view them as Israelites since this reading is consistent with the theme of God "signaling" the nations in order to gather Israelites back to Zion (cf. Isa 11:12; 14:1–2; 49:22–23; 60:4). Among the Israelites and Gentiles who return to Zion, God will elect "some of them" as "priests" and "Levites" ("And some of them also I will take for priests and for Levites, says the Lord"; 66:21). Third, the "priests" and "Levites" may refer to Gentiles or Jews.

---

65. John W. de Gruchy notes that there were three understandings of this hope depicted in OT prophetic passages: (1) the hope for the political reinstitution of the Davidic kingdom (Zech 9:9–10) through the coming of a political Messiah; (2) the apocalyptic hope (Dan 7:9) that the crisis of the present world would be redeemed with a new heavens and earth; or (3) a hope for a new Jerusalem. See de Gruchy, "New Heaven," 67.

66. John Goldingay believes it refers to Gentiles since the word "survivors" connects with Isa 45:20, where they are explicitly survivors of the nations. See Goldingay, *Isaiah 56–66*, 514. However, the word "survivors" also appears in Isa 4:2 commenting on those who "survived" God's judgment in Jerusalem. Edward Young argues that the context "demands" that the survivors refer to the Jews described in vv. 16–17. See Young, *Isaiah*, 532.

The phrase "some of them" could mean that some of the Israelite "brothers" included priests and Levites or that some Israelites from other tribes will serve as Levites.[67] Even if one were to view "some of them" as referring to Gentiles, this does not indicate that Gentiles replace Israel's tribal identification as Levites. Instead, it is more likely that Isa 65 fulfills the promise that Zion will function as a "house of prayer for all peoples," with both Israelites and Gentiles serving in Zion ("these I will bring to my holy mountain, and make them joyful in my house of prayer"; Isa 56:7).

In Isa 66, the messianic king will "signal" the nations (cf. Isa 11:10; 49:22; 62:10) by sending out "survivors" within Israel from Zion to the nations. Then, the nations will respond by bringing back the scattered Israelites ("sons" and "daughters") back to Zion, along with their "wealth" (cf. Isa 11:12; 14:1–2; 49:22; 60:3–5, 11). Despite the interpretative issues within Isa 66:19–22, what is clear is that a multinational kingdom is presented in this vision. There are territorial movement and national distinctions. The "wealth of nations" will flow to Zion, implying territorial movement. Also, the "survivors" will be sent from Zion and the nations will respond by bringing the "brothers" to Zion, implying national distinctions between Israelites and Gentiles.

Conclusion

There are three major themes presented in Isaiah's eschatological kingdom that contribute in depicting a multinational eschatological kingdom. First, God promises to reverse Zion's condition in order to establish it as his dwelling place (Isa 49:14–21; 51:2–4). Also, Zion is not portrayed as synonymous with Gentile nations but as a distinct territory with "gates." Second, Israel and Gentile nations are presented in the kingdom with national distinctions. God's promise of restoration for Israel includes a return to their land (Isa 60:21; 61:3), a reversal of the conditions of Zion, and a shift in the relationship between Israel and Gentile nations from submission to mutual submission to the Davidic king (Isa 11:14; 60:16; 62:8). Third, the messianic king's function in Zion depicts a multinational kingdom. He will restore Israel (Isa 11:12; 49:6), purify them (Isa

67. Croatto, "Exegesis de Isaiahs 56," 91–110; Klostermann, *Deuterojesaia*, 114. August Dillman argues that "some" may refer to Israelites who assist the priests as "Levites." See Dillmann, *Der Prophet Jesaia*, 542. Joseph Blenkinsopp adds that one's interpretation of "some of them" in v. 21 is dependent on one's view of "them" in v. 19. See Blenkinsopp, *Isaiah 56–66*, 315.

4:4), and "plant" them in their land (Isa 61:3). For Gentile nations, he will gather them to Zion to teach him his word (Isa 2:3), include them as his covenant people (Isa 19:24–25), reverse their physical infirmities (Isa 35:5–10), and bless them as his servants (Isa 56:2–6). The king will be a "light" to them (Isa 49:6) by bringing peace and justice to all nations (Isa 32:15–19) and nations with their kings will respond by bringing their "wealth" into Zion (Isa 60:11).

There are several kingdom visions that exhibit all three themes. Isaiah 11 describes a future Davidic king who will reign from Zion and establish a peace that is echoed in Isa 65. He will "signal" the nations to bring scattered Israelites back to Zion and establish a peace that unifies the cosmos and all peoples. Isaiah 60 correlates with Rev 21 in its description of Jerusalem. Jerusalem is portrayed as a distinct location from Gentile territories as evidenced by its "gates" and "borders." Isaiah 61 continues the motif of the "wealth of nations," affirming territorial and national distinctions between Israel and Gentiles. Gentiles will have distinct roles in Zion ("shepherds," "plowmen," and "vinedressers") from Israelites ("priests"; "ministers"). Isaiah 65 mentions nations and kings streaming to Jerusalem just as Isa 60:3 and Isa 2:2–3 predicted. Finally, Isa 66 synthesizes several themes from Isaiah. The messianic king will "signal" the nations (Isa 11:10; 49:22; 62:10) by sending out "survivors" from Zion to the nations. Then, the nations will respond by bringing scattered Israelites ("sons" and "daughters") back to Zion (Isa 11:12; 14:1–2; 49:22; 60:3–5, 11).

These kingdom visions provide textual details that lead to a multinational kingdom. A multinational kingdom is able to provide a more comprehensive picture that accounts for the details that Isaiah presents. As Michael Vlach concludes, "It appears that there is more to God's plans for nations than select members of each nation being saved. The nations of the world as a whole also appear headed for some form of restoration."[68]

---

68. Vlach, *Has the Church Replaced Israel?*, 171–72.

7

Conclusion

Summary of the Study

THE INTRODUCTION COMMENTED ON redemptive history as a way several biblical theologians interpret the canonical narrative. Many highlight the kingdom of God as the key theme that explains the direction of redemptive history. Since God redeems people from all nations into his kingdom, a question arises whether the kingdom is composed only of individuals or whether it includes a multinational structure as well. Some have argued that the NT reveals a new covenant community who will redefine national Israel. However, others have claimed that even in the OT, the prophets change the picture of the multinational kingdom into a multiethnic community, otherwise known as the NT church. Many have referenced Isaiah as evidence for their claim that the kingdom consummates with the new covenant community. However, I argue that Isaiah's eschatological visions are consistent with a multinational consummate order where Israelites and Gentiles are identified with national and territorial distinctions.

The first chapter examined anthropological studies regarding the definition of a nation. Although anthropologists do not agree on a definition of a nation because of the differences between a nation and nation-state, a consensus does exist that a historic homeland and dominant ethnic core are defining traits of a nation. These traits also apply to how ancient Israel defined themselves as a nation. Their identification with their historic homeland united successive generations together even when they were dispersed outside of their land. Although individual

Gentiles joined Israel, their dominant ethnic core remained Israelite. From an anthropological perspective, a historic homeland and dominant ethnic core are indispensable for any nation.

The second chapter presented observations about the biblical conception of a nation by examining the contextual uses of גּוֹי and its relationship with עַם, מִשְׁפָּחָה, אֻמָּה, and ἔθνος. Based on the contextual uses of these terms, there were two conclusions that are relevant for this book. First, there seems to be different characteristics, besides territory or governmental structure, highlighted when Israel is called a עַם, מִשְׁפָּחָה, or אֻמָּה.[1] While all three words can be applied to a nation, they usually refer to a subset group of a nation. Also, the overall conception of a nation within Scripture supports the anthropological perspective that a nation includes a homeland and dominant ethnic core.[2] Second, the narrative of God's kingdom, in both historical and prophetic texts, consistently labels Israel and Gentiles as גּוֹי. If the language describing the eschatological kingdom speaks of its dominion over גּוֹיִם, then it seems that a multinational consummate order seems more likely than a singular corporate reality of individuals.

The third chapter examined Gen 10–12 in order to establish a biblical foundation for a multinational kingdom. The Table of Nations shows that territorial and political distinctions are necessary in defining an ethnic group as a nation. The Tower of Babel narrative explains how a multitude of nations, listed in the Table of Nations, formed. How one interprets the Babel event is pivotal in how one will understand the Abrahamic covenant. If the Tower of Babel event is interpreted negatively, then the result of nations is a product of sin and the Abrahamic covenant reverses this result with a new "one people" concept called the kingdom of God. However, if the Babel event is interpreted as part and parcel to God's redemptive plan, then it fulfills God's purpose of creating a diversity of nations. When properly placed in its context, Gen 11 seems to indicate that a diversity of nations is a result of God's original mandate from creation. The Abrahamic covenant, in Gen 12, affirms this reading of Babel. God foretells, in this covenant, that Israel will become a great nation, who will possess land, in order to bless all the nations of

---

1. The word עַם seems to highlight Israel's covenantal relationship with Yahweh; מִשְׁפָּחָה stresses ethnic ties; and אֻמָּה highlights kinship within a nation.

2. Although different ethnicities may be found within a nation and land boundaries may shift over time, nations in both the OT and NT appear to have dominant ethnic cores and particular territorial locations.

the world. Also, the Abrahamic covenant provides a backdrop for a multinational kingdom theme which is developed throughout the OT canon.

The fourth chapter surveyed several passages from OT narratives, prophets, and Writings in order to examine whether a multinational kingdom, as first predicted in the Abrahamic covenant, is a consistent theme in the OT. After surveying this theme, there are several conclusions. First, God's multinational kingdom agenda continues for both Israel and Gentile nations. The dearth of Gentiles coming to Yahweh, during the OT narratives, does not reveal a failure on God's part to fulfill his kingdom agenda, but a reflection of Israel's incompetence to fulfill their mission as a light to the nations. Second, several OT prophecies predicted a time when both Israel and Gentile nations would worship Yahweh in his multinational kingdom (i.e., Egypt participating in the Feast of Tabernacles). A restored Zion, Israel, and Gentile nations are depicted in several prophesies. Third, the Writings explain the role of the Davidic king in the eschatological kingdom. What Yahweh has already done for Israel in the past will foreshadow what he will do for Israel and Gentile nations in the future. The salvation depicted in the Writings is made possible by Christ's death and resurrection and is realized at his return when he will reign over Israel and Gentile nations.

The fifth chapter analyzes Peter Gentry's intepretation of Isaiah's eschatological kingdom from *Kingdom through Covenant* (1st and 2nd editions), as a case study, since his arguments are indicative of how other scholars read Isaiah's visions. Several issues with Gentry's interpretation were highlighted. First, Gentry's assumption that national Israel functions as an OT type of the church underlines his interpretation of the Abrahamic covenant. Gentry argues that the use of גּוֹי, as opposed to עַם, in Gen 12:2, signifies that God will create a future kingdom or a "great nation," through Abraham, out of the chaos of Babel. Based on his view of typology, this "nation" will function as a type of Jesus and the NT church and the Abrahamic covenant blessings are applied to "many" nations.

Second, in his analysis of Isaiah's eschatological visions, Gentry assumes that the presence of Gentiles in the eschatological kingdom indicates that Jews and Gentiles unite to form a new "one people" concept. He claims that a "one in many" paradigm exists such that the blessings ascribed to the Servant apply to the many who identify with him, including Gentiles. The Abrahamic and Davidic blessings previously promised to national Israel are redefined by a future Davidic king who will bless the new covenant community known as the "servants of the Lord." However, several textual details within Isaiah consistently portray national and territorial distinctions between Israelites and Gentiles. Gentry also contends that Isa 65 depicts the new Jerusalem as coextensive with the new creation. Yet, a closer look at the details of Rev 21 and Isa 60, as well as the texts leading up to Isa 65, reveals that Isaiah consistently presents Zion as a distinct city within the new creation.

Third, Gentry applies a certain form of typology to Israel, where an escalation of a type results in its replacement or redefinition by an antitype. It seems that Gentry imposes his assumption of the metanarrative of Scripture into his exegesis of certain prophetic passages or may be reading these details as idiomatic expressions. The issue with Gentry's interpretation of Isaiah is not his affirmation of typology but his insistence that Isaiah portrays Israel as an OT type of a particular conception of an eschatological kingdom, even though the textual details do not seem to support his interpretation.

The sixth chapter presented a reading of Isaiah's eschatological visions as a multinational reality, composed not just of individuals, but of individuals with distinct ethnic and territorial affiliations. There were three major themes seen in Isaiah's eschatological kingdom visions. First, God promises to reverse Zion's condition in order to establish it as his dwelling place (Isa 49:14–21; 51:2–4). Zion is not portrayed as synonymous with Gentile nations but as a distinct territory. Second, Israel and Gentile nations are depicted with national distinctions. God's promise of restoration for Israel includes a return to their land (Isa 60:21; 61:3), a reversal of the conditions of Zion, and a shift in the relationship between Israel and Gentile nations from submission to mutual submission to the Davidic king (Isa 11:14; 60:16; 62:8). Third, the messianic king will bless both Israel and Gentile nations. He will restore Israel (Isa 11:12; 49:6), purify them (Isa 4:4), and "plant" them in their land (Isa 61:3). For Gentile nations, he will gather them to Zion to teach him his word (Isa 2:3), include them as his covenant people (Isa 19:24–25), reverse their physical infirmities (Isa 35:5–10), and bless them as his servants (Isa 56:2–6).

There are several kingdom visions that exhibit all three themes. Isaiah 11 describes a future Davidic king who will reign from Zion and establish a peace that is echoed in Isa 65. He will "signal" the nations to bring scattered Israelites back to Zion and establish a peace that unifies the cosmos and all peoples. Isaiah 60 portrays the new Jerusalem as a distinct location where Gentile nations and their kings bring their "wealth." Isaiah 61 continues the motif of the "wealth of nations," affirming territorial and national distinctions between Israelites and Gentiles. Isaiah 62 states that the messianic king will "signal" the nations to travel on a highway to Zion by revealing the city's glory. Isaiah 65 mentions nations and kings streaming to Jerusalem just as Isa 60:3 and Isa 2:2–3 state. Finally, Isa 66 synthesizes several themes from Isaiah. The messianic king will "signal" the nations (Isa 11:10; 49:22; 62:10) by sending out "survivors" from Zion to Gentile nations. The nations will respond by bringing scattered Israelites ("sons" and "daughters") back to Zion (Isa 11:12; 14:1–2; 49:22; 60:3–5, 11). The sending of "survivors" from Zion and the return of "brothers" portray territorial movement and national distinctions between Israelites and Gentiles. A multinational paradigm is able to provide a more consistent reading of the textual details seen in Isaiah's visions. Also, a canonical understanding of Gentile nations, specifically one that argues for a renewed multinational kingdom, preserves the integrity of Israel's identity and role.

Areas of Further Research

There are a number of areas for further research which logically issue from the current work. First, there needs to be a comprehensive examination of NT passages that portray the eschatological kingdom. As with any book, the scope did not allow for an exhaustive discussion on NT passages that comment on the eschatological kingdom. Examining whether the theme of a multinational kingdom is reinforced or reinterpreted in the NT is an area that merits further discussion.

Second, there needs to be a comprehensive examination and critique of the hermeneutics of those who assume that Israel functions as an OT type of the eschatological kingdom. The hermeneutical issue of typology was addressed, in chapter 5; however, further research on the nature of typology and how it functions regarding the relationship between Israel, Jesus Christ, and the church is warranted.[3] How typology applies to Israel in the OT should be further studied since it is this hermeneutical assumption that Gentry, along with others, apply in their reading of

3. Brent Parker argues that the relationship between Israel, Jesus, and the church is understood through a certain form of typology that includes escalation. He proposes that when typology is properly defined, then a new theological view distinct covenantal and dispensational theology, coined as "progressive covenantalism," becomes the solution to the ecclesiological problems found in covenant and dispensational theology and their understanding of typology. See Parker, "Israel-Christ-Church."

Isaiah's eschatological kingdom. Also, the topic of "prophetic idiom" and its validity is a topic that warrants further research.

Third, while this work focused on the national distinctions presented in the eschatological kingdom, a study on the territorial distinctions in the eschatological kingdom is important. Steven James, in his book, argued that there is a logical inconsistency in the arguments of recent new creationists regarding territorial particularity, which results in a kingdom conception that lacks consistency regarding descriptions of materiality in the texts.[4] Those who argue that the new Jerusalem is coextensive with the new creation should explain the exegetical and hermeneutical reasons for including or excluding territorial particularity in their respective conceptions.

Fourth, there has been a rising interest in the field of ecclesiology regarding the need of multicultural and multiethnic churches in the United States.[5] The church is the union of redeemed people of Christ and that union manifests itself in different local expressions worldwide. Since the local churches are expressions of this kingdom reality, then it seems that a multinational kingdom would provide a basis for a local church to express its constituents as a multinational congregation. One of the merits of recent scholarship about multiethnic churches is that it provides a biblical response to the sin of racism. In a similar way, a multinational kingdom may provide a biblical paradigm for churches to respond to the sin of nationalism.

Concluding Thoughts

In light of the conclusions drawn from this book, it seems that studying the nature of the eschatological kingdom would be profitable. The eschatological kingdom provides hope for the future reality that the church looks forward to with faith and reveals how God faithfully fulfills what he has promised for both Israel and the nations. It is my hope that this book plays a role in working toward a better understanding of God's redemptive plan for his people and how the church can live in the present age in light of the kingdom that will be fully consummated with the return of Christ. My prayer is that the church will continue to study the new creation with

---

4. See James, *New Creation Eschatology*.

5. See Brouwer, *Multicultural Church*; McIntosh, *Being the Church*; Deymz, *Healthy Multi-ethnic Church*; Piper, *Bloodlines*; and Emerson, *People of the Dream*.

all its intricacies in order to strengthen their resolve to endure the temporary tribulations they experience in the present world with joy. As the Apostle John, in Rev 22:20, declared, "Amen. Come, Lord Jesus." May we look forward to the day when King Jesus will reign in his multinational kingdom and wipe the tears of sorrow from our eyes forever.

Bibliography

Abernethy, Andrew T. *The Book of Isaiah and God's Kingdom: A Thematic-Theological Approach*. Downers Grove: InterVarsity, 2016.

Ahlstrom, Gosta W. *Who Were the Israelites?* Winona Lake, IN: Leiden, 1986.

Albright, W. F. "The Names *Shaddai* and *Abram*." *JBL* 54 (1935) 173–210.

Alexander, Joseph Addison. *Commentary on the Prophecies of Isaiah*. Grand Rapids: Zondervan, 1953.

Alexander, T. Desmond. *From Eden to the New Jerusalem: An Introduction to Biblical Theology*. Grand Rapids: Kregel, 2008.

———. *From Paradise to the Promised Land: An Introduction to the Main Themes of the Pentateuch*. Grand Rapids: Baker, 1995.

Allen, Ronald Barclay. "עַם." In *TWOT*, edited by R. Laird Harris et al., 676–77. Chicago: Moody, 1999.

———. "Psalm 87, A Song Rarely Sung." *BibSac* 153 (1996) 131–40.

———. *When Song Is New: Understanding the Kingdom of the Psalms*. Nashville: Nelson, 1983.

Allis, Oswald. T. *Prophecy and the Church*. Philadelphia: Presbyterian and Reformed, 1945.

Allison, D. C., Jr. *The New Moses: A Matthean Typology*. Minneapolis: Fortress, 1993.

Alt, Albrecht. "The Settlement of the Israelites in Palestine." Chapter 3 in *Essays on Old Testament History and Religion*, translated by H. A. Wilson. Oxford: Blackwell, 1966.

Alter, Robert. *The Art of Biblical Narrative*. Rev. ed. New York: Basic, 2011.

Amsler, Samuel. "Ou en est la typologie de l'Ancien Testament?" *Eisenbahntechnische Rundschau* 27 (1952) 75–81.

———. "צמח." In *TLOT*, edited by Claus Westermann and E. Jenni, 1085–87. Peabody: Hendrickson, 1997.

Anderson, Bernhard W. *Contours of Old Testament Theology*. Philadelphia: Fortress, 1999.

———. *Creation versus Chaos: The Reinterpretation of Mythical Symbolism in the Bible*. Philadelphia: Fortress, 1987.

———. *From Creation to New Creation: Old Testament Perspectives*. Minneapolis: Fortress, 1994.

———. "Tradition and Scripture in the Community of Faith." *JBL* 100 (1981) 5–21.

Armstrong, John. *Nations before Nationalism*. Chapel Hill: University of North Carolina Press, 1982.

Arndt, William. "ὅσιος." In BDAG, edited by Frederick William Danker, 728. 3rd ed. Chicago: University of Chicago Press, 2000.

Aster, Shawn Zelig. "Isaiah 19: The 'Burden of Egypt' and Neo-Assyrian Imperial Policy." *JAOS* 135 (2015) 453–70.

Atlas, George. "The Creation of Israel: The Cosmic Proportion of the Exodus Event." In *Exploring Exodus: Literary, Theological, and Contemporary Approaches*, edited by Brian S. Rosner and Paul R. Williamson, 30–59. Nottingham, UK: Apollos, 2008.

Baker, David L. *Two Testaments, One Bible*. Downers Grove: InterVarsity, 2010.

Barker, Patrick G. "Allegory and Typology in Galatians 4:21–31." *St. Vladimir's Theological Quarterly* 38 (1994) 193–209.

Barton, Stephen C. "The Unity of Humankind as a Theme in Biblical Theology." In *Out of Egypt*, edited by Craig Bartholomew, 233–60. Grand Rapids: Paternoster/ Zondervan, 2004.

Barrett, C. K. *Acts*. Vol. 1. ICC. Edinburgh: T. & T. Clark, 1994.

Bartholomew, Craig G. *Out of Egypt: Biblical Theology and Biblical Interpretation*. Edited by Craig Bartholomew et al. Scripture and Hermeneutics 5. Grand Rapids: Paternoster/Zondervan, 2004.

Bauckham, Richard. "The Restoration of Israel in Luke-Acts." In *Restoration: Old Testament, Jewish and Christian Conceptions*, edited by James M. Scott, 435–89. JSOTSup 72. Leiden: Brill, 2001.

Baumgartner, Walter. "גּוֹי." In *HALOT*, edited by M. E. J. Richardson, translated by Benedikt Hartmann, 1:182–83. 5 vols. Leiden: Brill, 2000.

———. "מִשְׁפָּחָה." In *HALOT*, edited by M. E. J. Richardson, translated by Benedikt Hartmann, 2:651. 5 vols. Leiden: Brill, 2000.

———. "אֻמָּה." In *HALOT*, edited by M. E. J. Richardson, translated by Benedikt Hartmann, 1:62. 5 vols. Leiden: Brill, 2000.

Bavinck, Herman. *Reformed Dogmatics*. Edited by John Bolt. Translated by John Vriend. 4 vols. Grand Rapids: Baker Academic, 2003–2008.

Baze, J. M., Jr. "A Dispensational Model: The Essentials-Part III." *CTJ* 3 (1999) 106–33.

Beale, G. K. *Handbook on the New Testament Use of the Old Testament: Exegesis and Interpretation*. Grand Rapids: Baker, 2012.

———. *A New Testament Biblical Theology: The Unfolding of the Old Testament in the New*. Grand Rapids: Baker Academic, 2011.

———. *The Temple and the Church's Mission: A Biblical Theology of the Dwelling Place of God*. Downers Grove: InterVarsity, 2004.

Beale, G. K., and Benjamin L. Gladd. *Hidden but Now Revealed: A Biblical Theology of Mystery*. Downers Grove: InterVarsity, 2014.

Beasley-Murray, George R. *Jesus and the Kingdom of God*. Grand Rapids: Eerdmans, 1986.

Beaulieu, Stephane A. "Egypt as God's People: Isaiah 19:19–25 and Its Allusions to the Exodus." *PRS* 40 (2013) 207–18.

Beers, Holly. *The Followers of Jesus as the 'Servant': Luke's Model from Isaiah for the Disciples in Luke-Acts*. Library of New Testament Studies 535. London: Bloomsbury T. & T. Clark, 2015.

Benton, Richard. "Aspect and the Biblical Hebrews Niphal and Hitpael." PhD diss. University of Wisconsin–Madison, 2009.

———. "Verbal and Contextual Information: The Problem of Overlapping Meanings in the Niphal and Hitpael." *ZAW* 124 (2012) 385–99.

Bergen, Robert D. *1, 2 Samuel*. NAC 7. Nashville: Broadman & Holman, 1996.

Berkhof, Louis. *Systematic Theology*. Rev. ed. Grand Rapids: Eerdmans, 1996.

Berlin, Adele. *The Dynamics of Biblical Parallelism*. Bloomington: Indiana University Press, 1984.

Bernasconi, Robert. "Who Invented the Concept of Race? Kant's Role in the Enlightenment Construction of Race." In *Race*, edited by Robert Bernasconi, 11–36. Malden, MA: Blackwell, 2000.

Beuken, W. A. M. "The Main Theme of Trito-Isaiah: 'The Servants of YHWH.'" *JSOT* 47 (1990) 67–87.

Bird, Michael F. "'A Light to the Nations' (Isaiah 42:6 and 49:6): Inter-Textuality and Mission Theology in the Early Church." *RTR* 65 (2006) 122–31.

Blaising, Craig A. "A Critique of Gentry and Wellum's Kingdom through Covenant: A Hermeneutical-Theological Response." *MSJ* 26 (2015) 111–27.

———. *Dispensationalism, Israel and the Church: The Serach for Definition*. Grand Rapids: Zondervan, 1992.

———. "The Future of Israel as a Theological Question." *JETS* 44 (2001) 435–50.

Blaising, Craig A., and Darrell L. Bock. *Progressive Dispensationalism*. Grand Rapids: Baker, 1993.

Blaising, Craig A., et al. Review of *Kingdom through Covenant: A Biblical Understanding of the Covenants*, by Peter Gentry and Stephen Wellum. Audio recording of ETS conference presentation, San Diego, November 19–21, 2014.

Blenkinsopp, Joseph. *Isaiah 40–55*. AB. New York: Doubleday, 2003.

———. *Isaiah 56–66: A New Translation with Introduction and Commentary*. AB. New York: Doubleday, 2003.

———. "The Servant and the Servants in Isaiah and the Formation of the Book." In *Writing and Reading the Scroll of Isaiah*, edited by Craig C. Broyles and Craig A. Evans, 155–75. Leiden: Brill, 1997.

Block, Daniel I. "The Privilege of Calling: The Mosaic Paradigm for Missions (Deut 26:16–19)." *BibSac* 162 (2005) 348–405.

Bock, Darrell L. *Acts*. BECNT. Grand Rapids: Baker Academic, 2007.

———. "Kingdom through Covenant: A Review by Darrell Bock." *Gospel Coalition*, September 11, 2012. https://www.thegospelcoalition.org/reviews/kingdom-covenant-darrell-bock/.

Bock, Darrell L., and Mitch Glaser. *The People, the Land, and the Future of Israel*. Grand Rapids: Kregel, 2014.

Boda, Mark J. "Figuring the Future: The Prophets and Messiah." In *The Messiah in the Old and New Testaments*, edited by Stanley E. Porter, 35–74. Grand Rapids: Eerdmans, 2007.

Boers, Hendrikus. *What Is New Testament Theology?* Philadelphia: Fortress, 1979.

Boice, James Montgomery. *Psalms 42–106*. 2 vols. Grand Rapids: Baker, 1996.

Botterweck, G. Johannes, and Helmer Ringgren, eds. *Theological Dictionary of the Old Testament*. Translated by Geoffrey W. Bromiley. 14 vols. Grand Rapids: Eerdmans, 1974–2004.

Boyd, Steven W. "A Synchronic Analysis of the Medio-Passive-Reflexive in Biblical Hebrews Verbs." PhD diss., Hebrew Union College, 1993.

Brouwer, Douglas. *How to Become a Multicultural Church*. Grand Rapids: Eerdmans, 2017.

Bruce, F. F. *The Book of Acts*. Rev. ed. Grand Rapids: Eerdmans, 1988.

———. *The Epistle to the Galatians: A Commentary on the Greek Text*. NIGTC. Grand Rapids: Eerdmans, 1982.

———. *The Letter of Paul to the Romans: An Introduction and Commentary*. Grand Rapids: Eerdmans, 1989.

———. "Typology." In *NBD*, edited by D. R. W. Wood, 1214–15. 3rd ed. Downers Grove: InterVarsity, 1996.

Brueggemann, Walter. "The Book of Exodus." In *NIB*, edited by L. E. Keck, 1:677–981. Nashville: Abingdon, 1994.

———. *Isaiah 40–66*. Edited by Patrick D. Miller and David L. Bartlett. Louisville: Westminster John Knox, 1991.

Bruno, Christopher R. "'Jesus Is Our Jubilee' . . . But How? The OT Background and Lukan Fulfillment of the Ethics of Jubilee." *JETS* 53 (2010) 81–101.

Butterworth, Mike. "Zechariah." In *New Bible Commentary: 21st Century Edition*, edited by G. J. Wenham et al., 863–82. 4th ed. Leicester, UK: InterVarsity, 1994.

Caird, G. B., and L. D. Hurst. *New Testament Theology*. Oxford: Oxford University Press, 1994.

Carraway, George. *Christ Is God Over All: Romans 9:5 in the Context of Romans 9–11*. New York: T. & T. Clark, 2015.

Carroll, Mark D. "Blessing the Nations: Toward a Biblical Theology of Mission from Genesis." *BBR* 10 (2000) 18–35.

Carson, D. A. "Mystery and Fulfillment: Toward a More Comprehensive Paradigm of Paul's Understanding of the Old and the New." In *The Paradoxes of Paul*, edited by D. A. Carson et al., 393–436. Grand Rapids: Baker, 2004.

Cassuto, Umberto. *A Commentary on the Book of Genesis*. 3 vols. Jerusalem, IL: Magnes, 1984.

Chapman, Colin. *Whose Promised Land?* Tring, UK: Lion, 1983.

Charlesworth, James H. *The Messiah: Developments in Earliest Judaism and Christianity*. Minneapolis: Fortress, 1987.

Childs, Brevard S. *Biblical Theology in Crisis*. Philadelphia: Westminster, 1970.

———. *Biblical Theology of the Old and New Testaments: Theological Reflection on the Christian Bible*. Minneapolis: Augsburg Fortress, 1992.

———. *Isaiah: A Commentary*. OTL. Louisville: Westminster John Knox, 2001.

Chilton, Bruce. *Pure Kingdom: Jesus' Vision of God: Studying the Historical Jesus*. Grand Rapids: Eerdmans, 1996.

Chisholm, Robert B., Jr. "Evidence from Genesis." In *A Case for Premillennialism: A New Consensus*, edited by Donald K. Campbell and Jeffrey L. Townsend, 35–54. Chicago: Moody, 1992.

Christensen, Duane L. *Deuteronomy 21:10—34:12*. Rev. ed. WBC 6B. Dallas: Word, 2002.

———. "Nation." In *ABD*, edited by David Noel Freedman, 4:1037–49. New York: Doubleday, 1992.

Clark, David J., and Howard Hatton. *A Handbook on Zechariah*. UBSHS. New York: United Bible Societies, 2002.

Clements, Ronald E. "גּוֹי." In *TDOT*, edited by G. Johannes Botterweck and Helmer Ringgren, translated by John T. Willis, 2:426–33. 15 vols. Grand Rapids: Eerdmans, 1975.

———. "A Light to the Nations: A Central Theme of the Book of Isaiah." In *Forming Prophetic Literature: Essays on Isaiah and the Twelve in Honor of John D. W. Watts*, edited by James W. Watts and Paul R. House, 57–69. Sheffield: Sheffield Academic, 1996.

———. "The Timelessness of Nations." *Nations and Nationalism* 10 (2004) 35–37.

Clines, David J. A. *The Theme of the Pentateuch*. JSOTSup. Sheffield: Sheffield Academic, 2001.

Clowney, Edmund P. *The Church*. Contours of Christian Theology. Downers Grove: InterVarsity, 1995.

Cole, Robert L. *The Shape and Message of Book III*. JSOTSup 307. Sheffield: Sheffield Academic, 2000.

Collins, John J. *The Scepter and the Star: The Messiahs of the Dead Sea Scrolls and Other Ancient Literautre*. ABRL. New York: Doubleday, 1995.

Connor, Walker. *Ethnonational: The Quest for Understanding*. Princeton: Princeton University Press, 1994.

———. "A Nation Is a Nation, Is a State, Is an Ethnic Group, Is a . . ." In *Nationalism*, edited by John Hutchinson and Anthony Smith, 36–46. Oxford: Oxford University Press, 1994.

Conversi, Daniele. "Mapping the Field: Theories of Nationalism and the Ethnosymbolic Approach." In *Nationalism and Ethnosymbolism: History, Culture, and Ethnicity in the Formation of Nations*, edited by Athena S. Leoussi and Steven Grosby, 15–30. Edinburgh: Edinburgh University Press, 2007.

———. "Reassessing Theories of Nationalism: Nationalism as Boundary Maintenance and Creation." *Nationalism and Ethnic Politics* 1 (1995) 73–85.

Cosgrove, Charles H. "The Law Has Given Sarah No Children (Gal 4:21–30)." *NovT* 29 (1987) 219–35.

Cranfield, C. E. B. *The Epistle to the Romans*. ICC. Edinburgh: T. & T. Clark, 1979.

Craigie, Peter C. *Jeremiah 1–25*. WBC 26. Dallas: Word, 1998.

———. *Psalms 1–50*. WBC 19. 2nd ed. Nashville: Nelson Reference, 2004.

Creason, Stuart Alan. "Semantic Classes of Hebrew Verbs: A Study of Aktionsart in the Hebrews Verbal System." PhD diss., University of Chicago, 1996.

Croatta, Jose Severino. "La inclusion sociale en el program del Tercer Isaias: Exegesis de Isaiahs 56, 1–8 y 66, 17–24." *Revista Biblica* 60 (1998) 91–110.

———. "The 'Nations' in the Salvific Oracles of Isaiah." *VT* 55 (2005) 143–61.

Cruise, Charles E. "The 'Wealth of the Nations': A Study in the Intertextuality of Isaiah 60:5, 11." *JETS* 58 (2015) 283–97.

Culler, Jonathan. *Structuralist Poetics: Structuralism, Linguistics, and the Study of Literature*. Ithaca, NY: Cornell University Press, 1975.

Currid, John D. "Recognition and Use of Typology in Preaching." *RTR* 53 (1994) 115–29.

Dahood, Mitchell. *Psalms 51–100*. AB. Garden City: Doubleday, 1968.

Danker, Frederick William. "λαός." In BDAG, edited by Frederick William Danker, 586–87. Chicago: University of Chicago Press, 2000.

Davidson, Richard M. "The Eschatological Hermeneutic of Biblical Typology." *TheoRhēma* 6 (2011) 5–48.

———. *Typology in Scripture: A Study of Hermeneutical ΤΥΠΟΣ Structures*. Andrews University Seminary Doctoral Dissertation Series 2. Berrien Springs, MI: Andrews University Press, 1981.

Davies, G. I. "The Destiny of the Nations in the Book of Isaiah." In *The Book of Isaiah /
Le Livre d'Isaïe: Les oracles et leurs relectures; Unité et complexité de l'ouvrage*,
edited by Jacques Vermeylen, 93–120. Leuven: Peeters, 1989.

Davis, Ken. "Building a Biblical Theology of Ethnicity for Global Mission." *JMT* 7
(2003) 90–125.

De Boer, Martinus C. "Paul's Quotation of Isaiah 54.1 in Galatians." *NTS* 50 (2004)
370–89.

De Boer, P. A. H. *Second Isaiah's Message*. OtSt. 11. Leiden: Brill, 1956.

DeClaissé-Walford, et al. *Psalms*. NICOT. Grand Rapids: Eerdmans, 2014.

De Gruchy, John W. "A New Heaven and a New Earth: An Exposition of Isaiah 65:17–
25." *JTSA* 5 (1999) 65–74.

Dempster, Stephen. *Dominion and Dynasty: A Biblical Theology of the Hebrew Bible.*
Downers Grove: InterVarsity, 2003.

Deutsch, Karl W. *Nationalism and Social Communications*. 2nd ed. Cambridge: MIT
Press, 1966.

Deymz, Mark. *Building a Healthy Multi-Ethnic Church*. San Francisco: Wiley, 2007.

Dillmann, August. *Der Propphet Jesaia*. 5th ed. Leipzig: Hirzel, 1890.

Diprose, R. E. *Israel in the Development of Christian Thought*. Rome: Istituto Biblico
Evangelico Italiano, 2000.

Dobbs-Allsopp, F. W. "Biblical Hebrew Statives and Situation Aspect." *JSS* 45 (2000)
21–53.

Driver, G. R. "Isaiah 52:13—53:12: The Servant of the Lord." In *In Memoriam Paul
Kahle*, edited by M. Black and G. Fohrer, 90–105. Berlin: Verlag Alfre Topelmann,
1968.

Driver, S. R. *A Critical and Exegetical Commentary on Deuteronomy*. 3rd ed. ICC.
Edinburgh: T. & T. Clark, 1902.

Dumbrell, William J. *Covenant and Creation: A Theology of Old Testament Covenants.*
Nashville: Nelson, 1984.

———. *The End of the Beginning: Revelation 21–22 and the Old Testament*. Eugene, OR:
Wipf and Stock, 2001.

———. *The Faith of Israel: A Theological Survey of the Old Testament*. Grand Rapids:
Baker Academic, 2002.

———. "Paul and Salvation History in Romans 9:30—10:4." In *Out of Egypt*, edited by
Craig Bartholomew, 286–312. Grand Rapids: Paternoster/Zondervan, 2004.

———. "The Role of the Servant in Isaiah 40–55." *RTR* 38 (1989) 105–13.

———. *The Search for Order: Biblical Eschatology in Focus*. Eugene, OR: Wipf and
Stock, 2001.

Dunn, James D. *Romans 1–8*. WBC 38A. Dallas: Word, 2002.

———. *Romans 9–6*. WBC 38. Dallas: Word, 1988.

Durham, John I. *Exodus*. WBC 3. Dallas: Word, 1998.

Eaton, John H. *Kingship in the Psalms*. Studies in Biblical Theology. 2nd ed. Sheffield:
Sheffield Academic, 1986.

Eichrodt, Walther. *Theology of the Old Testament*. Vol. 1. Translated by John A. Baker.
OTL. London: SCM, 1961.

Ellis, E. Earle. "How the New Testament Uses the Old." In *New Testament Interpretation:
Essays on Principles and Methods*, edited by I. Howard Marshall, 199–219. Exeter,
UK: Paternoster, 1979.

Emerson, Michael O. *People of the Dream: Multiracial Congregations in the United States*. Princeton: Princeton University Press, 2006.

Engelsma, David J. "Herman Bavinck: The Man and His Theology." *PRTJ* 46 (2012) 3–43.

Enns, Peter. "Fuller Meaning, Single Goal: A Christotelic Approach to the New Testament Use of the Old in Its First-Century Interpretative Environment." In *Three Views on the New Testament Use of the Old Testament*, edited by Kenneth Berding and Jonathan Lunde, 167–217. Grand Rapids: Zondervan, 2008.

Erlandsson, Seth. "Exegetical Study of Isaiah 2:1–4—the Prophecy and Its Fulfillment." *WLQ* 104 (2007) 267–75.

Evans, Craig. "On the Unity and Parallel Structure of Isaiah." *VT* 38 (1988) 129–47.

Eze, Emmanuel Chukwudi. "The Color of Reason: The Idea of 'Race' in Kant's Anthropology." In *Postcolonial African Philosophy: A Critical Reader*, edited by Emmanuel Chukwudi Eze, 103–40. Cambridge, MA: Blackwell, 1997.

Fantuzzo, Christopher J. "True Israel's 'Mother and Brothers': Reflections on the Servants and Servanthood in Isaiah." In *Eyes to See, Ears to Hear: Essays in Memory of J. Alan Groves*, edited by Peter Enns et al., 106–24. Phillipsburg, NJ: Presbyterian and Reformed, 2010.

Fausset, A. R. *A Commentary, Critical and Explanatory, on the Old and New Testaments*. 2 vols. Hartford, CT: Scranton, 1878.

Feinberg, Charles. "The Place That Israel Holds in Prophetic Truth." *BibSac* 93 (1936) 449–55.

Feinberg, John S. *Continuity and Discontinuity: Perspectives on the Relationship between the Old and New Testaments*. Wheaton, IL: Crossway, 1988.

Fekkes, Jan. *Isaiah and the Prophetic Traditions in the Book of Revelation*. Sheffield: Sheffield Academic, 1994.

France, R. T. *Jesus and the Old Testament: His Application of Old Testament Passages to Himself and His Mission*. Vancouver: Regent College Publishing, 1998.

Frankel, David. *The Land of Canaan and the Destiny of Israel: Theologies of Territory in the Hebrew Bible*. Siphrut: Literature and Theology of the Hebrew Scriptures. Winona Lake, IN: Eisenbrauns, 2011.

Fritsch, Charles T. "Biblical Typology." *BibSac* 103 (1946) 293–305.

Fruchtenbaum, Arnold G. *Israelology: The Missing Link in Systematic Theology*. Tustin, CA: Ariel Ministries, 1994.

Fuller, Michael E. *The Restoration of Israel: Israel's Re-gathering and the Father of the Nations in Early and Jewish and Christian Perspectives*. Leiden: Brill, 2001.

Fullerton, Kemper. "Viewpoints in the Discussion of Isaiah's Hopes for the Future." *JBL* 41, "A Symposium on Eschatology" (1922) 1–101.

Fusco, Vittorio. "Luke-Acts and the Future of Israel." *NovT* 38 (1996) 1–17.

Gaffin, Richard. "Systematic and Biblical Theology." *WTJ* 38 (1976) 281–99.

Gellner, Ernest. *Nations and Natinoalism*. Ithaca, NY: Cornell University Press, 1983.

Gentry, Peter John, and Stephen J. Wellum. *Kingdom through Covenant: A Biblical-Theological Understanding of the Covenants*. Wheaton, IL: Crossway, 2012.

———. *Kingdom through Covenant: A Biblical-Theological Understanding of the Covenants*. 2nd ed. Wheaton, IL: Crossway, 2018.

———. "'Kingdom through Covenant' Authors Respond to Bock, Moo, Horton." Gospel Coalition, September 20, 2012. http://thegospelcoalition.org/article/gentry-and-wellum-respond-to-kingdom-through-covenant-reviews/.

George, Timothy. *Galatians*. NAC 30. Nashville: Broadman & Holman, 2001.

Gerleman, Gillis. "Der Gottesknecht bei Deuterojesaja." In *Studien zur alttestamentlichen Theologie*, 38–60. Franz Delitzsch Vorlesungen Neu Folge. Heidelberg: Verlag Lambert Schneider, 1980.

Gesenius, Wilhelm. *Gesenius' Hebrew and Chaldee Lexicon to the Old Testament Scriptures*. Translated by Samuel Prideaux Tregelles. New York: Wiley, 1888.

Giddens, Anthony. *Contemporary Critique of Historical Materialism*. Vol. 1. London: Macmillan, 1981.

Godet, Frédéric Louis. *Commentary on Romans*. 2 vols. Edinburgh: T. & T. Clark, 1881–82.

Goldingay, John. *Isaiah*. NIBC. Peabody: Hendrickson, 2001.

———. *Isaiah 56–66: A Critical and Exegetical Commentary*. ICC. New York: Bloomsbury / T. & T. Clark, 2014.

———. *Psalms 1–41*. Vol. 1. BCOTWP. Grand Rapids: Baker Academic, 2006.

———. *Psalms 42–89*. Vol. 3. BCOTWP. Grand Rapids: Baker, 2007.

———. *Psalms 90–150*. Vol. 3. BCOTWP. Grand Rapids: Baker, 2008.

———. *The Theology of the Book of Isaiah*. Downers Grove: InterVarsity, 2014.

Goldingay, John, and David Payne. *Isaiah 40–55*. Vol. 2. ICC. New York: T. & T. Clark, 2006.

Goldsworthy, Graeme. *According to Plan: The Unfolding Revelation of God in the Bible*. Grand Rapids: InterVarsity, 1991.

Goppelt, Leonhard. *Typos: The Typological Interpretation of the Old Testament in the New*. Translated by Donald H. Madvig. Grand Rapids: Eerdmans, 1982.

Gordis, Robert. "The Biblical Root *sdy-sd*." *JTS* 41 (1940) 34–43.

Gosse, Bernard. "Le quatrième livre du Psautier, Psaumes 90–106, comme rëponse àlëchec de la royautë Davidique." *Biblische Zeitschrift* 46 (2002) 239–52.

Grieve, Jerry A. "The Origin of Languages." *ATJ* 3 (1970) 14–20.

Grisanti, Michael A. "The Davidic Covenant." *MSJ* 10 (1999) 233–50.

———. "Israel's Mission to the Nations in Isaiah 40–55: An Update." *MSJ* 9 (2002) 39–61.

———. "The Relationship of Israel and the Nations in Isaiah 40–55." PhD diss., Dallas Theological Seminary, 1993.

Grogan, Geoffrey. *Psalms*. Two Horizons Old Testament Commentary. Grand Rapids: Eerdmans, 2008.

Grosby, Steven Elliot. *Biblical Ideas of Nationality: Ancient and Modern*. Winona Lake, IN: Eisenbrauns, 2002.

Grüneberg, Keith N. *Abraham, Blessing and the Nations: A Philogical and Exegetical Study of Genesis 12:3 in Its Narrative Context*. Berlin: de Gruyter, 2003.

Guibernau, Montserrat. "Anthony D. Smith on Nations and National Identity: A Critical Assessment." *Nations and Nationalism* 10 (2004) 125–41.

Gunkel, Hermann, and Joachim Begrich. *An Introduction to the Psalms: The Genres of the Religious Lyric of Israel*. Translated by James D. Nogalski. Mercer Library of Biblical Studies. Macon, GA: Mercer University Press, 1998.

Gunn, David M. "Deutero-Isaiah and the Flood." *JBL* 94 (1975) 493–508.

Gzella, Holger. "Voice in Classical Hebrews against Its Semitic Background." *Orientalia* 78 (2009) 292–325.

Hahn, Scott. *Kinship by Covenant: A Canonical Approach to the Fulfillment of God's Saving Promises*. AYBRL. New Haven: Yale University Press, 2009.

Hamilton, Victor P. *The Book of Genesis: Chapters 1–17*. NICOT. Grand Rapids: Eerdmans, 1990.

Hanson, Anthony Tyrell. *Studies in Paul's Technique and Theology*. Grand Rapids: Eerdmans, 1974.

Harmon, Matthew S. "Allegory, Typology, or Something Else? Revisiting Galatians 4:21—5:1." In *Studies in Paul's Letters: A Festschrift for Douglas J. Moo*, edited by Jay E. Smith and Matthew Harmon, 144–58. Grand Rapids: Zondervan, 2014.

Hasel, Gerhard. F. "The Remnant: The History and Theology of the Remnant Idea from Genesis to Isaiah." Andrews University Monographs V. Berrien Springs, MI: Andrews University Press, 1972.

Hays, Daniel J. *From Every People and Nation: A Biblical Theology of Race*. Downers Grove: InterVarsity, 2003.

Hays, Richard B. *Echoes of Scripture in the Letters of Paul*. New Haven: Yale University Press, 1989.

Hayes, John H., and Stuart A. Irvine. *Isaiah the Eighth Century Prophet*. Nashville: Abingdon, 1987.

Hendrickson, William. *Exposition of Paul's Epistle to the Romans*. BNTC. Grand Rapids: Baker, 1953–2001.

Hertz, Frederick. *Nationality in History and Politics*. London: Kegan Paul, Trench, Trubner, 1944.

Hoehner, Harold W. "Israel in Romans 9–11." In *Israel, the Land, and the People*, edited by H. Wayne House, 145–69. Grand Rapids: Kregel, 1998.

Holladay, William L. *Jeremiah: A Commentary on the book of the Prophet Jeremiah (Chapters 1–25)*. Hermeneia. Philadelphia: Fortress, 1986.

Hooker, Joy. *Isaiah and Imperial Context: The Book Of Isaiah in the Times of the Empire*. Edited by Andrew T. Abernethy et al. Eugene, OR: Wipf and Stock, 2013.

Horton, Michael S. *The Christian Faith: A Systematic Theology for Pilgrims on the Way*. Grand Rapids: Zondervan, 2011.

Hoskins, Paul M. *Jesus as the Fulfillment of the Temple in the Gospel of John*. Paternoster Biblical Monographs. Eugene, OR: Wipf and Stock, 2006.

Howe, E. Margaret. "Nations." In *Baker Encyclopedia of the Bible*, edited by Walter A. Elwell and Barry J. Beitzel, 2:1527–30. 2 vols. Grand Rapids: Baker, 1988.

Huey, F. B. *Jeremiah, Lamentations*. NAC 16. Nashville: Broadman & Holman, 1993.

Hugenberger, G. P. "Introductory Notes on Typology." In *The Right Doctrine from the Wrong Texts?*, edited by G. K. Beale, 331–41.Grand Rapids: Baker, 1994.

Irons, Charles Lee. "Prophetic Idiom." http://www.upper-register.com/papers/prophetic-idiom.pdf/.

Isaacs, Elcanon. "The Origin and Nature of Parallelism." *AJSLL* 35 (1919) 113–27.

Jacobson, Thorkild. "The Assumed Conflict between Sumerians and Semites in Early Mesopotamian History." *JAOS* 59 (1939) 485–95.

James, Steven L. *New Creation and the Land: A Survey of Contemporary Perspectives*. Eugene, OR: Wipf & Stock, 2017.

Jamieson, Robert. "Genesis." In *A Commentary, Critical, and Explanatory on the Old and New Testaments*, edited by Robert Jamieson et al., 17–47. Peabody: Hendrickson, 1997.

Janzen, Gerald J. "On the Moral Nature of God's Power: Yahweh and the Sea in Job and Deutero-Isaiah." *CBQ* 56 (1994) 458–78.

Jenni, Ernst. *Studien zur Sprachwelt des Alten Tesaments II*. Stuttgart: Kohlhammer, 2005.

Jones, Christopher M. "'The Wealth of Nations Shall Come to You': Light, Tribute, and Implacement in Isaiah 60." *VT* 64 (2014) 611–22.

Kaiser, Otto. *Isaiah 1–12*. Translated by John Bowden. 2nd ed. Philadelphia: Westminster, 1981.

Kaiser, Walter C., Jr. "An Assessment of 'Replacement Theology': The Relationship Between the Israel of the Abrahamic-Davidic Covenant and the Christian Church." *Mishkan* 21 (1994) 9–20.

———. "The Blessing of David: The Charter for Humanity." In *The Law and the Prophets: Old Testament Studies Prepared in Honor of Oswald Thompson Allis*, edited by John H. Skilton, 298–318. Philadelphia: Presbyterian and Reformed, 1974.

———. *Mission in the Old Testament: Israel as a Light to the Nations*. Grand Rapids: Baker, 2000.

Kaminsky, Joel, and Anne Stewart. "God of All the World: Universalism and Developing Monotheism in Isaiah 40–66." *HTR* 99 (2006) 139–63.

Kebede, Aschalew. "How Can the Concept of Universalism and Nationalism in the Book of Isaiah Be Reconciled?" PhD diss., New Orleans Baptist Theological Seminary, 2002.

Keener, Craig S. *Acts: An Exegetical Commentary*. Vol. 2. Grand Rapids: Baker Academic, 2013.

Kidner, Derek. *Psalms 1–72*. Vol. 1 of *Psalms*. TOTC. Downers Grove: InterVarsity, 1973.

Klein, George L. *Zechariah*. NAC 21B. Nashville: Broadman & Holman, 2008.

Klein, William W. *The New Chosen People: A Corporate View of Election*. Grand Rapids: Zondervan, 1990.

Klostermann, August. *Deuterojesaja, Hebraisch und Deutsch, mit Anmerkungen*. Munich: Beck, 1893.

Koehler, Ludwig, and Walter Baumgartner. "עַם." In *HALOT*, edited by M. E. J. Richardson, translated by Benedikt Hartmann, 2:837–39. 5 vols. Leiden: Brill, 2000.

Köstenberger, Andreas J. *New Dictionary of Biblical Theology*. Edited by T. Desmond Alexander and Brian S. Rosner. Downers Grove: InterVarsity, 2000.

Köstenberger, Andreas J., and Peter T. O'Brien. *Salvation to the Ends of the Earth: A Biblical Theology of Mission*. NSBT 11. Downers Grove: InterVarsity, 2001.

Kohn, Hans. *American Nationalism: An Interpretive Essay*. New York: Macmillan, 1958.

Konradt, Matthias. *Israel, Church, and the Gentiles in the Gospel of Matthew*. Waco, TX: Baylor University Press, 2014.

Kraus, Hans-Joachim. *Psalms 1–59: A Commentary*. CC. Translated by Hilton C. Oswald. Minneapolis: Augsburg, 1988.

Kugel, James. *The Idea of Biblical Poetry: Parallelism and Its History*. New Haven: Yale University Press, 1981.

Kuyper, Abraham. *Encyclopedia of Sacred Theology: Its Principles*. New York: Scriber, 1898.

Ladd, George Eldon. *Jesus and the Kingdom*. New York: Harper & Row, 1964.

———. *The Presence of the Future: The Eschatology of Biblical Realism*. Grand Rapids: Eerdmans, 1974.

———. *A Theology of the New Testament.* Grand Rapids: Eerdmans, 1974.

Lampe, Geoffrey H. "Typological Exegesis." *Theology* 56 (1953) 201–8.

Lee, Chee-Chiew. "גּוֹיִם in Genesis 35:11 and the Abrahamic Promise of Blessings for the Nations." *JETS* 52 (2009) 467–82.

Leoussi, Athena S., et al. *The Call of the Homeland: Diaspora Nationalisms, Past and Present.* IJS Studies in Judaica Series 9. Boston: Brill, 2010.

Leoussi, Athena S., and Steven Grosby. *Nationalism and Ethnosymbolism: History, Culture, and Ethnicity in the Formation of Nations.* Edinburgh: Edinburgh University Press, 2007.

Levenson, Jon D. *Creation and the Persistence of Evil.* San Francisco: Harper & Row, 1988.

Lindsey, F. Duane. "Zechariah." In *The Bible Knowledge Commentary: An Exposition of the Scriptures,* edited by John F. Walvoord et al., 1545–72. Wheaton, IL: Victor, 1983.

Lipinski, Edward. "עַם." In *TDOT,* edited by G. Johannes Botterweck and Helmer Ringgren, translated by John T. Willis, 11:163–77. 15 vols. Grand Rapids: Eerdmans, 1975.

Liverani, Mario. "Nationality and Political Identity." In *ABD,* edited by David Noel Freedman, 1031–37. London: Doubleday, 1992.

Lohfink, Norbert. "The Concept of 'Covenant' in Biblical Theology." In *The God of Israel and the Nations: Studies in Isaiah and the Psalms,* translated by Everett R. Kalin, 11–32. Collegeville: Liturgical, 2000.

———. "Covenant and Torah in the Pilgrimage of the Nations: The Book of Isaiah and Psalm 25." In *The God of Israel and the Nations: Studies in Isaiah and the Psalms,* translated by Everett R. Kalin, 33–84. Collegeville: Liturgical, 2000.

———. *Das Jüdische am Christentum: Die verlorene Dimension.* Freiburg, Germany: Herder, 1987.

———. "'Israel' in Jesus 49:3." In *Wort, Lied und Gottespruch: Beitrage zu psalmen und Propheten,* edited by J. Schreiner, 217–29. Echter: Katholisches Bibelwerk, 1972.

Lohfink, Norbert, and Erich Zenger. *The God of Israel and the Nations: Studies in isaiah and the Psalms.* Translated by Everett R. Kalin. Collegeville: Liturgical, 2000.

Longenecker, Richard N. *Galatians.* WBC 41. Dallas: Word, 2002.

Longman, Tremper, III. "The Messiah: Explorations in the Law and Writings." In *The Messiah in the Old and New Testaments,* edited by Stanley E. Porter, 13–34. Grand Rapids: Eerdmans, 2007.

Lowth, Robert. *Isaiah: A New Translation with a Preliminary Dissertation and Notes.* London: Tegg, 1848.

Lundström, Gösta. *Kingdom of God in the Teaching of Jesus.* Richmond, VA: John Knox, 1963.

MacKay, John. *Isaiah.* Vol. 2, *Chapters 40–66.* EP Study Commentary. Darlington, UK: Evangelical, 2009.

MacRae, Allan. "Paul's Use of Isaiah 65:1." In *The Law and the Prophets: Old Testament Studies Prepared in Honor of Oswald Thompson Allis,* edited by J. H. Skilton, 369–76. Philadelphia: Presbyterian and Reformed, 1974.

Marcus, Joel. "Mark and Isaiah." In *Fortunate the Eyes that See,* edited by David Noel Freedman and A. B. Beck, 449–66. Grand Rapids: Eerdmans, 1995.

———. *The Way of the Lord: Christological Exegesis of the Old Testament in the Gospel of Mark.* Louisville: Westminster John Knox, 1992.

Marshall, I. Howard. "An Assessment of Recent Developments." In *It Is Written: Scripture Citing Scripture; Essays in Honor of Barnabas Lindars*, edited by D. A. Carson and H. G. M. Williamson, 1–21. Cambridge: Cambridge University Press, 1988.

Mathews, K. A. *Genesis 1–11:26*. NAC 1A. Nashville: Broadman & Holman, 1995.

Maur, Christian. "ῥίζα." In *TDNT*, edited by Gerhard Kittel and Gerhard Friedrich, translated by Geoffrey W. Bromiley, 6:987–89. Grand Rapids: Eerdmans, 1964.

McCarthy, D. J. "'Creation' Motifs in Ancient Hebrew Poetry." *CBQ* 29 (1967) 393–406.

McComiskey, Thomas Edward. *The Minor Prophets: An Exegetical and Expository Commentary*. Edited by Thomas McComiskey. Grand Rapids: Baker, 1998.

McDougall, Donald Gordon. "Revelation 21:9 to 22:5: Millennium or Eternal State?" ThM thesis, Talbot Theological Seminary, 1969.

McIntosh, Gary L. *Being the Church in a Multi-ethnic Community: Why It Matters and How It Works*. Indianapolis: Wesleyan, 2012.

McIntosh, John A. "Mission Dei." In *Evangelical Dictionary of World Mission*, edited by A. Scott Moreau, 631–33. Grand Rapids: Baker Academic, 2000.

McKenzie, John L. *Second Isaiah*. AB. Garden City: Doubleday, 1968.

McNicol, Allan J. *The Conversion of the Nations in Revelation*. New York: T. & T. Clark, 2011.

Meek, James A. *The Gentile Missoin in Old Testament Citations in Acts: Text, Hermeneutic and Purpose*. Library of New Testament Studies 385. New York: T. & T. Clark, 2008.

Melugin, Roy F. *The Formation of Isaiah 40–55*. Beihefte zur Zeitschrift fur die alttestamentliche Wissenschaft 141. Berlin: De Gruyter, 1976.

———. "Israel and the Nations in Isaiah 40–55." In *Problems in Biblical Theology: Essays in Honor of Rolf Knierim*, edited by Henry T. C. Sun and Keith L. Eades, 249–64. Grand Rapids: Eerdmans, 1997.

Merkle, Benjamin. "A Typological Non-Future-Mass-Conversion View." In *Three Views on Israel and the Church: Perspectives on Romans 9–11*, edited by Jared Compton and Andrew David Naselli, 161–208. Grand Rapids: Kregel Academic, 2018.

Merrill, Eugene H. *Deuteronomy*. NAC. Nashville: Broadman & Holman, 1994.

———. *Everlasting Dominion: A Theology of the Old Testament*. Nashville: Broadman & Holman, 2006.

———. *An Exegetical Commentary: Haggai, Zechariah, Malachi*. Chicago: Moody, 1994.

Merrill, Eugene, and Roy B. Zuck. *A Biblical Theology of the Old Testament*. Chicago: Moody, 1991.

Mettinger, Tryggve. *In Search of God: The Meaning and Message of the Everlasting Names*. Minneapolis: Fortress, 2005.

Meyer, Jason C. *The End of the Law: Mosaic Covenant in Pauline Theology*. NACBT. Nashville: Broadman & Holman, 2009.

Middleton, J. Richard. *A New Heaven and a New Earth: Reclaiming Biblical Eschatology*. Grand Rapids: Baker Academic, 2014.

Moessner, David P., et al. *Paul and the Heritage of Israel: Luke's Narrative Claim upon Paul and Israel's Legacy*. New York: T. & T. Clark, 2012.

Moltmann, Jürgen. *Theology of Hope: On the Ground and the Implications of a Christian Eschatology*. London: SCM, 1967.

Moo, Douglas J. "Creation and New Creation." In *BBR* 20 (2010) 39–60.

———. *The Epistle to the Romans*. NICNT. Grand Rapids: Eerdmans, 1996.

―――. *Galatians.* BECNT. Grand Rapids: Baker, 2013.

―――. "Kingdom through Covenant: A Review by Douglas Moo." *Gospel Coalition*, September 12, 2012. http://thegospelcoalition.org/article/kingdom-through-covenant-a-reivew-by-douglas-moo/.

Moore, Thomas S. "The Lucan Great Commission and the Isaianic Servant." *BibSac* 154 (1997) 47–60.

Morgenstern, Julian. "The Suffering Servant—a New Solution." *VT* 11 (1961) 406–31.

Motyer, Alec J. *Isaiah: An Introduction and Commentary.* TOTC. Downers Grove: InterVarsity, 2009.

Mowinckel, Sigmund. *He That Cometh.* Oxford: Oxford University Press, 1958.

Muilenburg, James. "Introduction to and Exegesis of the Book of Isaiah, Chapters 40–66." In *The Interpreter's Bible*, edited by George A. Buttrick, 5:381–419. New York: Abingdon, 1955.

Myers, Allen C. *The Eerdmans Bible Dictionary.* Grand Rapids: Eerdmans, 1987.

Nelson, Richard D. *Deuteronomy: A Commentary.* Louisville: Westminster John Knox, 2002.

Niccaci, Alviero. "Analyzing Biblical Hebrew Poetry." *JSOT* 74 (1997) 77–93.

Ninow, Friedbert. *Indicators of Typology within the Old Testament: The Exodus Motif.* Friedensauer Schriftenreihe: Reihe I, Theologie, Band 4. Berlin: Lang, 2001.

Noisette, Christiane. "Abraham ou le chemin de la foi." *Theophilyon* 16 (2011) 149–69.

Noonan, Benjamin J. "Abraham, Blessing, and the Nations: A Reexamination of the Niphal and Hitpael of Brk in the Patriarchal Narratives." *Hebrew Studies* 51 (2010) 73–93.

North, Christopher R. *Isaiah 40–55: Introduction and Commetnary.* Torch Bible Commentaries. London: SCM Press, 1952.

Noth, Martin. "Gott, König, Volk im Alten Testament." *ZTK* 47 (1950) 157–91.

Odendall, Dirk H. *The Eschatological Expectation of Isaiah 40–66 with Special Refernce to Israel and the Nations.* Nutley, NJ: Presbyterian and Reformed, 1970.

Ollenburger, Ben. *Zion, the City of the Great King: A Theological Symbol of the Jerusalem Cult.* Sheffield: JSOT, 1987.

Oswalt, John N. *The Book of Isaiah: Chapters 1–39.* NICOT. Grand Rapids: Eerdmans, 1986.

―――. *The Book of Isaiah: Chapters 40–66.* NICOT. Grand Rapids: Eerdmans, 1998.

―――. *Isaiah.* NIVAC. Grand Rapids: Zondervan, 2003.

Pao, David W. *Acts and the Isaianic New Exodus.* BSL. Grand Rapids: Baker Academic, 2002.

Parker, Brent Evan. "The Israel-Christ-Church Typological Pattern: A Theological Critique of Covenant and Dispensational Theologies." PhD diss., Southern Baptist Theological Seminary, 2017.

Pedersen, Johannes. *Israel: Its Life and Culture.* London: Oxford University Press, 1920.

Penny, Robert L. *The Hope Fulfilled: Essay in Honor of O. Palmer Robertson.* Phillipsburg, NJ: Presbyterian and Reformed, 2008.

Perrin, Nicholas. "Messianism in the Narrative Frame of Ecclesiastes?" *Revue Biblique* 108 (2001) 37–60.

Perrin, Norman. *The Kingdom of God in the Teaching of Jesus.* Philadelphia: Westminster, 1963.

Pillai, C. A. Joachim. *Apostlic Interpretation of History: A Commentary on Acts 13:16–41.* Hicksville, NY: Exposition, 1980.

Piper, John. *Bloodlines: Race, Cross, and the Christian.* Wheaton, IL: Crossway, 2011.

Polhill, John B. *Acts*. NAC 26. Nashville: Broadman & Holman, 1992.

Poulsen, Frederik. *God, His Servant, and the Nations in Isaiah 42:1–9*. Tübingen: Mohr Siebeck, 2014.

Rad, Gerhard von. *Genesis*. Rev. ed. Philadelphia: Westminster, 1972.

———. *Old Testament Theology*. 2 vols. Translated by D. M. G. Stalker. New York: Harper and Row, 1962–65.

———. "Typological Interpretation of the Old Testament." Translated by John Bright. *Intrepretation* 15 (1961) 174–92.

Ramsdell, T. J. "The Missionary Future in the Book of Isaiah." *Biblical World* 10 (1897) 190–97.

Rendtorff, Rolf. "'Covenant' as a Structuring Concept in Genesis and Exodus." *JBL* 108 (1989) 385–93.

———. *The Covenant Formula: An Exegetical and Theological Investigation*. Translated by Margaret Khol. OTS. Edinburgh: T. & T. Clark, 1998.

Reyburn, William David, and Euan M. Fry. *A Handbook on Genesis*. UBSHS. New York: United Bible Societies, 1997.

Ribbens, Benjamin J. "Typology of Types: Typology in Dialogue." *JTI* 5 (2011) 81–95.

Ridderbos, Herman. *The Coming of the Kingdom*. Translated by Raymond O. Zorn. Phillipsburg, NJ: Presbyterian and Reformed, 1975.

Robertson, O. Palmer. *The Christ and the Covenants*. Phillipsburg, NJ: Presbyterian and Reformed, 1980.

———. *The Israel of God: Yesterday, Today, and Tomorrow*. Phillipsburg, NJ: Presbyterian and Reformed, 2000.

Roehers, Walter R. "The Typological Use of the Old Testament in the New Testament." *Concordia Journal* 10 (1984) 204–16.

Rogers, Jeffrey S. "Table of Nations." In *Eerdmans Dictionary of the Bible*, edited by David Noel Freedman, 1271–72. Grand Rapids: Eerdmans, 2000.

Routledge, Robin. "The Exodus and Biblical Theology." In *Reverberations of the Exodus in Scripture*, edited by R. Michael Fox, 187–210. Eugene, OR: Pickwick, 2014.

Ryan, William F. J. "The Church as the Servant of God in Acts." *Scripture* 15 (1963) 110–15.

Rydelnik, Michael. "The Jewish People: Evidence for the Truth of Scripture." In *The People, the Land, and the Future of Israel: Israel and the Jewish People in the Plan of God*, edited by Darrell L. Bock and Mitch Glaser, 253–68. Grand Rapids: Kregel, 2014.

Sandys-Wunch, John, and Laurence Eldredge. "J. P. Gabler and the Distinction between Biblical and Dogmatic Theology: Translation, Commentary, and Discussion of His Originality." *SJT* 33 (1940) 133–58.

Sasson, J. M. "On Choosing Models for Recreating Israelites Pre-Monarchic History." *JSOT* 21 (1981) 3–24.

Saucy, Mark. *The Kingdom of God in the Teaching of Jesus in 20th Century Theology*. Dallas: Word, 1997.

Saucy, Robert L. *The Case for Progressive Dispensationalism: The Interface between Dispensational & Nondispensational Theology*. Grand Rapids: Zondervan, 1993.

Schmidt, Karl Ludwig. "εθνος." In *TDNT*, edited by Gerhard Kittell, Geoffrey W. Bromiley and Gerhard Friedrich, 2:369. Grand Rapids: Eerdmans, 1964.

Schnabel, Eckhard J. *Acts: Exegetical Commentary on the New Testament*. Edited by Clinton E. Arnold. Grand Rapids: Zondervan, 2012.

Schnackenburg, Rudolf. *God's Rule and Kingdom*. New York: Herder & Herder, 1968.

Schökel, Luis Alonso. "Isaiah." In *The Literary Guide to the Bible*, edited by Robert Alter and Rank Kermode, 165–83. Cambridge: Harvard University Press, 1987.

Schreiner, Thomas R. *Romans*. BECNT 6. Grand Rapids: Baker, 1998.

Schultz, Richard L. "Intertextuality, Canon, and Undecidability: Understand Isaiah's 'New Heavens and the New Earth' (Isaiah 65:17–25)." *BBR* 20 (2010) 19–38.

Schweizer, Eduard. "The Concept of the Davidic 'Son of God' in Acts and Its Old Testament Background." In *Studies in Luke-Acts: Essays in Honor of Paul Schubert*, edited by Leader E. Keck and J. Louis Martyn, 186–93. Nashville: Abingdon, 1966.

Scobie, Charles H. H. *The Ways of Our God*. Grand Rapids: Eerdmans, 2003.

Scott, James M. *Paul and the Nations: The Old Testament and Jewish Background of Paul's Mission to the Nations with Special Reference to the Destination of Galatians*. WUNT 84. Tübingen: Mohr, 1995.

Scott, J. Julius, Jr. "Gentiles and the Ministry of Jesus: Further Observations on Matt 10:5–6; 15:21–28." *JETS* 33 (1990) 160–69.

Sherwood, Aaron. *Paul and the Restoration of Humanity in Light of Ancient Jewish Traditions*. Boston: Brill, 2013.

Silva, Moisés. "Galatians." In *Commentary on the New Testament on the Use of the Old Testament*, edited by G. K. Beale and D. A. Carson, 785–813. Grand Rapids: Baker, 2007.

Simon, Ulrich E. "Konig Cyrus und die Typologie." *Judaica* 11 (1955) 83–89.

Skilton, John H. *The Law and the Prophets: Old Testament Studies Prepared in Honor of Oswald Thompson Allis*. Philadelphia: Presbyterian and Reformed, 1974.

Smelik, K. A. D. "Distortion of Old Testament Prophecy: The Purpose of Isaiah XXXVI-XXXVII." In *Crises and Perspectives*, edited by A. S. van der Woude, 70–93. Leiden: OTS, 1986.

Smith, Anthony D. "Basic Themes of Ethno-Symbolism." In *Ethno-Symbolism and Nationalism: A Cultural Approach*, 23–40. Oxford: Routledge Taylor and Francis Group, 2009.

———. *Chosen Peoples: Sacred Sources of National Identity*. Oxford: Oxford University Press, 2004.

———. "Chosen Peoples: Why Ethnic Groups Survive." *Ethnic and Racial Studies* 15 (1992) 436–56.

———. *The Ethnic Origins of Nations*. New York: Blackwell, 1986.

———. *Ethno-symbolism and Nationalism: A Cultural Approach*. Oxford: Routledge Taylor and Francis Group, 2009.

———. *Nation and Nationalism in a Global Era*. Cambridge: Polity, 1995.

———. *The Nation in History: Historiographical Debates about Ethnicty and Nationalism*. Cambridge: Polity, 2000.

———. *Nationalism*. Edited by John Hutchinson and Anthony D. Smith. Oxford: Oxford University Press, 1994.

Smith, Daniel L. *The Religion of the Landless: The Social Context of the Babylonian Exile*. Bloomington, IN: Meyer Stone, 1989.

Smith, Gary V. *Isaiah 1–39*. NAC 15A. Nashville: Broadman & Holman, 2009.

———. *Isaiah 40–66*. NAC 15B. Nashville: Broadman & Holman, 2009.

Smith, Ralph L. *Micah-Malachi*. WBC 32. Dallas: Word, 2002.

Snaith, Norman H. *Isaiah 40–66: A Study of the Teaching of the Second Isaiah and Its Consequences*. Studies on the Second Part of the Book of Isaiah. VTSup 14. Leiden: Brill, 1967.

Snyder, Louis. *The Meaning of Nationalism*. New Brunswick, NJ: Rutgers University Press, 1954.

Soulen, Kendall. *The God of Israel and Christian Theology*. Minneapolis: Fortress, 1996.

Speiser, E. A. *Genesis*. AB. Garden City: Doubleday, 1964.

———. "People and Nation of Israel." *JBL* 79 (1960) 157–63.

Stalin, Joseph. "The Nation." In *Nationalism*, edited by John Hutchinson and Anthony D. Smith, 18–20. Oxford: Oxford University Press, 1994.

Steinmann, Jean. *Le livre de la consolation d'Israel et les prophetes du retour de l'exil*. LD 28. Paris: Cerf, 1960.

Stone, John, and Polly Rizova. "The Ethnic Enigma: Nationalism, Racism and Globalization." In *Nationalism and Ethnosymbolism: History, Culture, and Ethnicity in the Formation of Nations*, edited by Athena S. Leoussi and Steven Grosby, 31–41. Edinburg: Edinburgh University Press, 2007.

Stuart, Douglas K. *Exodus*. NAC 2. Nashville: Broadman & Holman, 2006.

Swartley, William M. *Israel's Scripture Traditions and the Synoptic Gospels: Story Shaping Story*. Peabody: Hendrickson, 1994.

Sweeney, Marvin A. "Eschatology in the Book of Isaiah." In *The Book of Isaiah: Enduring Questions Answered Anew; Essays Honoring Joseph Blenkinsopp and His Contribution to the Study of Isaiah*, edited by R. J. Bautch and J. T. Hibbard, 179–95. Grand Rapids: Eerdmans, 2014.

Tate, Marvin E. *Psalms 51–100*. WBC 20. Dallas: Word, 2002.

Thompson, Alan J. *The Acts of the Risen Lord Jesus: Luke's Account of God's Unfolding Plan*. NSBT 27. Downers Grove: InterVarsity, 2011.

———. *One Lord, One People: The Unity of the Church in Acts in Its Literary Setting*. New York: T. & T. Clark, 2008.

Trimm, Charlie. "Did YHWH Condemn the Nations When He Elected Israel? YHWH's Disposition toward Non-Israelites in the Torah." *JETS* 55 (2012) 521–36.

Tsumura, David Toshio. "Verbal Grammar of Parallelism in Hebrew Poetry." *JBL* 128 (2009) 167–81.

Uehlinger, Christoph. "'Zeichne eine Stadt ... und belagere sie!' Bild und Wort in einer Zeichenhandlung Ezechiels gegen Jerusalem (Ez 4f)." In *Jerusalem Texte— Bilder—Steien. Zum 100. Geburtstag von hildi und Othmar Keel-Leu*, edited by Max Küchler and Christoph Uehlinger, 112–91. Novum Testamentum et Orbis Antiquus 6. Göttingen: Vandenhoeck & Ruprecht, 1987.

Van Groningen, G. "גּוֹי." In *TWOT*, edited by R. Laird Harris et al., 1:153–54. 2 vols. Chicago: Moody, 1980.

———. *Messianic Revelation in the Old Testament*. Grand Rapids: Baker, 1990.

Van Winkle, Dwight Wayne. "The Relationship of the Nations to Yahweh and to Israel in Isaiah XL–LV." *VT* 35 (1985) 446–58.

Vasholz, Robert. "The Character of Israel's Future in Light of the Abrahamic and Mosaic Covenants." *TrinJ* 25 (2004) 37–59.

Vlach, Michael J. *Has the Church Replaced Israel? A Theological Evaluation*. Nashville: Broadman & Holman, 2010.

———. "Have They Found a Better Way? An Analysis of Gentry and Wellum's *Kingdom Through Covenant*." *MSJ* 24 (2013) 10–12.

———. "A Non-Typological Future-Mass-Conversion View." In *Three Views on Israel and the Church: Perspectives on Romans 9–11*, edited by Jared Compton and Andrew David Naselli, 21–74. Grand Rapids: Kregel Academic, 2018.

―――. "What Does Christ as 'True Israel' Mean for the Nation Israel? A Critique of the Non-Dispensational Understanding." *MSJ* 21 (2012) 43–54.

Vos, Geerhardus. *Biblical Theology: Old and New Testaments*. Grand Rapids: Eerdmans, 1948.

Wagner, J. Ross. "The Heralds of Isaiah and Mission of Paul: An Investigation of Paul's Use of Isaiah 51–55 in Romans." In *Jesus and the Suffering Servant: Isaiah 53 and Christian Origins*, edited by William H. Bellinger Jr. and William R. Farmer, 193–222. Harrisburg, PA: Trinity, 1998.

―――. *Heralds of the Good News: Isaiah and Paul "in Concert" in the Letter to the Romans*. NovTSup 101. Leiden: Brill, 2003.

Wallace, Robert E. *The Narrative Effect of Book IV of the Hebrew Psalter*. SBL. New York: Lang, 2007.

Walter, Nikolaus. "εθνος." In *EDNT*, edited by Horst Robert Balz and Gerhard Schneider, 1:381–83. 3 vols. Grand Rapids: Eerdmans, 1990.

Waltke, Bruce K., and M. O'Connor. *Introduction to Biblical Hebrew Syntax*. Winona Lake, IN: Eisenbrauns, 1990.

Ware, Bruce. *God's Greater Glory*. Wheaton, IL: Crossway, 2004.

Watts, John D. W. *Isaiah 1–33*. WBC 24. Rev. ed. Nashville: Nelson, 2005.

―――. *Isaiah 34–66*. WBC 25. Rev. ed. Nashville: Nelson, 2005.

Watts, Rikk. "Echoes from the Past: Israel's Ancient Traditions and the Destiny of the Nations in Isaiah 40–55." *JSOT* 28 (2004) 481–508.

―――. *Isaiah's New Exodus and Mark: Isaiah's New Exodus in Mark*. BSL. Grand Rapids: Baker, 2000.

Webb, Barry G. *The Message of Isaiah: On Eagle's Wings*. Bible Speaks Today. Downers Grove: InterVarsity, 1996.

Weber, Max. *Ancient Judaism*. Translated by Hans H. Gerth and Don Martindale. Glencoe, IL: Free, 1952.

―――. "The Nation." In *Nationalism*, edited by John Hutchinson and Anthony D. Smith, 21–25. Oxford: Oxford University Press, 1994.

Weiser, Artur. *Introduction to the Old Testament*. Translated by D. Barton. London: Darton, Longman & Todd, 1961.

Weiss, Johannes. *Die Predigt Jesu vom Reiche Gottes*. Göttingen: Vandenhoeck und Ruprecht, 1892.

Wellhausen, Julius. "Israel." In *Prolegomena to the History of Anicent Israel*, 446–584. Gloucester, MA: Peter Smith, 1881; reprint 1973.

Wenham, Gordon J. *Exploring the Old Testament: A Guide to the Pentateuch*. Vol. 1. Downers Grove: InterVarsity, 2003.

―――. *Genesis 1–15*. WBC 1. Dallas: Word, 2002.

Westermann, Claus. *Genesis 1–11*. Translated by John J. Scullion. Minneapolis: Fortress, 1994.

―――. *Genesis 12–36: A Continental Commentary*. CC. Translated by John J. Scullion. Minneapolis: Fortress, 1995.

―――. *Isaiah 40–66*. OTL. Philadelphia: Westminster, 1969.

White, Marsha. "Uriah." In *Eerdmans Dictionary of the Bible*, edited by David Noel Freedman et al., 1348. Grand Rapids: Eerdmans, 2000.

Whybray, Norman R. *Isaiah 40–66*. New Century Bible. London: Oliphants, 1978; reprint, Grand Rapids: Eerdmans, 1987.

Wilderberger, Hans. *Isaiah: A Continental Commentary*. 3 vols. Minneapolis: Fortress, 1991–2002.

Williamson, H. G. M. "The Concept of Israel in Transition." In *The World of Ancient Israel: Sociological, Anthropological and Political Perspectives*, edited by R. Clements, 141–62. Cambridge: Cambridge University Press, 1989.

———. *Variations on a Theme: King, Messiah, and Servant in the Book of Isaiah*. Carlisle, UK: Paternoster, 1998.

Williamson, Paul R. *Sealed with an Oath: Covenant in God's Unfolding Purpose*. NSBT. Downers Grove: InterVarsity, 2007.

Wilson, Gerald Henry. *The Editing of the Hebrew Psalter*. SBL Dissertation series. Chico, CA: Scholars, 1985.

———. *Psalms*. NIVAC 1. Grand Rapids: Zondervan, 2002.

Wisdom, Jeffrey. *Blessing for the Nations and the Curse of the Law: Paul's Citation of Genesis and Deuteronomy in Galatians 3:8-10*. Tübingen: Mohr Siebeck, 2001.

Wolff, Hans Walter. "The Hermeneutics of the Old Testament." In *Essays on Old Testament Hermeneutics*, edited by Claus Westermann, translated by Keith Crim, 160–99. Richmond, VA: John Knox, 1963.

———. "The Kerygma of the Yahwist." *Interpretation* 20 (1966) 131–58.

Wolters, Al. "The Messiah in the Qumran Documents." In *The Messiah in the Old and New Testaments*, edited by Stanley E. Porter, 75–89. Grand Rapids: Eerdmans, 2007.

Woudstra, Marten H. "Israel and the Church: A Case for Continuity." In *Continuity and Discontinuity: Perspectives on the Relationship between the Old and New Testaments*, edited by John S. Feinberg, 221–38. Wheaton, IL: Crossway, 1988.

Wright, Christopher J. H. *Knowing Jesus through the Old Testament*. Downers Grove: InterVarsity, 1992.

———. "Mission as a Matrix for Hermeneutics and Biblical Theology." In *Out of Egypt*, edited by Craig Bartholomew, 102–43. Grand Rapids: Paternoster/Zondervan, 2004.

———. *The Mission of God*. Downers Grove: InterVarsity, 2006.

Wright, Nicholas T. *The New Testament and the People of God*. Minneapolis: Fortress, 1992.

Young, Edward J. *The Book of Isaiah Chapters 19-39: The English Text, with Introduction, Exposition, and Notes*. NICOT. Grand Rapids: Eerdmans, 1969.

———. *The Book of Isaiah Chapters 40-66: The English Text, with Introduction, Exposition, and Notes*. NICOT. Grand Rapids: Eerdmans, 1972.

Youngblood, Ronald F. "1, 2 Samuel." In *The Expositor's Bible Commentary*, edited by F. Gaebelein, 3:553–1104. Grand Rapids: Zondervan, 1992.

Zaspel, Fred, and James M. Hamilton Jr. "A Typological Future-Mass-Conversion View." In *Three Views on Israel and the Church: Perspectives on Romans 9-11*, edited by Jared Compton and Andrew David Naselli, 97–140. Grand Rapids: Kregel Academic, 2018.

Zenger, Erich. "Zion as Mother of the Nations in Psalm 87." In *The God of Israel and the Nations: Studies in Isaiah and the Psalms*, translated by Everett R. Kalin, 123–60. Collegeville: Liturgical, 2000.

Zobel, Greifswald. "מִשְׁפָּחָה." In *TDOT*, edited by G. Johannes Botterweck and Helmer Ringgren, translated by John T. Willis, 9:79–85. 15 vols. Grand Rapids: Eerdmans, 1975.

Scripture Index

CPSIA information can be obtained
at www.ICGtesting.com
Printed in the USA
BVHW050736210223
658736BV00030B/537